AF653900

Studies in Vedānta

Essays in Honour of Professor S.S. Rama Rao Pappu

Professor Rama Rao Pappu, who has been teaching philosophy in U.S. universities since the sixties has founded the 'International Congress of Vedanta' in 1986 at Miami University, Oxford, Ohio, USA. "The Vedanta Congresses initiated and organized systematically and selflessly by Dr. Pappu during the past nineteen years have played a very productive and positive role. It has stimulated serious studies, scholarly papers, and insightful exchanges on countless aspects of the enormously rich treasure-chest that we call Indian philosophy and tradition."

Andhra University Philosophical Studies, no. 5

Studies in Vedānta

Essays in Honour of Professor S.S. Rama Rao Pappu

Editors
P. George Victor
V.V.S. Saibaba

D.K. Printworld (P) Ltd.
New Delhi

Cataloging in Publication Data — DK
[Courtesy: D.K. Agencies (P) Ltd. <docinfo@dkagencies.com>]

International Congress of Vedanta (15th : 2005 : Visakhapatnam, India)
Studies in Vedānta : essays in honour of Professor S.S. Rama Rao Pappu / editors, P. George Victor, V.V.S. Saibaba.
p. 23 cm. — (Andhra University philosophical studies ; no. 5)
Proceedings of the Fifteenth International Congress of Vedanta, held at Visakhapatnam during 3-6 January 2005.
Includes bibliographical references.
Includes index.
ISBN 8124603502

1. Vedanta — Congresses. I. Rama Rao Pappu, S. S. II. Victor, P. George (Pasalapudi George), 1953- III. Saibaba, V.V.S. (Venkata Vadlamani Satya), 1947- IV. Title. V. Series: Andhra University philosophical studies ; no. 5.

DDC 181.48 22

ISBN 81-246-0350-2
First published in India in 2006
© Copyright for individual articles with the authors.

Proceedings of the Fifteenth International Congress of Vedānta held at Andhra University, Vissakhapatnam, India during Jan. 3-6, 2005.

All rights reserved. No part of this publication may be reproduced or transmitted, except brief quotations, in any form or by any means, electronic or mechanical, including photocopying, recording, or any information storage or retrieval system, without prior written permission of the copyright holder, indicated above, and the publishers.

The views expressed in this volume are those of the authors, and are not necessarily those of the editors or the publisher.

Published and printed by:
D.K. Printworld (P) Ltd.
Regd. Office: 'Sri Kunj', F-52, Bali Nagar
New Delhi-110 015
Phones: (011) 2545-3975; 2546-6019; *Fax:* (011) 2546-5926
E-mail: dkprintworld@vsnl.net
Website: www.dkprintworld.com

॥श्रीः॥

॥अभिनन्दनमालिका॥

एम० नरसिंहाचारी

श्रीमत्पप्पुकुलाब्धिसोमममलं निर्व्याजमन्दस्मितं
नानावेदरहस्यपूतरसना-सौजन्यधन्याशयम्।
प्राच्यैः पण्डितमण्डलैरपि तथा पाश्चात्त्यविज्ञैरपि
प्रख्यातैः परिकीर्त्यमानविभवं श्रीराममेनं श्रये॥१॥

अन्तर्जातीयवेदान्तप्रतिष्ठा विश्वतोमुखी।
यदुपज्ञं, भजे श्रीमद्रामारावुमहोदयम्॥२॥

समस्तविद्वन्मणिमण्डनेन
श्रीरामनाम्ना महिमोन्नतेन।
क्लृप्तास्सभाः सर्वदिगन्तराले
प्रभा अपूर्वाः जनयाम्बभूवुः॥३॥

यस्य द्वितीया परमद्वितीया
सार्थाभिधाना किल सूर्यकान्ता।
नित्यं यदीयोद्यमबीजजातं
फलोन्मुखं संतनुते नितान्तम्॥४॥

श्रीपप्पुरामाभिधमात्मनाथं
छायेव नित्यं परिषस्वजन्ती।
तस्य प्रशस्तेरपि मूलभूता
सीतेव रामस्य जगत्प्रसूतेः॥५॥

श्रीपप्पुरामः सुगुणाभिरामः
महोन्नतैः तात्त्विकभावजालैः।
आदर्शभूतः निरवद्यबोधः
विराजते विश्वहितप्रवृत्तिः॥६॥

ये वा दार्शनिकाः प्रसिद्धिमगमन् देशे विदेशेष्वपि
प्रज्ञादीपनिरस्तमोहतमसः योगीश्वरान् तान्बुधान्
श्रीमत्-शङ्कर-रामकृष्ण-सुविवेकानन्दमुख्यान् तथा
राधाकृष्णमुखान् विशेषविधया श्रीपप्पुरामोऽर्चयत् ॥७॥

प्रज्ञा बहुमुखी यस्य। सिता च निशिता तथा।
प्राच्य-पश्चिमतत्त्वानां सतत्त्वं स्फुटमीक्षते ॥८॥

वृद्धा युवानः श्रुतितत्त्वसक्ताः
जिज्ञासवः सर्वविधैकबन्धौ।
श्रीपप्पुरामे विहिताधमर्ण्याः
समस्तदिङ्मण्डलवासिनोऽपि ॥९॥

तेऽमी महान्तः स्वयशोवितानैः
विभूषिताशाः निरवद्यवेषाः।
सुसंस्कृताः कर्मणि, वाचि, चित्ते
श्रीरामरावः विलसन्तु शश्वत् ॥१०॥

अन्तर्जातीयवेदान्त-संस्थापकमहोदयाः।
अष्टादशसमास्तावत् असमाः निरवहन् सभाः ॥११॥

इदानीं तत्सभाध्यक्ष्यात् विरंस्यन्तीति हेतुतः।
मनो मे खिद्यते नूनम् अद्वितीया हि ते यतः ॥१२॥

आचार्यवर्यः विबुधाग्रगण्यः
निरञ्जनः निर्मलसत्प्रवृत्तिः।
श्रीरामरावाभिध एष जीयात्
विद्वत्सरोजातसहस्रभानुः ॥१३॥

आयुरारोग्यमक्षय्यं शुभसौख्यपरम्परा।
लभेतां दम्पती नित्यं दिव्यदम्पतिमानितौ ॥१४॥

मदीयपद्याम्बुजमालिकेयं
सौहार्दसौरभ्यसमृद्धियुक्ता।
धिनोतु रामं विबुधाग्रगण्यं
सदाभिनन्द्यं सुकृताभिवन्द्यम् ॥१५॥

Contents

Section - I
Vedānta Metaphysics

Section - II
Advaita Epistemology, and Ethics

Section - III
Schools of Vedānta, and Compositions

Section - IV
Vedānta and other Systems

Section - V
Vedānta and Global Parallels

Section - VI
Vedānta and Contemporary World

Preface

THE importance of societies and organizations, both formal and informal, for the promotion of scholarship, exchange of ideas and spread of knowledge needs no emphasis. Imagine a poet who finds no forum to read his work and no publisher to print and distribute his books. His world is indeed a lonely world, his creativity will find no recognition and he will have no admirers. Scholarship and creativity cannot flourish in the absence of societies, forums and organizations, which promote scholarship. Those who start academic societies and organizations do so with a vision; and the International Congress of Vedānta is the product of such a vision.

When Professor Rama Rao Pappu, who has been teaching philosophy in U.S. universities since the sixties realized that scholars of Indian Philosophy in the West were studying texts and conducting research in relative isolation, or at most with negligible interaction at professional Western philosophical associations, he had a vision to start a forum which will bring together Indian Philosophy scholars on a common platform. Professor Rama Rao Pappu has organized for the first time a panel on 'Perspectives on Vedānta' during the "Midwest Conference on Asian Affairs, October 11-13, 1985." Later on he translated his vision into reality with the founding of the 'International Congress of Vedānta' in 1986 at Miami University; and over the past two decades, he had organized sixteen such conferences. One of the special features of these conferences was the celebration of the life and assessment of the contributions of various Indian philosophers, ancient and modern, like Śaṅkarācārya and Jñāneśvara, Radhakrishnan and Vivekananda, Sri Aurobindo and Krishnamurti. Though Professor Pappu is a scholar pursuing his own scholarship in Indian and Comparative Philosophy, Philosophy of Law and Ethics, he takes pride in assembling the scholars together in the forum he named 'International Congress of Vedānta.'

'Global Understanding with Vedāntic Spirit' has been the motto and tradition of the Philosophy Department of Andhra University, starting from the foundation head, Professor Sailaswar Sen, inculcated in the works of Padma-bhushan P.T. Raju and Padma-vibhushan K. Satchidananda Murty. Accordingly Professor Rama Rao Pappu thought it fit to organize the "Fifteenth International Congress of Vedānta" at Andhra University in Visakhapatnam during January 3-6, 2005 with local assistance from the faculty of the departments of Philosophy, Sanskrit and Physics, and Prof. George Victor assuming the role of the Conference Director. The conference was a great success. It was during the conference, the Andhra University's philosophy faculty expressed a desire to honour Professor Rama Rao Pappu by presenting him a festschrift in his honour for his contributions to advance Vedāntic studies in particular and Indian philosophy and culture in general around the world. This idea was also supported by professors V. V. Raman, George A. James, J. S. R. L. Narayana Moorty, Klaus Witz, R. Puligandla, Patricia Reynaud, and Sarada Purna Sonty from USA, and professors A. Ramamurty, Godabarisha Mishra, and K. Srinivas in India. A festschrift to Professor Pappu by the Andhra University faculty was also thought fitting because Visakhapatnam is his hometown, and great academicians of Vedānta like S. Radhakrishnan, P. T. Raju, K. Satchidananda Murty, and Saileswar Sen taught at Andhra University.

Most of the essays included here are revised papers presented at the "Fifteenth International Congress of Vedānta," in addition to the invited essays contributed by Prof. Pappu's friends and admirers. Space limitation however has prevented the inclusion of all the papers presented in the Vedānta Congress; and language limitations also made it impossible to include several excellent papers presented in Sanskrit. Starting from the analytic explanations, the essays in this volume have been arranged in six sections covering Vedānta Metaphysics, Advaita Epistemology and Ethics, Schools of Vedānta, Other Indian Systems to Global Parallels and Contemporary World. Covering the entire gamut of Vedānta philosophy, the essays were written by both young and senior scholars of India and America.

We have included *Studies in Vedānta: Essays in Honour of Professor S.S. Rama Rao Pappu* in the "Andhra University Philosophical Studies" series, which was started a few years ago to expound the spiritual and ethical issues of our tradition and its contemporary relevance. Volumes already published in this series include *Life and Teachings of Ādi Śaṅkarācārya*, *Saints and Gurus*, *Social Relevance of Philosophy*, and *Teaching Philosophy in the Twenty-first Century*. The last volume consists of the Proceedings of an international conference "Teaching Philosophy in the Twenty First Century" which was jointly organized at Andhra University by Professor Rama Rao Pappu and Professor George Victor.

Our special thanks are due to Professor A. Ramamurty, University of Hyderabad and Professor Godabarisha Mishra, University of Madras for selecting and scrutinizing the papers. Professor V.V.S. Saibaba has made considerable editing of the essays and even changing the title of the essays in some cases. Professor P. George Victor has procured the papers and formalized the contents. Being the editors of this volume, while the former took care of transliteration problems, the latter has made changes in the translation of Sanskrit words and was responsible for the overall editorial tasks. The administrative help given by professors S. Satyanarayana, T. Christanandam, and S. D. A. Joga Rao, and the executive assistance of Dr. G. Veerraju and Mr. B. Ravi Babu are immense. We would be failing in our duty if we do not express our thanks to Mr. B. Raju for typing the entire manuscript. We are extremely grateful to Shri Susheel K. Mittal, Director, D. K. Printworld, New Delhi for undertaking the publication.

EDITORS

Prologue
Rama Rao Pappu and the Legacy of Vedānta Congress*

V.V. Raman

> This is the same land where wisdom made its home before it went to any other country, the same India whose influx of spirituality is represented on the material plane by rolling rivers like oceans, where the eternal Himālayas, rising tier over tier into their snow-caps, look as it were into the very mysteries of heaven.

So thundered Swami Vivekananda over a century ago, reminding his fellow citizens about the ancient and rich roots of Indic visions, and telling them that we must remember the blood that courses in our veins, and from that understanding, we must build an India that would be greater and stronger than what she had ever been. These were not mere words of self-affirmation. That was an inspiring call to enter into the modern world even while being anchored to our heritage, wisdom of our seers, and the vitality of a culture that has withstood for centuries the shocks of foreign invasions, and a series of upheavals in manners and customs.

---

* Keynote Address of the "Fifteenth International Congress of Vedānta," Andhra University, Visakhapatnam, January 3-6, 2005.

Our own age has, undoubtedly, been enriched in a thousand ways by the knowledge and benefits that have accrued from science, and all the creature comforts that have ensued from technology. But it is no secret that industrial civilization has engendered a plethora of perilous problems, ranging from pollution and threats of global warming to personal anguish, culture wars, and slippery moral frameworks. Now, as never before, some of the meaningful perspectives of Vedānta could serve to heal the psychological stress and spiritual crises that afflict the world. The multiple paths to religious fulfilment, enshrined in the Vedic aphorism of Truth being one and described by the learned in many ways, could well serve as a motto for a United Nations Declaration on Religious Freedom. The Upaniṣadic insight that every conscious entity is a reflection of the creative Cosmic effulgence, as encapsulated in the Upaniṣadic great saying "*tat tvaṁ asi*" is not only a lofty assessment of what we are; but it has immense potential, when internalized, for evoking the very best in us, goading us to caring, compassion, and respect for fellow humans, for the spark of divinity is in one and all of us.

Yet, while India has been making significant technical, scientific, and economic progress as a modern nation, not many educated people of Indic heritage, whether within India or beyond, are very clear about the stature and substance of the rich treasures of sublime thought and weighty wisdom to which they are legitimately heirs to. On the other hand, Vedāntic insights have been seeping into Europe for more than a couple of centuries now. We have all read about the exhilaration of Schopenhauer and other Western thinkers of the nineteenth century, about the massive efforts of Max Müller to translate the sacred books of the East, whatever his motives, and about American Transcendentalists like Ralph Waldo Emerson and Henry Thoreau.

Ever since Swami Vivekananda's memorable speech in Chicago in 1893 for which he has been commemorated in a street bearing his name near the building where he spoke, Hindu thought in general and Vedānta in particular have caught the attention of vast numbers of people beyond the shores of India: scholars, students and the general public alike. Scores of universities and colleges in the West have been offering courses on various aspects of Indian culture, philosophy and religion. Numerous scholarly journals, hundreds of books and thousands of articles have been published on the subject. Not all of these are to our full satisfaction, and quite a few of the materials contain misrepresentations and distortions, unintended or intentional, malicious and just mistaken, for which committed activists of Indic traditions are appropriately chastising them these days. Nevertheless, scholarly interest in Indology and in Vedānta has not abated in any way. If anything, they have been on the rise, and will most likely continue to do so, barring some catastrophic episode that would cut off all interest for anything Hindu in the West as of now a most unlikely occurrence.

Many saints and sages of our tradition have reminded us that spiritual evolution does not result from scholarly analyses and philosophical debates. However, for the preservation and propagation of a culture's messages and insights we need scholars and philosophers, we need hearty exchanges, healthy debates, and erudite commentaries. The works of scholars sustain, nourish, and serve to enrich further a people's heritage. Among the factors that have contributed to a resurgence of scholarly interest in Vedānta are a series of conferences on various aspects of the subject, initiated in 1986 at Miami University in the heart of America. Named after an American Indian tribe that once lived in that region of Ohio, Miami University was established in 1809 in the little town of Oxford, with gorgeous buildings adorning its 2000-acre idyllic campus.

Only a small group of philosophers teaching at the university attended the first Vedānta Congress, as it was called. The second one, held in 1988, had a well defined theme: it was a celebration of S. Radhakrishnan, perhaps the most illustrious Indian philosopher of the twentieth century whose serene eloquence and erudite writings served the cause of Indic studies in Western academia, just as the spirited oratory of Vivekananda attracted people beyond the ivory tower to the taste and experience of Hindu spiritual life. John Galbraith of Harvard University who had once served as U.S. Ambassador to India inaugurated the 1988 event. On other occasions, scholar-dignitaries like P.K. Kaul, Karan Singh, and Abid Hussain, and Swamijis from the Vedāntic Society of New York and the Paramarthaniketan of Rishikesh, graced the meetings. In each succeeding meeting, more and more scholars began to participate from different universities in the United States. Participants came from Canada, Europe, India, and other places too. Soon it became the International Congress of Vedānta.

The Congress dedicated to Radhakrishnan was so successful that the next one centered on the philosophy of Ādi Śaṅkara: 1990 was reckoned as the 800th anniversary of the sage who, as we all know, is the foremost saint-philosopher of the Hindu world. The following congress in 1992 was to commemorate Swami Vivekananda's visit to the United States during which the dynamic disciple of Sri Ramakrishna took American audiences by storm by his extempore outpourings on the richness and loftiness of Hindu thought. One year they explored the thoughts of Sri Aurobindo who moved with ease from poetry to politics, from profound philosophy to mature mysticism. Another year was dedicated to Jiddu Krishnamurti, whom Annie Besant had once declared to be a new messiah, but who turned out to be one of the most original and spiritually emancipated souls of the twentieth century. Yet another year, scholars explored the teachings of Sant Jñāneśwara, the great practitioner and exponent of the *Bhakti* tradition. Congresses were also devoted to non-personal themes such the *Bhagavad-Gītā*, the major epics, and the *dharma-śāstras*. So it is that every two years, scholars have been gathering in the peaceful surroundings of Miami University, discussing about the Vedas and Vedānta.

The papers presented in the meetings add up to a massive corpus of scholarly perspectives and informed commentaries on various aspects of Indic thought, for they also included Buddhism, Vedānta and Physics, and so on.

The Vedānta Congress became international in another sense also, for it has been held in Port of Spain, Trinidad, whose large population of Indic heritage received us all with warm embraces; in Rishikesh, that ancient and vibrant spiritual center near the source of the Gaṅgā and at the foothills of hoary Himālayas; in Chennai where the much admired nightingale of India, M.S. Subhalakhsmi treated us all one evening to a musical feast; and in Hyderabad, which enjoys a special place of affection in the hearts of quite a few people here. And now we are meeting in this great city of Visakhapatnam in the precincts of a university, which counts with pride its historical association with none other than S. Radhakrishnan, the brightest gem in the philosophical crown of Mother India.

How did the Vedānta Congress originate? The idea of the congress was the brainchild of one individual. He is S.S. Rama Rao Pappu, who is Professor of Philosophy at Miami University. I have run into some of his students and colleagues in different places, and I have heard them express only the highest regard for him as a teacher and as a person. Pappu has also authored or edited works with such titles as *Gandhi and America's Educational Future*; *Indian Philosophy: Past and Present*; *Dimensions of Karma: Perspectives on Vedānta*; and *New Essays in the Philosophy of Sarvapalli Radhakrishnan*. He is also an associate editor of *Darśanamulu* and *Matamulu*. In 1998 the Indian Council of Philosophical Research, New Delhi nominated him as a Distinguished Visiting Professor. He was also appointed as a Visiting Professor to Wittenberg University in the USA. He has received several honorary awards including the Distinguished Educator Award of Miami University. He is in every sense a true scholar. In addition to all this, he is a man of disarming simplicity, with never a tinge of pride or self-importance. He is invariably cordial and friendly; always ready to give a helping hand to the attendees of these conferences and to others too.

Congresses of such recurrence and magnitude do not sprout out automatically. They come about from careful planning and meticulous organization. The credit for putting together the details, which transform ideas into reality and visions into actuality, also goes to Pappu. But I suspect his consistent success in these is largely due a very charming and devoted wife in the person of Srimati Suryakantham. Anyone who has attended a Vedānta Congress at Miami University has experienced the gracious hospitality of Mrs. Pappu who has invariably treated us all to sumptuous Indian feasts, whether home-cooked or catered. There is little doubt that her unfailing support to Pappu has been giving him considerable energy and enthusiasm in the execution of his grand undertaking.

Rumors are going around to the effect that Pappu is contemplating retirement from his duties as professor at Miami University within the next few years. How fortunate that it is taking place in this city and university with which Pappu's own life is intimately associated.

Any observer of the international political scene knows that in the twenty-first century India is destined to play a major role in determining the course of world history. She will emerge as a world power with all the might of more than a billion people, only some of whose capacities are being harnessed today. This nation will undoubtedly assert itself with economic, industrial and military strength. But more importantly, if she does not let go of the nuggets of wisdom of the sage-poets of yore who have guided her through the ages, then she will become a beacon to the rest of the world on the moral and spiritual planes as well. For this to happen, the perennial philosophy implicit in Vedāntic visions must be periodically articulated and propagated, even as the tangible results of modern science that emerged in the West have been made universal by the protagonists of modern science.

In this context, the Vedānta Congresses initiated and organized systematically and selflessly by Prof. Pappu during the past nineteen years have played a very productive and positive role. It has stimulated serious studies, scholarly papers, and insightful exchanges on countless aspects of the enormously rich treasure-chest that we call Indian philosophy and tradition. And for having initiated and nourished it for almost two decades, we are all very deeply grateful to Professor S.S. Rama Rao Pappu, and his constant companion Mrs. Suryakantham Pappu. I wish to take this opportunity to convey to them both, on behalf of all who have been enriched by these congresses, our most heart-felt appreciation for all they have done.

Section - I
Vedānta Metaphysics

1

The Paradigm of the Metaphysic of Experience
A Study of Gauḍapāda's Māṇḍūkya-kārikā

Srinivasa Rao

IN most of the schools of Indian philosophy, especially the *Āstika* schools, our everyday empirical experience is taken at its face value. Its truthfulness is taken for granted, and it is assumed not to possess any kind of metaphysical significance. It is only *Vijñānavāda* Buddhists who questioned the truthfulness of waking experiences. Gauḍapāda went very much farther than Vijñānavādins and resorted to a thoroughly metaphysical interpretation of all the three states of human experience like waking, dream and deep sleep. He postulated non-dual consciousness as the basis of these three states. He also proposed a radically metaphysical meaning for the ordinary terms *svapna* (dream) and *nidrā* (sleep). He interpreted "dream" as misperceiving the nature of non-dual reality and "sleep" as being completely unaware of the same non-dual reality. When both such "dream" and "sleep" are overcome, there would be a realization of *ātman*, which is *Brahman* — the non-dual Consciousness. Thus, by metaphysically interpreting the empirical concepts of dream and sleep, Gauḍapāda introduces a paradigm shift, which is both warmly accepted and hotly challenged in Vedānta philosophy. This paper is an exploration of this new paradigm of the metaphysic of our experience offered by Gauḍapāda.

It is a very curious fact of Indian philosophical history that while nearly all schools of philosophy take the whole of our empirical experience entirely at its face value and do not, for that reason, offer any kind of metaphysic of it, only the Buddhist philosophers of the *Vijñānavāda* school and Gauḍapāda, an early commentator on the *Māṇḍūkya Upaniṣad*, attempt to ground our everyday empirical experiences metaphysically. The radically revolutionary character of Gauḍapāda's *Māṇḍūkya-kārikā* is powerfully demonstrated through the very forceful Advaita metaphysic of experience offered by it. Of course, the grounding offered by Gauḍapāda and the Buddhists are radically different. Therefore, it is also yet another curious fact that the very radical character of both these attempts was so completely misunderstood and their differences so completely missed, that it became standard practice among Indian philosophers to identify Advaitins like Gauḍapāda and Śaṅkara with *Vijñānavāda* Buddhists and label them as "crypto-Buddhists" (*Pracchanna Bauddha*).

One outstanding difference between all other *Āstika* schools of philosophy and Advaita is that while the *Āstika* schools take everyday experience as an almost unquestioned basis for the development of their metaphysical world-views, Advaita queries the very nature of our everyday experience in its entirety before attempting any formulation of its own world-view. In other words, while the other schools do not offer any general metaphysic of everyday experience, Advaita tries to offer such a metaphysic. In all other schools, everyday experience is of course analyzed philosophically, but it is done primarily with an epistemological focus. That is, experience is categorized into perception, inference, and verbal testimony and so on. Then, it is also a fact that all these categories of experiences are part of our waking experience in general, and all human beings universally have such waking experiences. Nevertheless, this waking experience itself — in its most general form — is not subjected to any philosophical analysis in any of the *Āstika* schools. The same holds good in the cases of dream and sleep also, which are equally universal human experiences. This entire range of human experience from waking to sleep comes to be studied and analyzed in the Advaita tradition; and this analysis is usually called "the science of the three states of experience" (*avastha-traya-vijñāna*). This analysis can be said to embody what may be called the "metaphysic of experience." Gauḍapāda is a pioneer in developing such a metaphysic of experience and his famous *Māṇḍūkya-kārikā* is a classic statement of the Advaitic metaphysic of experience.

Gauḍapāda brings about a paradigm shift in the philosophical approach to human experience by offering his metaphysic of experience in his *Kārikā* on the *Māṇḍūkya Upaniṣad*. Gauḍapāda is of course not unique in taking note of the three states of experience because they are already noticed and analyzed even in the very early Upaniṣads themselves. While the treatment of the three states of experience in the other Upaniṣads like the *Bṛhadāraṇyaka Upaniṣad* is somewhat brief as well as scattered, in the *Māṇḍūkya Upaniṣad* it is equally brief but is also very unified, focused and distinctly metaphysical. In his *Kārikā*, Gauḍapāda takes the analysis found in the *Māṇḍūkya Upaniṣad* to newer metaphysical heights thus far unknown in the Upaniṣadic tradition. In my opinion, while the *Māṇḍūkya Upaniṣad* may be said to contain a very brief *philosophical description* of consciousness and its states, Gauḍapāda's *Kārikā* on this Upaniṣad may be said to contain a *metaphysical interpretation* of this Upaniṣadic description. It is in giving a metaphysical interpretation of the Upaniṣadic statements that Gauḍapāda offers an absolutely new — and also hitherto non-existent-metaphysic of experience and thereby brings about a paradigm shift in the Indian philosophical approach to the understanding and interpretation of everyday human experience.

Until the advent of Gauḍapāda, waking was waking, dream was dream, and sleep was sleep not only for ordinary people but also even for all philosophers of the *Āstika* schools. These states were regarded as mere physical — or, if you so prefer, psychological — occurrences; and none of them were taken to imply anything metaphysical. There is of course a lot of discussion and debate concerning dream experiences done by many philosophers of different schools in the pre-Gauḍapāda period, but they are not done from any metaphysical point of view. These debates centre around questions like whether dream cognitions are presentative or representative in character, whether they are real or illusory in nature, and if so, in what way they are different from either perceptions or illusions experienced in the waking state, whether dreams are simply recollections that are either true or false, and similar largely epistemological and marginally metaphysical issues. There is indeed a wealth of detail available in this body of literature concerning how exactly dream cognitions differ from every other conceivable type of cognition, and also very varying and insightful explanations of dream phenomena, but no attempt whatever at providing a metaphysical foundation for them.

Even among the Upaniṣads, only *Māṇḍūkya Upaniṣad* has taken a different view in grounding the three states of experience in a metaphysical reality which it simply designates as the "fourth" (*caturthaṁ*), but also clearly identifies with *ātman*: *caturthaṁ manyante sa ātmā sa vijñeya* (*Māṇḍūkya Upaniṣad*, 1.7). Basing himself on this Upaniṣad, Gauḍapāda radically changed our understanding of the three states by pointing out, for the first time, that all the three have deep metaphysical significance. The Upaniṣad had made it clear that whatever each one of the three states itself was, the "fourth" one was *not any of them* because this "fourth" was transcending them all.

Since the "fourth" was clearly declared by the Upaniṣad to be the "*ātman* which is to be known" (*sa ātmā sa vijñeyaḥ, Māṇḍūkya Upaniṣad* 1.7), it was also clear that the *ātman* was not in fact known in its true form in any of the three states although it lay underneath all the three. That is, the *ātman* is not revealed in the three states but something else is revealed instead. In the waking state, the external world is revealed. The presentation of this external world is suppressed in dream and a separate internal world is revealed instead. Neither of these two worlds is revealed in deep sleep during which we are not aware of anything. However, the *ātman* equally underlies all these three states of waking, dream and sleep.

If the underlying reality of *ātman* is accepted, we can see that what happens in the waking and dream states is metaphysically very similar. In both of them, the underlying *ātman* is not perceived, but something else is perceived in its place, i.e., the external world and the internal world respectively. In deep sleep also, neither the *ātman* nor anything else like the external or internal worlds is perceived and therefore there is no knowledge of anything. In this way, the facts concerning the three states of universal human experience like waking, dream and deep sleep come to be interpreted metaphysically by Gauḍapāda as constituting a commonly present ignorance of the true nature of *ātman*.

We all normally regard dream experience as illusory. The things seen in a dream are regarded as non-existent. *Bṛhadāraṇyaka Upaniṣad* says that in the dream state, there are no chariots, but chariots are seen. Therefore, "dream" may be described as a case of illusion, misapprehension, or the seeing of things that do not really exist. After accepting this, the next step Gauḍapāda takes is surprising. He declares that what we all normally regard as the waking state is also nothing but "dream" because in that state also we misapprehend the sole reality, the ever-existing *ātman*, as the "external world." Since the *ātman* alone is what exists according to Gauḍapāda, whether we perceive a chariot in the waking state or perceive it in the dream state, it is the same. Both are cases of misapprehension and there is no difference between the two from the metaphysical point of view. This metaphysical non-difference between the waking and dream states forms the soul and substance of the entire second chapter of his *Kārikā* called "the chapter on illusion" or *vaitathya prakaraṇa.*

The similarity between waking and dream states does not end in their both being states of misapprehension of the true nature of reality. Misapprehension is possible only when there is not only a failure to apprehend the true nature of a thing but also something else is apprehended instead. Therefore, the two states of waking and dream are also metaphysically similar in yet another respect, viz. both of them being states in which there is no awareness of the true nature of ultimate reality. Since deep sleep is a general state of not being aware of anything including the *ātman,* it is also, like waking and dream, characterized by the non-apprehension of the true nature of reality. Therefore, while the non-apprehension of the true nature of reality characterizes all the three states uniformly, the misapprehension of the true nature of reality is restricted only to the states of waking and dream. Gauḍapāda chooses to use the word *svapna* or dream to characterize our misapprehension of *ātman,* and the word *nidrā* to characterize our non-apprehension of *ātman.* Thus, he endows the ordinary expression "dream" or *svapna* with a new metaphysical meaning, viz. misapprehension of the true nature of ultimate reality. Likewise, he also endows the ordinary expression "sleep" (*nidrā*) with an equally new metaphysical meaning, viz. the non-apprehension of the true nature of ultimate reality. He says tersely, *anyathā gṛhṇataḥ-svapno nidrā tattvaṁajānata; viparyāse tayo kṣīne turīyaṁ padamasnute* (*Māṇḍūkya Kārikā* 1.15), which means: while dream is misapprehension of reality, sleep is its non-apprehension. When these two forms of wrong knowledge are eliminated, the *turīya* state is realized.

Such a metaphysical reinterpretation of the meaning of the ordinary terms *svapna* and *nidrā* enables Gauḍapāda to give a new metaphysical interpretation of the three states of human experience in such a way that it naturally and ultimately leads to a non-dual ultimate Reality. If the three states of ordinary human experience are now approached and analyzed from the standpoint of the newly formulated metaphysical meanings, the two states of waking and dream which are called *viśva* and *taijasa* by the *Māṇḍūkya Upaniṣad*, turn out to be states in which the ultimate reality is both not apprehended and wrongly apprehended. We may empirically distinguish between waking and dream and hold the former to be a correct apprehension and the latter alone to be incorrect. However, from a metaphysical point of view, there is no difference between the two. Since there is no knowledge of any kind in the state of sleep (which is called *prajñā* by the Upaniṣad), the misapprehension of ultimate reality, or *svapna* in the metaphysical sense, is of course totally absent in it, but there is still found in it *nidrā* or the metaphysical non-apprehension of ultimate reality. Therefore, only that state in which both such metaphysical *svapna* and *nidrā* are completely absent, is called *turīyā*, the "fourth." Once again, Gauḍapāda puts this point equally tersely: *svapna nidrā yutāvādya prajñāsta svapna nidrāyā; na nidrāṁ naiva ca svapnaṁ turye paśyanti niścita* (*Māṇḍūkya Kārikā* 1.14) which means: the first two, *viśva* and *taijasa*, are characterized by dream and sleep; *prajñā* is characterized by sleep without dream. Those who are sure of the nature of reality see neither dream nor sleep in the *turīya*.

Now, it is not difficult to see the difference between Gauḍapāda and the Vijñānavāda positions. The Vijñānavādins confine their analysis to just waking and dream which are both dynamic states of consciousness. They totally exclude the sleep state in which the modifications of consciousness cease completely. We do not also find in their writings the kind of metaphysical interpretations of the concepts of dream and sleep offered by Gauḍapāda. The kind of *śāśvata ātmavāda* advocated by Gauḍapāda is anathema to all Buddhists including the Vijñānavādins although the Vijñānavādins are also Advaitavādins like Gauḍapāda. It is the partial similarity that is at the root of the mistaken charge by many theistic Vedāntins that the Advaitins are concealed Buddhists (*pracchanna bauddha*).

Now, it is not also difficult to see why Rāmānuja, Madhva and several other theistic Vedāntins refused to accept Gauḍapāda's metaphysic of experience. All the theistic schools require the dualism of the Deity and the devotee. The *bhakti*-practices of all theistic schools are founded on this dualism. But the new metaphysic of experience offered by Gauḍapāda provides no scope whatever for this or any other type of dualism. That is because, there is no way the metaphysic of human experience as formulated and embedded in Gauḍapāda's *Māṇḍūkya-kārikā* can be detached from the thesis that pure, attributeless consciousness or *nirguṇa Brahman* alone is the ultimate reality. Such *nirguṇa* reality logically blocks the finality or the legitimacy of any form of theism. Therefore, very naturally, the theistic Vedāntins are not at all inclined to accepting the kind of the metaphysic of empirical experience offered by Gauḍapāda. Since the very logical exposition of the new metaphysic of Gauḍapāda very much rests on his thesis of the metaphysical equivalence of the waking and the dream states, the only way left open for the theistic Vedāntin to reject the new metaphysic is to reject this equivalence.

But those who have carefully read the *Māṇḍūkya Kārikā* know that the thesis of equivalence of waking and dream contained in it is indeed very strong. In fact, even Rāmānuja found that thesis to be so formidable that in order to reject it he had to finally reject, even the commonly accepted belief that dreams are unreal. That is, Gauḍapāda's argument was: (a) Dreams are unreal, (b) Waking experiences are exactly like dreams. Therefore, (c) Waking experiences are unreal. Since (b) was supported by irrefutable arguments based on the very natures of waking and dream experiences, Rāmānuja chose to reverse Gauḍapāda's argument and its consequences by replacing (a) by a startling new proposition "Dreams are real." This enabled him to change (c) into "Waking experiences are real" thus preserving the reality of waking experiences and ultimately blocking the way for the acceptance of the truth of non-difference and non-duality.

Thus, even common sense realism of regarding dreams as illusory experiences is given a go by Rāmānuja just in order to avoid the so-called *māyāvāda* or illusionism arising out of the acceptance of the Advaita metaphysic of experience. It very much seems that the only way Rāmānuja could successfully banish what he thought to be the illusionistic metaphysics of Advaita was to banish the very idea of illusion from our ordinary discourse by endorsing with approval of the famous dictum "All experiences are valid" (*anubhūt-pramā*). Therefore, the theistic Vedāntins like Rāmānuja and his fellow travellers find no alternative but to firmly refuse to entertain the idea of Advaita even in their dreams, because in their attempts to finally avoid Advaita, they have made even dreams quite real!

2

The Viability of Non-Duality

J.S.R.L. Narayana Moorty

My aim in this paper is to show that there is no inherent incompatibility between non-dual experience and the phenomenon of thinking. Non-dual living can include thinking and moreover, to reverse the coin, thinking can even occur in the process of dissolution of duality.[1]

There is an apparent problem in conceiving non-dual living. Thinking, being a conceptual activity, seems to be a mental operation which involves contrasts both in terms of the object (of thinking) contrasted with what it is not, and in terms of the object contrasted with the subject, i.e., as involving an implicit or explicit reference to the self. If these contrasts necessarily create a division and duality between the self and the world, and if thinking is essential even for a liberated person in order to operate in this world, then the problem seems to be, how can the liberated man be said to exist in a state of non-duality and yet use dualistic thinking in order to deal with his world, other people, and himself?

---

1. For some of the remarks in this paper I am indebted to the teachings of U.G. Krishnamurti. Some others are based upon my observations of the way he lives. Of course, in no case, what I say here should be attributed to him.

I will attempt to resolve this problem by showing that the process of thinking creates more than one type of duality to be specific, what I shall call merely conceptual (or cognitive) duality, on the one hand, and affective and existential dualities, on the other. It is to claim that in the state of non-duality a person is free from affective and existential dualities, while I will also claim that conceptual (or cognitive) duality is innocuous and quite compatible with non-duality in an affective and existential sense. Even though in deep states of *samādhi* one is probably free of even conceptual duality, one could be in a non-dual state in waking consciousness and yet employ dualistic thinking. Such a dualism can nevertheless be clearly distinguished from the emotionally "dualistic" thinking where one is painfully aware of oneself as separate from the world and other selfs.[2]

I

What is Duality?

Simply defined, duality is two-ness, and may be conceived in three types, as stated below:

A) COGNITIVE DUALITY

Perceiving a chair as different from a table, and thinking about an object, both employing concepts, involve cognitive duality.

---

2. See David Loy's *Nonduality*, (New Haven, 1988) for a discussion of the different sorts of non-duality. In fact, this paper can be construed as a footnote to his book. David Loy does not mention "affective" or "existential" non-dualities in his classification, but I think they are crucial in the understanding of liberation. He does, however, mention non-duality in thinking and action. Unlike David Loy, in this paper I understand thinking is necessarily dualistic, although I do claim that it is not incompatible with the state of liberation.

When I see a chair and recognize it as such, I see it, at least implicitly, as distinct from things other than chairs, and also as other than myself. This may also be accompanied by an implicit awareness (perhaps made explicit in a later act of reflection) of my seeing. The same sort of awareness goes on when I am in the purely mental realm of thinking about things. This duality is what I shall call cognitive duality. However, the mere fact that a chair is perceived as different from a table is not the sort of duality that matters for purposes of liberation, although the same mental functions also produce other sorts of duality, which are relevant. To repeat, the mere fact of perceiving a chair as different from a table, or perceiving that there are many things in the world, or seeing that people, you and I, are different from one another and from the world, do not by themselves constitute the problem of bondage. No one has renounced the world to become free from this sort of duality.

B) AFFECTIVE DUALITY

When there is a consciousness of the object as distinct from oneself (either implicitly or explicitly) and when there is an interpretation of such consciousness as pleasant or painful, we have what could be called affective duality. Affective duality is inherent in the process of desire or avoidance. Affective duality is considered a problem only when it connotes a consciousness of pain, a sense of uneasiness at the least, something that one resists. The disappointment felt in not succeeding at or not possessing what one wanted, creates a consciousness of the pain one has, a pain that one would like to avoid. Other dualities (perceptual or cognitive duality and duality in action) play a significant role in the life of the person striving for liberation only on the assumption that affective duality is a problem.

When a person merely perceives something, there is no sense of separation in his mind between himself and what he perceives. However, recognition of the object of perception implies employing a concept. He classifies it, makes a judgment about it. He may desire such an object, based on his experience of it, or he may wish to avoid it (or remain indifferent to it). In desire (or avoidance), there is an implicit awareness of oneself as separate from the object of one's desire (as lacking it). Then he acts to fulfill his desire. If he obtains what he desires, then he plays with it, cherishes it, and soon goes on to some other object and repeats the process. When there is an obstacle in the process of obtaining what one desires, there is a keen consciousness of oneself as separate from the object one desires. This is accompanied by a sense of tension, pain or uneasiness, and there is an attempt to avoid this consciousness of separation (and the accompanying pain). Before, any implicit awareness of separation (or duality) was not a problem. Now duality has become a problem one has to resolve. I see the object as something I must have, or as something, I must avoid. At this level the self or ego exists, although shortly, in the sense that there is a consciousness of oneself as lacking something, as having achieved something, as being hurt, and so on.

Affective duality is not always seen as something painful. When it is seen as pleasant, it is when one has solved the problem of a previous affective duality by achieving the object of a desire, and thereby has gained temporarily a sense of achievement. In addition, the process of desiring itself can seem to be pleasant as when it presents the prospect of fulfilment, or when one fantasizes the fulfilment of desire in some fashion or other. Nevertheless, my claim is that any affective duality, regardless of how it is seen, involves a sense of alienation[3] and uneasiness, and hence in itself is a problem, although it is not seen as such except at the level of existential duality. At the level of existential duality, one is not so much enchanted with the goals of one's desires as much as with the process of seeking them. Then one may be well aware of the accompanying weariness and the underlying alienation.

C) EXISTENTIAL DUALITY

Ordinarily, we attempt to transcend this affective duality by focusing on the world and trying to change the situations in it, or by trying to "improve" ourselves, so that we can eventually get what we want. But, when somehow the problem of "affective" duality is not solved (either I still have not got what I wanted, or getting what I wanted only left me with a sense of vague dissatisfaction, weariness or alienation, with a sense of meaninglessness of the goals I have been seeking), I am left with a more profound sense of separation between myself and the world (or the people and situations in it), or between myself and my life or existence. This is when we say the person is experiencing "existential duality." Although existential duality is only an extension or continuation of affective duality, it is at this level that duality is felt at its keenest. Existential duality is synonymous with *saṁsāra* or suffering. When a person seeks liberation, it is generally at the level of existential duality that he does so. Of course, even at this stage a person may not see duality as suffering. When he does, he may still not see the suffering as something that can be totally dissolved by the process of liberation.

---

3. I argued elsewhere that underlying the process of desire or avoidance (both of which together I called becoming) there is a sense of alienation. The Existentialists would perhaps call this alienation "anguish." See my paper, "Radhakrishnan on Buddha's Silence" in the *Radhakrishnan Centenary Volume*, ed. By S. Parthasarathi and D.P. Chattopadhyaya, Oxford University Press, Delhi, 1989, p. 115ff.

Thinking Underlies Affective and Existential Dualities

Thinking can only operate through concepts. Conceptualization through the recalling of a past experience as pleasant or unpleasant, the consequent formation of an image of it as desirable (if it was pleasant), and the thinking of oneself as not having it, the perception of something as means to achieving it, and so on are all mental processes necessary for the formation of affective and existential dualities. However, the thought process here is not merely cognitive; it is at the same time affective and conditional. When we label (or describe) a thing, all the knowledge related to that thing is also brought to bear upon it in such a way that the description of the thing is translated into our value scales of pleasure and pain and then elaborated upon. The thing is then seen as something to be sought after (for one's pleasure or happiness or fulfilment) or something to be avoided. If our subsequent non-attainment of the object of desire and the frustration in our attempts to achieve it are seen as such from the point of our past expectations, then such consciousness brings forth affective duality, which is seen as painful, which may in some individuals culminate in existential duality. The consciousness of the attainment of the objects of desire is not something, which we resist as painful. Hence, it does not present a problem of duality.

Affective and Existential Dualities Imply the Ego[4]

Our thinking process also creates the notion of the self or ego, the "idea" of oneself as currently being happy or unhappy,

---

4. I am not pretending here to give an explanation as to the "whys" and "wherefores" of the tendency on the part of an experience to repeat itself, or as to the metaphysical origins of the phenomenon or "illusion" of the ego. I am satisfied with describing it and explaining how it is possible to live without it.

and as having to be happy or fulfilled in the future, and the consequent notion of "time." Even if one has, for instance, solved the current problem of pain, the memory of the pain still leaves an emotional "scar" on one's psyche. Similarly, one is not merely satisfied with the achievement of a current goal; one attributes the achievement to oneself and feels proud of it. The achievement is now seen as flowing from one's "potency" or "potentiality."

The ego is a sense of oneself as a continuous person to which are attributed all experiences, actions, the body, and various other qualities. The ego always goes beyond the present experience. Our conscious existence is in reality nothing but a collection of thoughts each followed by other thoughts. Some previous thoughts and memories become the objects of present thoughts. When a previous memory becomes an object of a present thought, there is consciousness of the memory, there is an attribution of it to the self, and a feeling that one is still in pain or pleasure. Thus a sense of continuity, which is perceived to be the self or ego, is created. Thoughts of the future, which are memories modified by our desires in a way that they anticipate events, also create continuity by a similar process. Present actions, performances, achievements, and the qualities one notices or others notice about oneself, are all followed by thoughts attributing them to the self, or feelings that one is the source of them.

This notion of the ego or self exists even at the level of affective duality as a momentary implicit or explicit awareness of self. However, beyond this implicit awareness of self in consciousness and thinking, and apart from the mere awareness of oneself in the present self-consciousness as the subject or self that experiences the world, there is a life of the more generalized or "long-term" ego, constantly gathering knowledge and experience, seeking fulfilment, meaning, ultimate and permanent happiness, a union with reality, and so forth. Existential duality is a problem only because we are governed by the long-term ego. Each thought, as it were, thinks for the whole self. Moreover, it seeks permanent happiness not for itself, but for the whole self. It is as if the whole of the knowledge we have accumulated operates through each thought, and seeks fulfilment for the self, although the single thought may be only seeking a particular goal or object.

Objectively speaking, the ego is nothing but a tendency to think, believe, and behave as if one were a permanent entity continuing in time, lacking a certain fulfilment, and having to be fulfilled, and having certain qualities, experiences, beliefs, hopes, fears, projects, potentialities, destiny, and so forth. Even more specifically, the ego is inertia created by the tendency on the part of an experience to linger on and repeat itself. If there is no desire or urge to repeat an experience of the past (or to avoid a painful one) then there is no self or ego, nor is there a consciousness of the self. The experience repeating itself looks upon itself as an object, as something to be desired or avoided, and also upon itself as a self, lacking what it desires. It then tries to strive for the object or become it. The generalized notion of the ego is only an extension of this primitive ego or self. A series of experience is put together, on the one hand, as the world (the object) and, on the other, as the ego or the self. To release the object is also to release the subject to that extent. Each thought builds the self, and it seems as though it is the self that builds (or causes) further thought about the same situation. The ego is not, however, dissolved by removing this or that particular goal or expectation. It will in fact seek out a goal, or even invent one, whenever it feels a lack or vacuum in its present consciousness.

The Process of Attachment Creates the Ego and Affective and Existential Dualities

The mere mental functions of thinking do not explain the ego or our affective and existential dualities. The tendency on the part of man to hold on to all that he attributes to himself is the additional element that is needed to explain how the ego and the affective and existential dualities are created and maintained. This holding on or grasping manifests itself in our feeling that what we are attached to is essential to our identity, happiness or well-being. In other words, to be attached to something is to be identified with it, whether positively or negatively. If "I" were identified with something positively, I would seek it, and treat it as necessary for my happiness and well-being. On the other hand, if "I" were identified with something negatively, I would seek to avoid it, and treat it as a threat or an obstacle in the way of my well being and happiness.

Thoughts going "back" in memory and actively recalling a past event, and attributing it to the self takes place only because one feels "attached" to the object or event in question, and to a certain image of oneself that one has created for oneself in the past. We of course interpret our attachment to these thoughts as ourselves going out and seeking, but never see ourselves as merely a series of thoughts, having their own momentum, and mechanically seeking fulfilment. While our attachments create the ego, the ego once formed renews old attachments, and in the process of seeking their fulfilment, it forms new attachments. These in turn further shape and strengthen the ego, thus creating a perpetual spiral of an increasingly complex ego fuelled by an increasing number of attachments.

Contrary to attachment, to be detached from something is to see and live as if that thing makes no difference to one's identity, happiness or well being. When one is detached from something, then there are no thoughts going back or forward seeking fulfilment either in fantasy or in actuality (by seeking pleasure and avoiding pain). When we are free from attachments, we are free from the continuity of the ego, and the consequent affective and existential dualities. Then our living is at least affectively and existentially speaking non-dual. The other sorts of non-duality are not a problem.

A clear distinction in analysis is not generally made between merely functional thinking or cognitive processes as such and the processes of thinking, which includes attachment and which creates the notion of the self and the affective and existential dualities that the notion of the self implies. The consequence is to assume that to be free from the ego or the self and its concomitant problems is to be free from even the cognitive processes such as thinking. I submit that these two are not synonymous.

There are several reasons why seers and philosophers might have felt that merely functional thinking and thinking which includes attachment are the same. First, in states of *samādhi* or total absorption no thinking whatsoever occurs. Second, thinking seems to be dualistic and divisive, since it involves the use of concepts. And third, thinking seems to be necessarily involved in the formation of desire and avoidance. While all these reasons are true, they do not necessitate equating cognitive with affective and existential dualities.

II

There are two contexts in which the role of thinking in non-dual living is especially relevant: thinking as used in day-today dealings with the world, and thinking as used in meditation as part of the process of "deconstruction" or dissolution of affective and existential duality.

Day-to-day living: When one becomes free from the urge to repeat an experience of the past or to avoid a painful one, then one can become free from the notion of the self. However, the rest of the mental processes, including the cognitive and affective ones, can still remain such that one can live and function in this world, without at the same time being subject to the psychological problems of worry, fear, pride, anger, depression, loneliness, and so forth. The ego can occur as a momentary counterpart of a thought, and one can experience momentary pleasure, fear, or anger, without attributing those experiences to the self. Hence, the ego as a continuous entity is not put together, and hence does not arise. Also, there is no continuous ego because one no longer has the urge to become, the urge to fulfill oneself through something other than oneself, since any response to an object in an environment (or a mental object) exists only as a momentary state (however short or long the "moment" is). And since there is no continuity between one such state and the next one, or attachment to any of them, the long-term ego or self cannot arise and does not exist to create the deeper problems of duality. It is existential duality (generated by the long-term ego) that creates sorrow or suffering in life, and not the momentary pleasures and disappointments of daily life. The latter, even when they are perceived as such and dealt with when they occur, would not be attached to a long-term self, and hence would not present a problem.

If the momentary responses to the world are not connected to a long-term self, then the particular responses, not only the pleasures and pains, but even the thoughts, which accompany them, would not have the "weight" which they normally have.

As the Zen Buddhists would say, then thoughts would be free "to come and go." When there is no need (whether "need" is defined in terms of "survival" or the "situation on hand") for dealing with the present situation, then there is no occasion for thought. Then one focuses on any aspect of the environment which "draws" his attention (without even naming it), or simply is withdrawn into a *samādhi* until some other situation or needs of living bring him into consciousness and prompt him to deal with the environment. When the process, which translates our knowledge and all we notice in the environment into the pleasant and the painful, is gone, the center, which puts together our experiences and attributes them, the "I," is also gone. Each thought may occur, bringing with a momentary (implicit) consciousness of itself, but does not refer the characteristics of the situation (or action or whatever is the object of one's awareness at the moment) to the self. Hence, affective or existential dualities are not created. Then one might act as if he has no "biography," character, or purpose in one's life. There is no continuity in one's consciousness or behavior. The person is moved by whatever is the immediate situation on hand.

When there is no putting together of the object or of the self beyond the needs of the immediate situation, then when responses occur, thoughts and actions are spontaneously brought to bear upon the situation, which demands attention; yet there is no referring to the self. To an observer, the person may seem to recognize the objects, to respond to them through an ego or self, be angry, laugh, converse philosophically, and so forth. Yet, for the person himself such distinctions do not arise. He becomes, as it were, part of the natural processes, which are interacting with one another. Any desire that might occur at the moment is limited to the means one has at one's disposal to achieve the end desired. Any ego that appears in a particular interaction is purely limited to the moment. There would be no "ulterior" for one's actions. As the Zen Buddhists would say, he eats when he is hungry and goes to bed when he is sleepy.

Spontaneous responses to the environment do not require "dualistic" thought or "active" memory. Being free from the self or the ego, one is moved by one's surroundings, seeing no reason to move by himself. Of course, some knowledge is operating in "reading" the situation in whatever way it is read, but as there is no attachment, the knowledge does not create an anticipatory "build-up" of thought or expectation. Memory helps him to recognize the situation and respond to it appropriately. But there is no active recall in terms of reminiscing, nor is there an active modifying of the past into the future through the seeking of pleasure or avoiding of pain, as we normally do in fantasizing and worrying. There is no fantasizing, no reminiscing, and no "movement of pleasure or pain."

Any pursuit in life, which requires continuity of action, occurs only when the situation itself reminds the person of the need to pursue with no prior deliberation or contemplation. For example, my hunger (or whatever situation reminds me of my need to eat) and the subsequent need to make a living are enough to prompt me each day to go to school and pursue a course of study. There is no need for a constant envisaging in one's mind of the prospect of getting a degree, and the pleasure and bounty it is supposed to bring, or of the disappointments, one might feel if one fails at one's efforts at making a living. The person is so flexible that he constantly readjusts himself to the ever-changing world and its situations.

III

Meditation: The second context in which the role of thinking in non-dual living is relevant is when it is used in meditation as part of the process of dissolving duality.[5] No meditation is completely successful without developing a sense of total detachment. If attachment is the source of affective and existential duality, then detachment is a necessary condition for, although not a means to, non-duality. Detachment has two aspects to it: acceptance and renunciation. Acceptance is to let whatever happens to oneself be, not to attempt to change it into something else, not to regard it as something to be overcome. Renunciation is to let go of all the fascinations and attractions that one is attached to. These attachments are not always to "positive" things. For example, one may have an attachment to one's anger or hatred to a person. To renounce that is to let it go.

---

5. Strictly speaking, there are no means to achieve non-duality, for before thinking ever occurred we already were in a state of non-duality to begin with, and any means such as thinking, having to conceive non-duality as a goal, would only create further duality between the person and the goal. If thinking is an aid, it can only be one in the sense that it removes the impression that there is a goal of non-duality "out there" to be reached or achieved by countering the sense of duality. Only thinking can act as an antidote to thinking. Thus, thinking helps the rediscovery of one's true "natural" state. Of course, meditation and detachment cannot be regarded as a means to achieving liberation either. To regard them as a means is to attempt to deliberately create an effect or result through the means. And that implies a certain duality between oneself and the liberation one is trying to create through these means, as if liberation is something apart from oneself. However, detachment can be construed as a necessary condition for the removal of the duality that already exists, i.e., the feeling that liberation is "out there" for us to achieve. When our attachment toward this goal or any other goal goes, then nothing needs to be achieved. We are (and we always have been) what we are seeking for.

In the thinking process of becoming free from duality, letting my fear, guilt or anger out, I can dissolve my duality. If I am resisting or trying to avoid these, I also have my resistance as attachment. For instance, when I am dualistically separated from a person or situation, I resist the person or situation through my anger, guilt or fear. I normally become reflectively aware of my own anger, guilt, pain or fear and resist that. In contrast, in meditation, accepting my fear, accepting the threatening object, and accepting even my resistance to the fear can dissolve my sense of duality. I let them all be. If I cannot accept something, then I learn to accept the non-acceptance of it. That is, I learn to accept things at whatever level I am capable of.

If, on the other hand, my duality is created by the awareness of my non-attainment of an object or goal, which I cherish, I accept that non-attainment and my resistance to it. I can let the object of my attachment go by realizing how duality, and the consequent alienation, is created by attachment. I realize that the satisfaction of the needs of living has little to do with being attached to objects. Alternately, I can let go of my resistance to the object's non-attainment. I let go of my fear of losing things I am attached to. This is a movement of renunciation, a detachment in my consciousness. A freedom from the objects I am attached to, or the detachment is accompanied by the process of thinking. In other words, dualism of thought by itself is not the problem here. When I let things be, although I am aware of the object as an object, as well as my response to it, I am able to let my response be without putting up any further resistance to it. And thus, I attain a level of reflection without generating further subject-object duality.

For instance, I am dualistically aware of a painful disturbance within myself. I am also aware of the particular attachments, which have created this disturbance. My realization so far has been that it is my attachments that cause my disturbance; and that as long as I hold on to them my disturbance will remain. I also realize that I cannot renounce my attachments with an expectation to achieve any result. I can only let my attachments go and let my disturbance be. Any consequence of this I accept as a possibility. I may be freed from my disturbance; but then I may become disturbed again, or in a different fashion. Any detachment that occurs thus is not the result of a willful act, and thus does not create further attachment. Before, I was aware of my disturbance dualistically (affectively speaking), but now though I may still be aware of my disturbance, I am no longer resisting it. Therefore, there is no duality in an affective sense. If I notice that I am still resisting the disturbance, then I let my resistance be, and not resist that. Thus, I am non-dualistically aware of my disturbance. Although conceptually dualistic thinking may still be occurring, it now occurs in the general context or environment of non-duality.

I may not succeed in developing such a movement of detachment until I renounce, through reflection, my attachments to certain basic objects of desire such as reputation, money, power, achievement, sex, knowledge, as well as the fear of not attaining them, and the fear of death or non-being. (Such fundamental detachment, once developed, is what perhaps enables one to be detached from particular objects without effort.) Indeed, I may have to become free from the very attachment to living itself, and from the very urge to become. But one cannot make a goal of developing such a detachment either, for that too would be a self-centered goal, and hence will only result in further affective duality. Indeed, there may well be times when one cannot develop detachment, and attachments keep recurring. Then one is forced to develop a detachment toward the very urge to detach oneself. I must ultimately become free from the very idea of "freedom." In other words, one cannot attempt to use detachment as a means, a method or technique to create a certain result or effect.

To repeat, the role of thinking in "deconstructing" duality is clear. It is by means of thought that we "see" that it is attachment and the consequent "seeking," which cause duality. We are thus disillusioned with attachment and the process of striving for goals. We are disillusioned to the degree of abandoning all goals (including the goal of being free from all goals) and the seeking, which we use to reach those goals. It is not that we are disillusioned first and then that disillusionment leads to the abandonment of goals. The very disillusionment is simultaneously a renunciation of our goals and of our process of seeking them. Thus, it is itself not a deliberate process of goal seeking. This is how thought, to use David Loy's expression, "deconstructs"[6] itself. Then there is a total acceptance of one's emptiness, or whatever we see we are. Whatever facts we see about ourselves, we are able to let them be. We accept ourselves without any attempt to change ourselves into something better. When such total detachment occurs then duality dissolves itself.

Is such "deconstructive" thinking free from ego-centered motivation? If it is not, is it not dualistic, and therefore does it not create further dualism instead of dissolving the dualism that is already there? It is true that such thought operating in meditation is dualistic, being borne out of a consciousness of one's condition and out of the desire to be free from it. However, since it operates without any attempt to change the given into something other than the given, such thought does not "construct" the ego. Instead, since it attempts to "accept" (by allowing to happen) whatever is given, it "deconstructs"

---

6. See: Chapter 6 on "Deconstruction of Dualism" in David Loy, *Nonduality*, (New Haven, 1988).

the duality it operates upon, while at the same time, having no other object to become, it dissolves or deconstructs itself in the process. Until such deconstruction occurs, thinking not only must operate dualistically, but must perpetuate the dualism that is already there.

In such a process of detachment in meditation, from the point of view of the subject, there is no distinction between means and ends, since the whole approach is based on letting go of an object one is attached to, without seeking a further end. Because of such a detachment, there is no interest even in liberation. If there is no goal one is seeking, then there is a willingness to accept one's *saṁsāra* as *nirvāṇa*, and the search ends. From the point of view of the person who practises meditation, there is no difference between *saṁsāra* and *nirvāṇa*. *Saṁsāra* is *nirvāṇa* and *nirvāṇa* is *saṁsāra*.

Being free is where I end up if and only if being free is how I start. I may have achieved this by the mechanism of thought, but the process and the end result are non-dual. I may have to do this repeatedly, and consequently I may appear to be making progress from an outside observer's point of view. However, from my own point of view, in the process of meditation, either I am always here in the dualistic world, making distinctions between *saṁsāra* and *nirvāṇa*, or I am "there" where there is neither here nor there. When I am liberated, I have no awareness of my liberation. Then there is neither *saṁsāra* nor *nirvāṇa*. There may be a moment when such non-dual liberation is once and for all final and complete, but I would not be concerned about it.

IV

Philosophically one could still ask the question whether cognitive non-duality should be a part of liberation along with affective and existential non-dualities. The answer to this question is that, there is no model as to how a liberated person does or should live, and that whether or not his living includes occurrences of cognitive non-duality is not a concern for the liberated person. For the essence of liberation is to be free from affective and existential dualities, from the concerns of the self and its "fulfilment." Liberation brings freedom from such concerns, including the concern of solving metaphysical problems. The liberated person knows by now fully well that metaphysical questions as to the true nature of reality or of oneself, the "whys" and "wherefores" of existence, are all generated from the alienation which is part of existential duality, and that thought, itself being dualistic, cannot solve those problems. On the other hand, it may well be that he does not achieve total unity (or non-duality) except in moments of *samādhi*. Even so, one cannot live all his life in such states of *samādhi*. Short of this, non-duality in living, in action, and in relationship makes perfect sense if it is understood as affective and existential non-duality.

3

Consciousness, Cosmology, and Science
An Advaitic[1] Analysis

R. Puligandla

THE purpose of this brief essay is two-fold: (1) to clarify what it is to study anything scientifically and show that consciousness cannot, in principle, be studied scientifically, and (2) to examine the aim and methods of cosmology and show that cosmology cannot, in principle, be a science. The essay can be read by ignoring any and all references to Advaita Vedānta (non-dualistic Vedānta). My reason for referring to Advaita Vedānta is simply the fact that these two truths were long ago discovered and taught by Advaita Vedānta, which is at once *Jñāna-Yoga* (The Way of Knowledge) and mysticism, unsurpassed and unsurpassable.

Since I wish to place my observations on cosmology and scientific study of consciousness in the overall context of Advaita Vedānta, I shall simply state in a clear and concise manner the central notions (not concepts) and propositions of Advaita Vedānta.[2] *Brahman* is ultimate reality, whose varieties

---

1. Advaita means non-dual; accordingly, "Advaitic" is to be understood as non-dualistic.
2. Advaita Vedānta means non-dualistic Vedānta, founded in the Upaniṣads. The term Vedānta refers to the concluding parts of →

of manifestation are the worlds of phenomena. What is a phenomenon? Here is the Upaniṣadic definition: "Phenomenon is anything that is or can in principle be an object of consciousness." All phenomena exist in time and some phenomena also exist in space. Thus, tables, chairs, stars, galaxies, bacteria, college professors, etc. exist in both space and time, whereas thoughts, emotions, feelings, dreams, etc. exist only in time. *Brahman*, ultimate reality, is unborn, uncreated, undying, and hence timeless, eternal, and immortal. *Brahman* is formless and hence nameless; *Brahman* is not to be mistaken for the God(s) worshipped by people. Never was there a time when *Brahman* was not, nor will there be a time when *Brahman* will not be. *Brahman* is neither a She nor a He but the That (*Tat*). *Brahman* cannot be captured by the senses and mind, for whatever can be perceived and conceived is always an object. *Brahman* is impartite — not made up of parts; for if *Brahman* were partite (composite), the parts would be fundamental and ultimate and not *Brahman*. No one can picture or visualize *Brahman*, for whatever one can picture and visualize is always, inevitably and ineluctably, an object. *Brahman* thus transcends the senses, mind, space, time, and causality. Let it be emphasized that to say that *Brahman* is transcendent is not to say that *Brahman* is beyond our ken and pale, and cannot be experienced. Rather, to say that *Brahman*

→ the Vedas (also known as the Upaniṣads). The Vedas are the sacred writings of the Hindu tradition. The Vedas are mistakenly referred to as scriptures. "Scripture" is a Western concept meaning word of God. The Vedas are not word of God. It is for this reason that the Vedas are correctly referred to as "sacred writings." There is a sense in which the Vedas can be looked upon as revelation. However, revelation is not to be understood as something revealed to the human being by some source or agency outside of the human being. Rather, it is self-revelation, meaning truth revealing itself to itself; that is, truth and to whom it reveals itself are one and the same, non-different.

is transcendent is to say that *Brahman* cannot be experienced as one alongside other phenomena (objects). *Brahman* is to be experienced (realized) in non-dual intuition, by rendering the senses and mind quiescent through *Yoga*, the goal of which is to attain total cessation of mental modifications (*cittavr̥tti nirodha*). To clarify these observations further, simply imagine a potter making cups, saucers, pots, jars, pans, etc. These objects can be destroyed (made to disappear) but the clay of which they are made continues to exist. That is, these objects depend for their existence on the clay, but the clay does not depend for its existence upon these objects. Further, a pot can be destroyed and made into a dish. What has changed? That which was hitherto called a "pot" is now called a "dish." Thus, all changes are changes only in form and name, but not in that of which the objects are but appearances (forms and names).

Ātman is pure, objectless consciousness and is not to be mistaken for the ego (*jīva*). The ego is an object — a psycho-physiological composite. Sensations, perceptions, thoughts, feelings, emotions, etc. are all objects of consciousness (phenomena). They constantly arise and pass away, but consciousness remains the same. No one can perceive consciousness as an object; one can only notice changes in the objects of consciousness but never in consciousness itself. Consciousness (*ātman*), like *Brahman*, is formless and nameless. Hence, no one can picture or visualize consciousness. Thus, everything we have said about *Brahman*, of course only negatively, can also be said of consciousness: unborn, uncreated, undying, timeless, eternal, and immortal. Consciousness (*ātman*) is always singular; it is therefore absurd to talk about *ātman*s. Just like *Brahman*, *ātman* (consciousness) is transcendent, in the sense that it cannot be captured by the senses and mind. Different *jīva*s (sentient beings) are simply different appearances of *ātman* under the limiting conditions (*upādhi*) of the body-mind complex. The consciousness of, say, a cat, cannot be distinguished from the consciousness of a human being. Cats and human beings differ only in the ranges of objects they can be conscious of. The ranges are a function of the psycho-physiological make-up, there being absolutely no difference in consciousness itself. In the Western tradition, "consciousness," "mind," "self," and "I" are used synonymously.[3] According to Advaita, mind is not consciousness, but only a subtle sense-organ; it is an information-processing instrument. To put simply, mind is a phenomenon, whereas consciousness is not a phenomenon. Mind is not a box containing thoughts; rather, mind is no more and no less than thoughts arising and passing away. Our sense of time is grounded in the dynamic of mind. Only when the mind is rendered wholly quiescent, will there be no sense of time.

One might now wonder whether according to Advaita, there are two ultimate realities, namely, *Brahman* and *ātman*, the former underlying the so-called external world and the latter the so-called internal world. According to Advaita, the very idea of two ultimates is absurd, in the sense of self-contradiction. *Brahman* and *ātman* are simply two different labels for one and the same ultimate reality. To put otherwise, *Brahman* and *ātman* are non-different, just as Washington, D.C. and the capital of the USA are one and the same, non-different. The clearest argument (demonstration) that *Brahman* and *ātman* are non-different is to be found in the briefest and most famous

---

3. Thus, for example, Descartes says in *Meditation II*: "What then am I? I am a thinking thing; if I cease to think, thereupon I shall altogether cease to exist." (Descartes, R. (tr.) 1958) But he also proclaimed, "I think, therefore I am." Thus for Descartes, thinking is both a necessary and sufficient condition for existence. An Upaniṣadic sage would have asked Descartes, "Your teaching is interesting; however, I wish to know how you came to know that you cease to exist on ceasing to think."

Māṇḍūkya Upaniṣad. For the purposes of this essay, I need not go into the argument.[4]

Before proceeding further, it should be emphasized that Advaita distinguishes the higher truth (*pāramārthika-satya*) and lower truth (*vyavahārika-satya*). This distinction was most clearly formulated in the *Muṇḍaka Upaniṣad* (1.1.4-6). Lower truths are the product of the activity of the senses and mind, whereas the higher truth transcends the senses and mind, all perceptions and conceptions. Thus, all rational scientific truths are lower truths — *Muṇḍaka Upaniṣad* (1.1.4-6). "Lower truth" does not mean falsehood; rather, it means truth certifiable by all inquirers who are constituted alike and conduct their inquiry according to a certain categorical framework. It is truly remarkable that the *Muṇḍaka Upaniṣad* regards even the Vedas, the sacred writings of the Hindu tradition, as lower truth, insofar as the Vedas are couched in language (percepts and concepts). Further, there are many lower truths, since there are many phenomena and categorical frameworks; in contrast, there is just one higher truth, since there is just the non-dual, ultimate reality transcending all percepts and concepts. In the case of every lower truth, truth and being are separable; to give an example, the proposition "this board is black" is true, because there is a certain state of affairs, namely, this board's being black; however, in the case of the higher truth, no such separation is possible, for here truth and being are non-different. The higher truth, unlike the lower truth cannot be experienced and certified through the senses and mind, but only through non-dual intuition, in which the tripartite distinction of the knower, known, and the act of knowing, simply vanishes away. To put directly, in the higher truth one's being is the truth. Let it be emphasized that lower truth

4. For a detailed presentation and critical discussion of the argument, see Puligandla, 1999.

is not to be disparaged and belittled, for it is valid in its own domain. That is, we should most rigorously continue our rational-scientific inquiries.

I come now to the scientific study of consciousness. In the last few years, spates of books have been published on the scientific study of consciousness. Some of these are under cognitive studies, others under neurophysiologic studies, and yet others under philosophical studies. But none of them seems to deliver the goods they promise, namely, the findings of scientific study of consciousness. In a very real sense, I am provoked to write this essay by these disappointing works.

What is it to study anything scientifically? Scientific study involves a categorical framework[5] — primitive (undefined) terms, defined terms, a system of logic, axioms and postulates, and a set of criteria by which to determine whether a problem is genuine and a proposed solution acceptable. However, I have not encountered a single author who articulates the categorical framework underlying his study. I therefore assume that these authors take for granted the prevailing framework underlying all modern scientific inquiries.

Different sciences study different kinds of phenomena, physical, chemical, biological, mental, emotional, economic, political, and so on. As has been clarified earlier, a "phenomenon" may be defined as anything that is or can in principle be an object of consciousness. All phenomena exist in time and some also exist in space. This definition is at the very heart of the prevailing understanding and practice of scientific inquiry. Whatever one studies scientifically is always, inevitably, a phenomenon — an object of consciousness. Thus, anything that is given as an object of consciousness can be

5. For a full clarification of categorical framework, see Puligandla, 1997.

studied scientifically and anything that can be studied scientifically is given as an object of consciousness. Being given as a phenomenon — an object of consciousness — is thus both a necessary and sufficient condition for its scientific study. Furthermore, the scientific study of anything results in a description of the object, its structure, its properties, and its relations to other objects.

It is a fundamental fact of the phenomenology of our experience that consciousness is never given to us as an object. Therefore, the inescapable conclusion is that, in principle consciousness cannot be scientifically studied, in the prevailing understanding and practice of "scientific study."

Not being aware of this fundamental fact of the phenomenology of our experience, many self-proclaimed scientists and philosophers use such absurd phrases as "the phenomenon of consciousness" and "the structure of consciousness." Consciousness is not a phenomenon, an object, and hence cannot have a structure, properties, and relations. Have you ever perceived your consciousness as an object, in order for you to be able to describe its structure, properties, and relations?

It is not surprising, then, that people who claim to scientifically study consciousness and write books only end up talking about their observations on synapses, neuronal circuits, various perceptual, linguistic, and emotional centers, and so on, all of which are objects of consciousness. When a physicist studies a certain particle, he/she clearly gives us all the above. A biologist scientifically studying, for example, a genome also does the same. This is true of all scientists. Likewise, anyone who claims to study consciousness scientifically should also give us a description of consciousness, its structure, properties, and relations to other objects. Otherwise, it is an empty claim.

In this context, I would like to dispel a serious misunderstanding concerning *Yoga*. Many people mistakenly think that *Yoga*, in its various forms, including Patañjali's *Yoga*, is a scientific study of consciousness. *Yoga* is not a scientific study of consciousness, but of various states of consciousness — objects of consciousness. The aim of *Yoga* is to study varieties of modes of consciousness, ordinary as well as extraordinary, and learn to render the mind quiescent and still in order to be consciousness without objects.

Am I then saying that consciousness cannot be studied scientifically? Yes, that is precisely what I am saying, insofar as "scientific study" means study of phenomena, objects. Am I suggesting that we cannot engage in scientific investigation as we actually conduct it? Certainly not. To the contrary, we should rigorously continue scientific inquiries by which to discover various phenomena, their structures, properties, and relations, hitherto unknown.

My thesis that consciousness cannot, in principle, be studied scientifically is to be regarded as an impotency-principle (an impotency-principle is a statement that something cannot, in principle, be done). Examples of the impotency-principle are the second law of thermodynamics, Heisenberg's uncertainty principle, Gödel's second incompleteness theorem, etc.

There is, however, an important and significant difference between my impotency-principle and the others: my impotency-principle is directly based upon the phenomenology of our experience, whereas the others are based on logico-empirical considerations. Let me emphasize, however, that these logico-empirical considerations themselves are fully founded and grounded in the phenomenology of our experience.

If someone has an argument, along with adequate evidence, to refute the impotency-principle I have proclaimed here, I should be most happy to hear. All that one needs to do to refute my thesis is to come up with a single counter-example of something that is scientifically studied but not an object of consciousness. In light of such a counter example, I am prepared to withdraw my thesis.

Let me now place the above observations on the scientific study of consciousness in the context of Advaita Vedānta or non-dualistic Vedānta. The pivotal message of Advaita Vedānta, as has been explicated earlier, is that ultimate reality, *Brahman*, of which the myriad worlds are appearances, is non-different from *ātman*, pure, objectless consciousness. Neither *Brahman* nor *ātman* can be perceived by the senses and mind—unperceivable and inconceivable but can only be experienced in non-dual intuition, *prajña*, by rendering the mind wholly quiescent and still, through various yogic techniques.

Why there is something rather than nothing cannot be explained by science. Explanation, demonstration, argument, proof, etc. belong in the domain of the dual; and since *Brahman* is that beside which nothing can in principle exist, the existence of the world in the last analysis, as Śaṅkara[6] long ago taught us, is *anirvachanīya* — indefinable and inexplicable. This is the reason for cosmologies becoming mere stories. Thus, no one can explain what caused the Big Bang; for space, time, and matter came into existence with the Big Bang, and therefore there cannot, in principle, be any talk of cause and effect prior to the Big Bang (if I may be permitted to use the term "prior"

6. Śaṅkara (seventh-eighth AD) is generally regarded as the founder of Advaita Vedānta i.e., non-dualistic interpretation of the Upaniṣads. He systematized and formulated the central insights of the Upaniṣads into Advaita Vedānta (non-dualistic Vedānta). It should, however, be noted that Bādarāyaṇa, Gauḍapāda, and Govindapāda, the predecessors of Śaṅkara, articulated the non-dualistic insights of the Upaniṣads.

here). Yes, cosmologists tell us that the Big Bang happened because of spontaneous quantum-fluctuations. But is this really an explanation? Certainly not. We cannot have, in principle, any initial conditions by which to explain the Big Bang; and even if we accept some explanation, as to how the Big Bang took place, that does not explain how the primordial singularity in which the Big Bang took place came to be. Let it be emphasized that the primordial singularity is neither spatial nor temporal, for space, time, matter, and causality come into being with the Big Bang. Hence, *Brahman*, ultimate reality, is inexplicable. Since *Brahman* is non-different from *ātman* pure, objectless consciousness, *ātman* too cannot be explained by science, for like *Brahman*, *ātman* cannot be an object of consciousness and therefore cannot be scientifically studied. Every discipline that is genuinely scientific will have laws, formulated by systematically studying the reproducible and repeatable (phenomena); and since the cosmos as a whole is not reproducible and replicable, cosmology cannot, in principle, be a science as "science" is understood and practised.

Since Advaita Vedānta, has its foundations in the Upaniṣads, the oldest recorded documents about mysticism, I hereby wish to make some pertinent observations on religion. It is to be emphasized that *Brahman* (*ātman*) is not God (*Īśvara*, creator, preserver, destroyer, and judge of the world). God is merely a conception of the inconceivable. Different religious traditions are centered around different conceptions of the inconceivable. Hence different religions and different Gods, each religion claiming that its own conception is the true and real conception and condemning other peoples' religions as false. No wonder, then, that people from one religious tradition try to convert others; and if conversion cannot be achieved through persuasion, they will resort to any means they deem fit, including violence. In this manner, arise religious wars, resulting in unspeakable bloodshed and horrors.

If unity were to be found among different religious traditions, it could only be found at the mystical level, never at the level of doctrines and dogmas; and all religious traditions have two sides, the exoteric (the public and visible) and the esoteric (the private, invisible and mystical). Mystical experience comes only by transcending doctrines, dogmas, and authorities. Doctrines, dogmas, and authorities only give you second-hand truth, which is always open to the assault of doubt and therefore can be lost. Only truth certifiable through one's own authentic experience is first-hand truth. Mystics from all traditions exhort us to attain the first-hand truth, by transcending all conceptions of ultimate reality, non-different from one's true being, *ātman*. Mysticism is marginal and peripheral in religious traditions controlled by central authorities. The Vedic (Upaniṣadic) tradition is unique in its emphasis upon the mystical experience and therewith first-hand truth. Hence, Advaita Vedānta is the mystical tradition, par excellence.

People should remain in the traditions they inherit and must earnestly pursue the way of the mystics and hence first-hand truth. Converting other people to one's own religious tradition is the highest violence and indignity one can inflict on other human beings. Converting people to one's own religious tradition is the hallmark of ignorance (*avidyā*). First-hand truth is too important to be left for others to determine. Consciousness (*ātman*) and ultimate reality (*Brahman*), not being phenomena (objects), are the higher truth and therefore cannot be scientifically studied.

To conclude, (1) consciousness cannot, in principle, be studied scientifically; (2) cosmology cannot, in principle, be a science, and (3) since Advaita Vedānta had long ago discovered and taught these two truths and consequently unflinchingly recommends the transcendence of all conceptions of ultimate reality (*Brahman, ātman*), Advaita Vedānta is at once *Jñāna-Yoga* (The Way of Knowledge) and mysticism, unsurpassed and unsurpassable, being the oldest of all mystical traditions of the world.

References

Descartes, R., (tr.), 1958, "Meditations on First Philosophy," tr. by Norman Kemp Smith, in *Descartes: Philosophical Writings*, New York: Modern Library.

Swami Gambhirananda, (tr.) 1977, *Brahma-Sūtra Bhāṣya of Śaṅkarācārya*, Calcutta: Advaita Asrama.

———, (tr.) 1977, *Eight Upaniṣads with the Commentary of Śaṅkarācārya*, vol. 2, Calcutta: Advaita Asrama.

Merrell-Wolff, F., 1973, *The Philosophy of Consciousness Without an Object: Reflections on the Nature of Transcendental Consciousness*, New York: The Julian Press.

Puligandla, R., 1997, *Jñāna-Yoga, The Way of Knowledge*, An Analytical Interpretation, Delhi: D.K. Printworld.

———, 1999, "The Message of the Māṇḍūkya Upaniṣad, A Phenomenological Analysis of Mind and Consciousness," in *Indian Philosophical Quarterly*, 25, pp. 221-31.

4

The Advaitic Understanding of Self and Human Rationality

K. Srinivas

I

HUMAN rationality at empirical level has two important dimensions, viz. moral and scientific. The modern man is completely under the sway of scientific rationality; and such an effect results in the erosion of basic human values, which are necessary for the overall development and furtherance of humankind. In such a situation, what becomes imperative is a careful and assiduous cultivation of values, which not only promote worldly comforts and material success but also an intellectual and moral/spiritual personality. The present crisis of man, in fact, is more mental than material. In spite of the fact that modern Western psychologists have done admirable work on human personality (empirical self) by reducing it to a series of behaviorist patterns or dispositions, they are yet to go a long way to get the kernel of truth. The frustration experienced by modern man is not merely due to sexual oppression as enunciated by the psychoanalysts like Freud, but due to the suppression of spiritual urges, which are an integral part of his personality. The unmitigated passion for scientific knowledge makes our modern education merely an art exclusively meant for a decent or comfortable living. However, it appears that the laws of nature do not seem to approve of this one-sided progress of human personality. Although the scientific achievements seem to alleviate the physical strains of the individuals by providing material comforts, they definitely result in an increasing poverty in the realm of higher human values. Thus, scientific rationality with its excessive emphasis on objectivity legitimizes our present form of education, which has mere material value. The lopsided development of human societies can be arrested only when we realize the importance of moral/spiritual values.

Unlike in the West, psychology in Indian philosophical traditions was not segregated from philosophy, which is primarily the philosophy of life. As an integral part of the latter, the former has much to offer in terms of overall personality development of an individual. Thus, its approach to human development is holistic rather than fragmentary or piecemeal. Human being in Indian philosophical traditions is regarded as a combination of spiritual and material components. The former represents the eternal metaphysical principle called the self (*ātman*/I — consciousness/spirit/being) and the latter the primordial matter, which is called *prakṛti*, constituted by *sattva*, *rajas*, and *tamas*. The bedrocks of the orthodox Indian philosophical traditions, the Upaniṣads contain speculations about the self as conscious principle. Those speculations form the basis for Indian psychology. However, they are not empty speculations about the highest reality. In fact, what is experientially encountered is rationalized. But in some cases what is rationalized from the source of authority or testimony (*śabda*) is experientially discovered. However, in either case the reflective thinking has become an instrument of speculation.[1] The distinctive feature of psychology in Indian philosophical traditions is that it distinguishes the Self from mind (*manas/antaḥkaraṇa*). The former is truly spiritual in its nature and the latter material or corporeal. Therefore, any attempt to reduce mind to spiritual substance would result in a meaningless exercise.

The self is the basic residue that the individual experiences when he gets behind all mental functions or modifications called *vṛttis*, which can be objectified. According to Indian psychology, self-realization in literal sense is possible. The possibility and desirability of such an experience forms the crux of the Indian psyche. Mind, unlike the self, belongs to lower order of reality and is the connecting link between the self and the world of nature. If this distinction between the self and mind is not noticed, the psychology of Indian philosophical traditions cannot be understood. Thus, one notices a total paradigm shift in understanding the psychology in Indian traditions as opposed to the Western psychology.

What we call human personality or empirical self or ego (*Jīva*) is the self, associated with the mind-body-sense complex. This empirical self or personality possesses reflective thinking, for it is conditioned or controlled by mind. Another salient feature of psychology in Indian philosophical traditions is that mind is understood more from within. Thus, it is inward rather than outward or behaviorist approach that makes the subject of experience completely conscious of its own actions. This inward approach may be called variously as intuition, self-reflection, and introspection. The choice is left to the respective philosophical traditions. Such an inward approach makes the individual more responsible and accountable for each of his

---

1. S.C. Chatterjee and D.M. Datta, An *Introduction to Indian Philosophy*, Calcutta: University of Calcutta, 1984, eighth edn., p. 8.

actions. In fact, this approach of psychology in Indian philosophical traditions differentiates education for life from education for mere living. The former is concerned with the overall development of human personality, and the latter is only interested in the material comforts of the individuals. The above introduction serves as a main backdrop of this paper. In this paper, I propose to take up the issues related to the analysis of the self as found in the Upaniṣads, which are the fountains of the orthodox Indian philosophical systems. In the process, the self is distinguished from the empirical self or human personality. Self-analysis and reflective thinking as found in the psychology of Indian traditions is also highlighted with a view to distinguish the approach of Indian psychology from that of the West.

II

According to the psychology of Indian philosophical traditions, only the self is treated as spiritual, and is considered the highest metaphysical principle to be realized. Hence, it is opposed to anything that is material or corporeal in its nature. Mind being a part of physical body cannot exist apart from the latter. But in the West, especially in the writings of Descartes, the chief attribute of the mind is thought and the matter is an extension. In other words, mind being non-material in its nature is treated as spiritual. Thus, it has an independent existence apart from matter (body). Descartes identified mind in its pure form with pure-ego (disembodied self). Such an approach to mind is unacceptable to the psychology of Indian philosophical traditions. Although there are subtle differences among the various systems of Indian philosophy in interpreting the nature of the self, except Cārvākas and Buddhists, what is generally agreed upon is that the self and mind are two distinct entities representing the higher and lower levels of world order. What is most striking in the psychology of Indian traditions is that, the self as pure consciousness operates through the medium called mind (*manas*).[2] In a way, the activities of mind come to a standstill if it is not associated with the self. Thus, the basic epistemic activity of human beings, which involves reflective thinking, is possible because of this conscious principle called the self. On the contrary, in the Western psychology mind is treated as a conscious principle responsible for cognitions and conations in general.

In the context of the analysis of the self in the philosophical traditions of India, the dictum "know thy self" becomes important for every reflective individual. Reflection as the essence of reason is always inward or internal. As mentioned earlier, barring Cārvākas and Buddhism that do not believe in the existence of the self, all other Indian philosophical systems are unanimous in their view that the self is different from mind (*manas*). Again, here when we talk about the self, the conscious principle called the self is different from the empirical self or ego. The latter is only a shadow of the former. One has to bear this distinction in mind. Regarding the self, which is the innermost essence of man, we come across the following injunction in the *Chāndogya Upaniṣad*.

> The self (*ātman*) which is free from evil, free from old age, free from death, free from grief, free from hunger and thirst, whose desire is the real, whose thoughts are true, he should be sought. Him, one should desire to understand, He who has found out and who understands that self; he obtains all worlds and desires.[3]

---

2. M. Hiriyanna, *Indian Philosophy of Values*, Mysore: Kavyalaya Publishers, 1975, p. 28.
3. *Chāndogya Upaniṣad*, 7. 7. 1; in S. Radhakrishnan (tr.), *The Principal Upaniṣads*, London: Allen and Unwin, 1953.

Therefore, the search for this ultimate metaphysical principle called the self is essentially a matter of going deeper and deeper into the very foundations of human existence.

In the third, fourth and fifth *mantras* of the *Māṇḍūkya Upaniṣad*[4] we come across an interesting explanation about nature of the self through the triple stream of experience (*avastha-traya-vicāra*), These three states of experience are waking (*jāgrat*), dream (*svapna*), and deep sleep (*suṣupti*). This Upaniṣad states that the self as a conscious principle is pervasive in all the three states of experience. A person can narrate his experiences provided he is conscious of them. In order to be conscious of his experiences he must possess consciousness. The self as conscious principle is called *Vaiśvanara* in the state of waking experience. In this state, consciousness is always oriented or directed towards some object or the other. Thus, it is always intentional. Therefore, we know consciousness as the consciousness of this or that object. The mind-sense complex is the aid or instrument through which this consciousness functions or operates to experience the objects of gross nature.

In the dream state, despite the fact that senses do not function, mind functions. Like in the waking state, even in the state of dream consciousness is intentional for it is oriented or directed towards the objects of dream, which are nothing but the impressions of our day-to-day waking experience stored in mind. They are only the impressions projected by mind. The self as a conscious principle is known as *Taijasa* in this state.

In the deep sleep state, along with senses, mind is also withdrawn. A person does not experience any object, internal or external, gross or subtle. But when he wakes up from the state of deep sleep he simply utters, "I had nice sleep." In

---

4. *Māṇḍūkya Upaniṣad*, 3. 4. 5.

other words, he did not know anything. There was no object presented to his consciousness. The absence of objects does not mean the absence of consciousness. It i.e. consciousness is present all through in the form of *prajña,* for otherwise the person concerned would not have uttered, "I had nice sleep." To quote from *Māṇḍūkya Upaniṣad:*

> That state is deep sleep where the sleeper does not desire any enjoyable thing, and does not see any dream. The third quarter is Prajña whose sphere is deep sleep, who remains one and undifferentiated who is a mass of mere consciousness who is full of bliss who experiences bliss, and who is the doorway to the experience (of the dream and waking states).[5]

What is remarkable in this analysis of the self is that it distinguishes deep sleep state from other two states of experience, namely, waking and dreaming. Unlike in waking and dreaming states, there are no objects to be presented to the consciousness in the state of deep sleep. The self as a conscious principle in deep sleep state is one, unified and undifferentiated. In other words, it is non-relational, non-intentional. The state of deep sleep can be termed as the state of bliss, which represents the true nature of the self. Although it is a state of bliss, it is not permanent since the state of deep sleep is not permanent. In spite of this fact that the self as conscious principle is present in all the three states, its presence is unnoticed by us. These three states of experience are transcended by the fourth state called *turīya*. The real nature of the self is known only in this state. The self as conscious principle transcends the ontological, theological, and other limitations. Therefore, it cannot be described positively as this or that.

---

5. *Ibid.*, 5.

Similarly, in the *Taittirīya Upaniṣad*[6] we come across an interesting analysis of the self as conscious principle. The empirical self or human personality is composed of five sheaths (*kośas*). They are — the sheath of matter (*Annamaya-kośa*), the sheath of life (*Prāṇamaya-kośa*), the sheath of conscious activity (*Manomaya-kośa*), the sheath of intelligence (*Vijñānamaya-kośa*), and the sheath of bliss (*Ānandamaya-kośa*). Each succeeding sheath is a self of the preceding sheath, which forms its body. As far as the empirical self or personality is concerned, the sheath of matter is responsible for physical and gross body, and the sheath of life for the five organs of action and the five *prāṇas*. The sheath of conscious activity is responsible for five organs of sense, and the sheath of intelligence for intellect (*buddhi*) and five sense organs. The sheath of bliss is responsible for the individual *a-vidyā* dissociated from the bodily and mental functions. The self is enveloped by all these five sheaths. Out of these the first sheath constitutes the gross body (*sthūla-śarīra*), the second, third and fourth constitute subtle body (*sūkṣma-śarīra*), and the fifth constitutes the causal body (*kāraṇa-śarīra*). The purpose of this analysis is to show that the self as conscious principle cannot be equated with matter, life, mind, and intellect. It is "different from and within that which consists of the understanding is the self, consisting of bliss."[7] Therefore, the self cannot be equated with any of the lower forms of the person exclusively, but is to be regarded as existing within the various layers of existence, giving them existence in the form of life while remaining distinct from them.

In the *Kena Upaniṣad*, the inquiry into the nature of the self takes the form of a search for an ultimate agent or doer of human activity. It is asked: "By whom willed and directed

---

6. *Taittirīya Upaniṣad*, 2.

7. *Ibid.*, 2. 5. 1.

does the mind light on its objects? By whom commanded does life the first, move? At whose will do (people) utter the speech? and what God is it that prompts the eye and the ear."[8] All these questions are answered with an emphatic assertion that there is a basic self that instructs the eye to colour, the ear to sound, the understanding to consciousness. And this self is "other than known and other than unknown."[9] The most important of the questions asked above is the question: What is that which directs all the human activities? It is not easy to answer this question as "there the eye goes not, speech goes not nor the mind; we know not we understand not how one can teach this."[10] Since the self is not an object known to the human subject, it cannot be apprehended by the eye, ear, and reason. It is the ultimate subject. It cannot be known, but can only be realized in total self-consciousness. This self is self-luminous. As an ultimate revealing principle of the presence and absence of objects, it is transcendentally *a priori*, and is known as the subject, but not in the sense of "knower" or "cognizer" (*jñāta* or *pramata*). It is a permanent subject. Anything other than the self is only an object. In the language of Wittgenstein[11] it can be called "the metaphysical subject." What is most striking in the above analysis of the self is that the self as conscious principle (transcendental "*I*") is to be distinguished from the empirical self (empirical "*I*"), which is bound by the limitations such as mind-body-sense complex. The Western psychologists equate this ego or empirical "*I*" with the self.

---

8. *Kena Upaniṣad*, 2.
9. *Ibid.*, 14.
10. *Ibid.*, 13.
11. The twentieth-century philosopher of language, Ludwig Wittgenstein calls the metaphysical subject Transcendental "I" in his *Tractates Logico-Philosophicus*. This metaphysical subject, according to him, is outside the bounds of this empirical world.

III

In contrast to the metaphysical subject (the self) mind is an entity that knows, feels, and wills. In our common parlance, it is treated as a subject opposed to all that is external to it. However, the psychology of Indian traditions is that they view mind as a subject in a limited or secondary sense. Because of its proximity to the ever-conscious principle (the self), mind becomes conscious. In other words, its consciousness is borrowed one. Hence it is endowed with cognitive power. The internal organ or mind (*antaḥkaraṇa/manas*)[12] performs four important functions (*vṛttis*). Depending upon its functions it is variously called mind (*manas*), intellect (*buddhi*), ego (*ahaṁkāra*), and the memory-stuff (*citta*). Although the internal organ is one single entity, its functions are four-fold. The function of *manas* is to doubt, analyze, or synthesize whatever is perceived by the senses. For instance, when an object is perceived by the senses, *manas* doubts whether it is this or that object. The function of *buddhi* is to make an assertion or to take a decision with regard to the status of an object given in sense-experience. For instance, the judgment "This is a pen" is the *result* of the decision of *buddhi*. The function of *ahaṁkāra* is to attribute "I"-ness, and that of *citta* is to present the given sense-experience in a unified appreciative mass. When an object is perceived, *manas* assumes the form of the object in question and offers it to *buddhi*. In turn, *buddhi* offers it to *citta*. Finally, *ahaṁkāra* appropriates it as a form of its own perception. Such a mechanism reveals the dynamic nature of the internal organ.[13]

---

12. According to Advaitins, internal organ (*antaḥ-karaṇa*) *is not* identical with mind (*manas*). In fact, mind is one of the functions (*vṛttis*) of internal organ.
13. P.T. Raju, "Nature of Mind and Its Activities," in Bhattacharya (ed.), *Cultural Heritage of India*, Calcutta: The Ramakrishna Institute of Indian Culture, 1983, p. 507.

The knowledge obtained by the functions of the internal organ can be communicated, for there is a subject to communicate it in the form of empirical self or human personality, and our language is so designed for this purpose. Our knowledge at this level is rational and relational. Therefore, every linguistic expression that we make represents whatever is grasped by our intellect through the internal organ. But behind all these functions there is the self or the transcendental "*I*." The knowledge obtained by means of internal organ is finite, relative, transient, mediate, and informative. The knowledge by mediation is empirical, pragmatic, and always presupposes subject-object polarity.

This secondary subject can be called human personality or empirical self or ego. As empirical individuals living in the world of actions, we have to discipline this ego or human personality. This results in self-analysis. The empirical "I," unlike the transcendental "I," is a composite of both spiritual and material elements. It derives its spirituality due to the presence of indwelling self, which is nothing but pure consciousness; and its materiality is due to the mind-body-sense complex, which is made up of the *guṇa*s called *sattva*, *rajas*, and *tamas*. The material element in empirical self obscures its spiritual nature due to ignorance (*a-vidyā*). Thus the empirical self is dragged into the world of action and are lured by the things of the world and attaches undue importance to them. Such a world of action requires a common ethical code as a measure to distinguish right actions from wrong ones. An ethical code becomes imperative and indispensable insofar as the world of action is concerned in which the human personality or empirical self acts as a moral agent.

In order to discipline the human personality or empirical self, the psychology of Indian traditions has recognized four basic human goals or aims (*puruṣārtha*s). They are — moral law (*dharma*), means of life (*artha*), enjoyment (*kāma*), and liberation (*mokṣa*). A reflective human personality is one who pays attention to these four human goals. He alone can lead an authentic life. He knows the meaning of life. These goals indeed make an empirical self or human personality a complete human being. *Dharma* literally means that which supports or bears. It is an over-arching principle that regulates the instrumental values called *artha* and *kāma,* which have mere extrinsic value. It is the moral duty of every individual to abide by *dharma* as a rule of human conduct. It provides us with the rules for settling social disputes and possible conflict, between individuals and groups to maintain harmony in the society. Thus, *dharma* has social significance.

But human beings cannot just live by righteousness and justice alone. They require material comforts (*artha*) and enjoyment of pleasures (*kāma*). *Artha* as one of the basic goals of human life refers to whatever means are necessary for human life. The emphasis is mainly on biological and social life. The acquisition of material wealth is permitted within the limits of *dharma.* It is the natural inclination of every human individual to strive after the satisfaction of the genuine desires. But these desires have to be regulated in the interest of society in which human beings live as an organic whole.

Mokṣa is the highest of all the goals. Every spiritual aspirant aims at this goal in order to free himself from the bondage of life and death. One has to realize that he is not merely body, merely biological life, merely social organism, and so on. One has to realize that he is not different from the Self. But, how can one realize this truth? There are various ways and means. The material adjunct in empirical self is the combination of three different tendencies called *sattva, rajas* and *tamas* that combine in varying proportions. *Sattva-guṇa* is responsible for intellectual activity, *rajas* for courage or chivalry, and *tamas* for dullness. Different personality types found among the empirical selfs are due to the varying combinations of these *guṇas*. It is important to notice here that the personality type belongs to each and every empirical self, which is psycho-physical in its nature. The way of discipline differs from one personality type to the other. Therefore, all the three ways — *karma, jñāna,* and *bhakti* are equally important for the self-realization.

Although it is held that hearing (*śravaṇa*), repetition (*manana*) and profound reflection (*nidhi-dhyāsana*) are pre-requisites for any spiritual aspirant, they can also be made mandatory for any type of learning process even in this world of action. One who follows this course of training would be successful in translating his ideals into concrete realities. And these ideals must be correlated with the basic human goals or aims (*puruṣārthas*) to make one's life meaningful and authentic rather than dry and purposeless. Ideals are not meant for reification, but must be realized as concrete realities, for otherwise they remain as utopian. The psychology of Indian philosophical systems is not interested in creating ideals for the sake of ideals. Its approach is praxis-oriented.

To conclude, in Indian philosophical systems we come across a different kind of psychology, which is *ātman*-centric. Unlike the Western psychologists, the psychological approach in Indian traditions is inward rather than outward. This approach mainly aims at distinguishing what is eternal from what is non-eternal. It emphasizes more on the ideals of life to lead a life of wisdom rather than the life of mere material comforts. Indian philosophical traditions offer different philosophies of life to suit the temperament and inner constitution of the individuals. The psychology behind these philosophies of life is to realize internally, through reflective thinking, the meaning and purpose of human life. Therefore, it is a total misconception if one thinks that Indian philosophical traditions are more interested in constructing obscure and abstruse metaphysical theories, which are empty claims about the nature of ultimate reality, world, and human being. It is only through personal experience (*anubhūti*) that one can judge the veracity of these theories.

Section - II
Advaita Epistemology, and Ethics

5

Śaṅkara Vedānta on Śruti, Tarka, and Adhyāsa

Bijayananda Kar

ŚAṄKARA has mainly propounded the Advaita perspective of Vedānta, while commenting upon the source books of Vedānta-*Brahma-Sūtra*, the Upaniṣads and the *Bhagavad-Gītā*. To understand his philosophic position, it is of prime necessity to read his commentaries. However, while going through the Sankarite expressions, one comes across different meanings, which, at least, appear mutually inconsistent. For instance, his statement that *Brahman* alone is real seems to be incoherent with the admittance of three grades of reality — *paramārthika, vyavahārika* and *pratibhāsika*. There are other issues which can neither be solved nor resolved and are simply being confined to the texts. Therefore, in the Indian philosophic tradition, more emphasis has been given to analytical and critical reasoning (*samīkṣātmaka vivecanā*) through *bhāṣya*s (commentaries) than on simply being restricted to the original texts. In that way, change or modification is rather inbuilt in the philosophic trend in India, which paved the way for innovation and creativity. Thereby it differed from uncritical dogmatism and authoritarianism.

In certain quarters it is held that reason in Śaṅkara has never occupied the primary position; and for them its role is considered to be secondary; and its relevance is admitted insofar as it helps to understand the scriptures (*Śruti*). In that case, what was the necessity for Śaṅkara to advance arguments/reasoning to criticize the rival philosophic viewpoints? Moreover, Śaṅkara himself has remarked clearly that *Śruti-vākya*s (sentences of the scriptures) cannot change one thing into another thing, and has nothing to do with the matters of the empirical world. *Vidyā* (knowledge), according to him, is the knowledge of empirical objects as it is *vastu svarūpa avadhāraṇa* but not what the scripture holds. For Śaṅkara empirical knowledge is not based dogmatically on any scriptural source, as scriptures are valid only insofar as what is not found in the physical world? Thus, Śaṅkara's approach to *Śruti* is (as also true to Indian philosophical setting) never unconditional but conditional; it is critical and not dogmatic. What he clearly indicates is that Vedānta, if rationally and critically viewed, must be Advaitic, and not anything else. Furthermore Śaṅkara (like others) does not take all the Vedānta *vākya*s (sentences of the scriptures) into consideration, but made use of those sentences and selections, which are suitable to his own philosophical position. As a commentator, his aim is to establish the philosophical position by taking recourse to *pramāṇa* or standard of validity to establish Advaita perspective of Vedānta.

Of course, while referring to *pramāṇa*s, the ordinary modes of knowledge such as sense perception, and inference, etc., were not dealt within the Advaita philosophical context. Such modes were not considered because those were considered useless and misleading, and have their own sphere of use and application in the empirical context. However, reasoning, in a deeper technical sense, is rather employed in the Advaita *darśana*, all through. There is no dogmatic, trans-rational backing of the *Śruti* passages; rather Śaṅkara never discarded reason. However, bare ratiocination (*ku-tarka*) is avoided. To reject reason outrightly and to succumb to blindfaith or dogma may be the concern of a stubborn theist and a rigid atheist (iconoclast), but that is never so for a philosopher. At least a philosopher is well aware of the logical boundaries of faith and reason. That is why to expose Advaita *darśana* in a trans-rational footing, according to me, is to do disservice it. Further, while following the track of reason, if a *dārśanika* (Śaṅkara Advaita is included) falls outside the track of reason, there is nothing wrong to point out that to remain critical on that specific issue.

Some have systematically made confusion between the concept of reality and truth (at least in some writings on Indian philosophy). Even in Sanskrit usage, though terms like *sat* and *satta* have the common root (*as*), the logical implication in both cases is strikingly different, and the *dārśanika*s are not unaware of that. Similar is the case with the terms like *mukti* and *mokṣa*. Both of them have the common root *muc*. While *mukti* is common, and adopted by many classical Indian philosophers for explaining their account of liberation, *mokṣa* remains a technical concept, befitting the typical philosophical standpoint of Advaita. However, later on, both the terms are used indiscriminately in certain writings.

Let us consider, for instance, Śaṅkara's statement *yat viṣaya buddhi na vyabhicārati tat sat*, which says that wherever the intellect prevails on a subject, there shall not be any unsubstantial, incorrigible, interpolation. Though popularly it is held in certain circles to be a criterion of reality, it is misleading for the simple reason that truth or falsity is applicable to what is asserted, while reality or unreality is applicable to what appears. We do distinguish between real and appearance by having certain criteria. There is nothing wrong and improper to state the rope to be real and the rope appearing as snake is appearance and not real. The ordinary and usual way of distinguishing between the real and the appearance is never questioned by him. He never challenges the objectivity of rope and the subjectivity of snake.

The Advaita philosophical stand is, if the snake-cognition is illusory appearance and not real, then the appearance of rope too is also conditioned and never be free from limiting adjuncts. That is how one can never know the object as it is, and that is how, from a logical perspective the sceptical arguments against the validity of empirical knowledge are advanced by Śaṅkara. His challenge is not factual but logical. Śaṅkara never denies the actuality of the world phenomena with all its diversities and multiplicities. It is very much real on its own account; and only for his typical philosophical position (Advaita *dṛṣṭi*), the challenge has been made. *Paramārtha* is to be understood in a philosophic and technical sense, not denouncing the world as illusion as popularly (rather superficially) treated; and Advaita, for that, has been unduly castigated. It is to be marked that the Advaitin raises certain conceptual issues at the technical field, i.e., epistemology. If one declares snake-perception as mere appearance, then why rope-perception be regarded as real and not appearance? Is it not that rope-perception also means rope appearance? If appearance is common to both the veridical and illusory perceptions, then why is one held as real and the other as illusory? In other words, the point that rose in the circle of *darśana* is not perceptual but conceptual. Śaṅkara challenges the conceptual setting and offers a prescription that *satya* must be so defined and must not have any change or interpolation (*vyabhicāra*). It must be *a-vyabhicāri*. Neither rope is true (*sat*/*satya*) nor snake is false (*a-satya*/*mithyā*); but to state rope as rope is *satya* and to state rope as snake or anything other than rope is *mithyā*. This is what is implied by Śaṅkara's saying; *atasmin tad buddhi*; and the rival philosophers too accept this.

That is the reason why in the classical Indian philosophic context, never it is stated that object is either *sat* or *asat*, it is the cognitive content, i.e., statement/judgment which is either said to be *jñāna* proper (*satya*) or it is *mithyā*. To put in a word, there is the acceptance of the expression: *mithyā-jñāna* but not *mithyā-vastu*. The whole discussion of error in Indian philosophical context is very much plausible and significant in the epistemic front and it has been unnecessarily, rather misleadingly extended to an ontological level (in certain quarters) by adopting (rather mis-adopting) a material mode of speech.

It is said that knowledge is a judgment, whether true or false; and even a false judgment refers to a real object. Śaṅkara's expression *avabhāṣa* is interpreted by Vacaspati (Bhamati) as that appearance which is terminated or depreciated (*avasanna* or *avamata*) is illusory cognition. Now the formulation: illusory cognition may be misleading, if it is treated that the appearance in this context is *mithyā* or wrong. Appearance of rope as snake is not wrong. Sometimes the rope does appear as snake. Even after the illusory cognition is withdrawn, the rope appears as snake. The difficulty lies in the judgmental level when the appearance is mis-rendered, i.e., what appears in a grade may not be appropriate according to another criterion. The appearance is neither true nor false; but the judging of the appearance as "A" or "not A" is either true or false. In fact, truth or falsity belongs to the judging aspect and not to the presentational aspect. The Advaitin does not object the ordinary notion between truth and falsity, but he challenges the criteria on which such concepts are applied. If snake-judgment is withdrawn on its being sublimated, then the rope-judgment can also be challenged on the ground of its sublimation. Hence any judgmental formulation, based on the coupling of *viṣaya* (predicate) and *viṣayī* (subject) is from the root improper and inappropriate. This is pointed out when it is held that the coupling of two opposing entities gives rise to error, *mithyeti bhavituṁ yuktaṁ*. Thus, it can be seen that the Advaitic challenge is rooted in the logico-linguistic conceptual source and not on the factual plane. To say that *jagat-mithyā* does not have any factual bearing, and the world in fact, is never regarded to be illusory (*mithyā*) — is a misleading interpretation. *Mithyatva* or falsity of the world is significant in the epistemic judgmental level and to put it in ontology in the manner in which it has been made in certain quarters is to mess its philosophic profundity.

Prakāśātman has brought to focus the valid point (that is implied by Śaṅkara himself) by holding that the erroneous relation in performing actions by the doer and enjoyer (*anarthaśca pramatrta pramukhaṁ kartr̥tva bhoktr̥tvaṁ*) constitutes *Adhyāsa* (superimposition). This is important, for it thereby brings to the focus the Advaita message that *Adhyāsa* virtually refers to a rectification in the valuation perspective, i.e., critically viewing *ahaṁbhāva* (egoistic feeling of possessiveness) that gives rise to the evils of life (*anartha*). *Anartha* may mean negation of object or meaning; but, in the present context, it signifies ills of life from the valuation perspective. Śaṅkara does not suggest escape from the worldly living status, but a re-look to life with a sense of detachment (*anāsakta*) but neither non-involvement/indifference (*udāsīna*) nor non-activity (*akarmānyata*).

It is said that the theory of in-determinability of Advaita is set to explain the phenomenon of erroneous cognition and its object. Such a remark is not philosophically warranted. This view appears to be compelling only when one treats the object of illusion as either existent (real) or non-existent (unreal) or both; and finds difficulty in one of these alternatives. But the rope-snake is neither a physical existent object nor even a metaphysical entity. Rope appears as snake because of misjudging. It is not that snake appears and the rope does not appear. Both occur in the sense-field; but mistake lies in judging one as another. It seems that in-determinability refers to the ordinary empirical judgment from a typical Advaita point of view. According to that, the judgment can neither be treated as true nor false, nor both true and false, and hence indeterminable. It seems to have a point of resemblance with the current saying that no synthetic/empirical judgment is true.

Usually *Adhyāsa* refers to superimposition of the characteristics of certain object seen before on the present object, due to memory. This is the ordinary account more or less accepted and has been endorsed without critical analysis. Though Śaṅkara has used the term *pūrva dṛṣṭī,* there is no need of confusing one physical object with another existing physical object. Confusion is at the conceptual plane. Somebody, without actually seeing snake before but understanding the meaning of the word "snake" can mistake rope as a snake. Even if the sandy steppe has nothing similar to water, yet it is misperceived or misjudged as water. Therefore, the confusion is not on the physical but on the conceptual plane, which is logically sound and convincing. As such, a *dārśanika* (philosopher) is to bring out his point by way of making a dive into the depth of language and not confined to surface. Here *adhyāsa* or error, which is due to misjudging, need not be traced to certain objective source, and its existential status need not be pursued. That is not warranted, unless one uses the concept (rather misuses) "existence" in an unfamiliar fanciful manner.

Some post-Śaṅkara Vedāntins have referred to three levels of truth, i.e., *Paramārtha satyaṁ, artha-kriyā-sāmarthya satyaṁ* and *a-vidyā-upādhikā satyaṁ*; those give rise to the three levels of reality. But it is cogent to raise the question here as to whether Śaṅkara can consistently admit these three levels of reality at the face of non-dualism. If the ultimate is construed in terms of *nirguṇa, nirākāra, nir-avayava* and with no description whatsoever, then where is the scope of conceiving *Brahman* (the ultimate real) as three-fold? Precisely speaking, a non-dualistic philosophical position can never accommodate different levels of reality in any sense of the term. It is notable that Prakāśātman has used the term, *satya,* which has distinct significance and has no implication of existence unless one becomes rigid to include that meaning.

Conceding to the prevalent use that truth and falsity of judgments (*vicāra*) may be differently used contextually, for instance, when someone identifies X as X, then such judgment is true and there is no scope for any doubt. It is, then, absolutely true. The analogy through which the Advaitin tries to explain "That thou Art" gives the clear indication that the identity is meant for clarification and illumination; and thereby it releases tension and anxiety. Thus, it is stated that, it leads to a state of peace (*śānti*), tranquility (*tuṣṭi*) and liberation (*mokṣa*). All this, in the Advaita context, has a clear reference to certain distinct valuation undertone in the sense that it has the direction towards the cessation of evils of life (*anartha*). In this connection, Śaṅkara's statement that *Brahma-jñāna* is the result of *niḥśreyas* is notable.

6

Tat tvaṁ asi
Understanding in the Tradition of Śaṅkara

Godabarisha Mishra

Introduction

FOR Śaṅkara, *Śruti* is the pre-eminent *pramāṇa* (means of knowledge) which teaches (1) the nature of the supreme Self, and (2) the identity of the supreme Self and the individual self. The context of *Tat tvaṁ asi* (that thou art) refers to the second type of *Śruti* statements, which identifies the individual self with the supreme Self. In this *mahā-vākya* (great sentence), the primary meaning of the terms *tat* is *Brahman* that is viewed as the source of the universe and *tvaṁ* is *jīva*, who is *ātman* conditioned by body-mind-complex. The secondary sense of the word *tat* is pure consciousness, which is existence, consciousness and bliss and that of the word *tvaṁ* is pure consciousness, which is the witness of the states of waking, dreaming and deep sleep.

Traditionally, the Advaitic understanding of *Tat tvaṁ asi* is derived from the exclusive-non-exclusive secondary signification (*jahadajahallakṣaṇa*), which gives us a recollection of *Brahman-ātman* identity, known from the Upaniṣads. What is meant by here is that the nature of *Brahman* is known through the *Śruti* statements and definitions given like "*Brahman* is existence, consciousness and bliss," and "*Brahman* is the source, place of sustenance and dissolution of the world." At the end, the teacher relates *Brahman* to the individual self as enunciated in the statement *Tat tvaṁ asi.*[1] A different method of interpretation is adopted for the derivation of the meaning of this sentence because the primary sense of the terms is incompatible in view of the contradictions present in them. In post-Śaṅkara tradition, it was Sarvajñātman who advocated that exclusive implication (*jahallakṣaṇa*) is sufficient to understand the meaning of *Tat tvaṁ asi*. In the *Vedānta-paribhāṣā*, Dharmarāja gives totally a different interpretation to the meaning of *Tat tvaṁ asi*. He says that it is through the primary meaning, we can derive the meaning of identity of *tat* and *tvaṁ*; and that implication is not necessary. The paper discusses the different types of interpretation of *Tat tvaṁ asi* in the tradition of Advaita and brings out their relative hermeneutic merit in the understanding of the sense of identity.

The Context and the Problem

The tradition of Advaita, starting from Śaṅkara, has accepted that understanding the meaning of *Tat tvaṁ asi* is one of the direct means for liberation. In the context of this understanding, we come across several exegetical formulations in the tradition of Advaita in the post-Śaṅkara period. The problem of this essay relates to one of the recent essays titled "The Self of Being and the Being of Self: Śaṅkara on *Tat tvaṁ asi*" by Julius Lipner[2] where the learned author tries to provide evidence that in the context of the derivation of the sense of identity between individual self and the supreme Self, the

1. *Chāndogya Upaniṣad*, 6. 8. 7.
2. Cited from: *New Perspectives on* Advaita Vedānta, *Essays in Commemoration of Professor Richard De Smet, S.J.*, Edited by Bradley J. Malkovsky, Brill, Leiden, 2000. pp. 51-69.

Advaitin's application of *jahadajahallakṣaṇa* (exclusive non-exclusive implication) needs to be sorted out. Lipner disagrees with Van Buitenen and Mayeda in their interpretation of the term *tat,* since both of them have used *lakṣaṇa* (what he terms hermeneutic surgery) for both the terms *tat* and *tvaṁ.* His argument is that according to Śaṅkara, in *Tat tvaṁ asi* (that thou art), the term *tvaṁ* (thou) needs to be understood in an excised form, dropping its empirical connotation of "a suffering agent self." This is not required in the case of *tat* (that) which need not be subjected to such semantic surgery since it connotes the self-luminous Self. Professor Lipner's point of reference is only to the writings of Śaṅkara; and hence my giving justification from post-Śaṅkara writers in support of *lakṣaṇa* (= character implied) for both the terms is not proper. I would like to analyze only as to what are the factors that prompted such analysis in the tradition and what are the problems if we accept the analysis proposed by Professor Lipner.

What would be the possible problem that would arise if we do not apply *lakṣaṇa* for both the terms? One question that must have prompted such an analysis is that if we do not apply *lakṣaṇa,* the word *tat* would give us the direct meaning as *Brahman* which becomes verbal (*śabda-vācya*). As "you" the pronoun in a statement stands for the person who is addressed, similarly, the word *that* would qualify *Brahman.* Now if we say *Brahman* is qualified by a word like *that,* then it goes against the spirit of Advaita since *Brahman* is not qualified at all. It is *śabda-vācya,* and cannot be known through the expressive sense of the words. I shall explain as to how this problem has been addressed in Śaṅkara as well as in the post-Śaṅkara tradition.

Meaning and Method

In Indian semantics, meaning is accepted to be of four types. Those are: 1. *abhidhā* (primary one, actual), 2. *lakṣaṇa* (secondary one, character), and 3. *vyañjanā* (suggestion), 4. *tātparya* (purport or the meaning derived). For the purpose of this essay, I will deal with the first two types of meanings, which have bearing on Advaita hermeneutics and the fourth one *tātparya*, which is dealt with by the post-Śaṅkara Advaitins for meaning derivation. Through the *jāti* (particularity or genus), *guṇa* (quality), *kriyā* (activity) and, *saṁbandha* (relation) which exists in the sense, one can derive the primary meaning of a term. The word "pot" conveys the object-pot because it has the particularity called "potness;" and the word cook conveys a person who knows the act of cooking. In the case of "blue-lotus," blue is the quality of the lotus where the signification is through the *guṇa*. Finally, in the king's son relates to a boy through a relation of being a son to the king. *Brahman*, which is one without a second, is spoken of as transcending both speech and mind and is free from qualities (*guṇa*s), since it is non-dual and therefore it cannot have any particular character (*lakṣaṇa*). It is non-relational and neither operates nor is operated in any activity. Hence, it cannot be primarily signified by the words because we do not know how to derive the meaning different than the ways specified above. There is another reason why *Brahman* is not conveyed by the words. When we refer to pot, we presuppose a significant relation between word and its meaning. This relation between the word and its sense can be known through some means of knowledge, like perception etc. In other words, we need to involve *pramāṇa* (means of knowledge) to come to be aware of this presupposition, and in all the cases of means of knowledge, there is the involvement of mind. *Brahman* is not comprehended by the mind and hence it cannot be known through any means of knowledge and hence the significant relation of the words to its sense, namely *Brahman*, if at all, cannot be comprehended through the primary sense.

The problem then would be, if words cannot signify *Brahman* primarily (actuality or reality), then secondary sense (characteristics) can be had only in the case of a word, which has a primary meaning. Then how *Brahman*, which cannot have the primary meaning of such words, conveys some meaning? Here, Advaita invokes the distinction of realities saying that primary meaning of the word *tat* is like any other word, implying *satya*, *jñānam*, etc. which is neither the phenomenal reality nor *Brahman*, but the blend of the two.[3] Hence, there is the necessity of the secondary sense (characteristics) for both the words.

So the incompatibility of primary sense is considered as an essential condition for resorting to secondary sense (characteristics). The actual referent of the word, sometimes, has to be taken as different from the usual one, but in some way connected with it. This function of the word, denoting a referent different from its usual meaning is known as *lakṣaṇa* (characteristics). The Vedāntins along with the *Mīmāṁsāka*s consider that the secondary meaning (= *lakṣaṇa*) of a word is known through a kind of reasoning similar to *arthāpatti* (presumption). For example, in the sentence, "The boy is a lion" the primary meaning of an animal is not sufficient to derive the meaning and therefore a secondary meaning (characteristics = *lakṣaṇa*) has to be taken through an immediate inference as in postulation (*arthāpatti*) we get the meaning that the boy is one who has the character of courage similar to a lion.[4] There is a transfer of meaning in the case of *lakṣaṇa*

3. Sarvajnatman in his *Saṁkṣepa-śarīraka* says that "One form of reality is present in the ether, etc., another form is present in the self; and the third is in a blend of these two. Of these three, it is the "that" is the primary sense of the word *satya*," Verse, 1. p. 178
4. This is explained through *gauṇi vṛtti*, which is a signification derived from the knowledge of similarities of qualities. When the primary →

(character) as in the example given here. In all kinds of metaphoric transfer, there is an affinity between the primary (actual) and the secondary (characteristics implied) meanings. In accordance with the degree of intimacy between the primary and secondary meanings, the secondary senses are divided into three types. Those are *jahallakṣaṇa*, *ajahallakṣaṇa* and *jahadajahallakṣaṇa*. The first type relinquishes the primary sense and the sense connected with the primary sense has to be taken. The example given is "the village on the Ganges" where the word "Ganges" means the bank of the river and not the river itself. In the second type, *ajahallakṣaṇa*, the primary sense is not completely excluded, but only specified by context or restricted by its syntactic function, extended by the inclusion of another sense. The example is "The red is running" where the red as an adjective adds to it the substantive horse in the context of a war to become meaningful. The Advaitin accepts a third variety of secondary sense where both of the above secondary senses are used to interpret the *mahā-vākya* like *Tat tvaṁ asi* (that thou art). This variety is conceived of on the analogy of the sentence "This is that Devadatta" where the meaning is construed by dropping the determinants like time and space, which condition the two seemingly different Devadattas.

→ sense of a sentence is atypical then one of the words constituting that sentence conveys some other sense; and this is known as *gauṇi-vṛtti*. In case of "The boy is a lion," the term lion signifies a boy, who has the qualities of valor and the like, which are conveyed as the qualities of the primary sense of the word lion. Some like Kumarila distinguish this *gauṇi-vṛtti* from *lakṣaṇa-vṛtti* saying that in *lakṣaṇa*, a word conveys another sense connected with the primary sense, like the village for Gaṅgā, or Horses for red, whereas in *gauṇi-vṛtti*, a word conveys another sense having the same qualities present in the primary meaning. Refer: *Tantra-vārtika* of Kumarila, Anandashrama Sanskrit Series, Poona, p. 334.

There is yet another problem, which may be raised here. It is known that a word could secondarily (characteristics) signify a sense which is known through other means of knowledge as related to its primary sense. In the sentence, "This is that Devadatta" the term "this" signifies the person Devadatta as this is known through recognition as related to primary sense — the person as seen in some place and time earlier. Hence, if *Brahman* is to be secondarily signified, then it should be known through some other *pramāṇa* (means of knowledge) as related to the primary sense of the words. Since *Brahman* is not known through any means of knowledge, it cannot be known as related to the primary sense of the words. Thus, how can it be secondarily known? It is answered that, it is required that the relation of the primary sense to the sense, which is to be secondarily signified, to be known, it is not necessary that such a relation should be known through means of knowledge. Madhusūdana answers this question saying that in *Tat tvaṁ asi, ātman* is secondarily signified by the word *tvaṁ*. Here the primary sense of the word is a blend of *ātman* and the mind. Its relation to *ātman*, which is secondarily signified, is known through self-luminosity of *ātman*, not by any means of knowledge. Similarly *Brahman* is secondarily signified by the word *tat* and here the primary meaning of the word *tat* is *Īśvara*, which is a blend of consciousness and *māyā-a-vidyā*.[5] Hence, the term *tat* would secondarily signify *Brahman* as the relation between this (*Brahman*) and the primary sense of the term which is known through a logical exercise than any consideration of means of knowledge.

An objection related to the earlier one also may be raised here that *Brahman* being supra-relational cannot be related to

5. Madhusudana says that the relation of the primary sense of the words to *Brahman* is known through *tarka*. Here *tarka* is not a *pramāṇa* but it is a subsidiary.

primary sense and cannot be secondarily signified. The Advaitin's position is that there cannot be any relation between *Brahman* and the primary sense of the terms, but still we can have the secondary signification in case of *Brahman* since there is an illusory relation between *Brahman* and the blend of empirical entities and *Brahman*. Madhusūdana[6] reiterates this saying that for the secondary signification in case of *Brahman*, we may accept a relation between the primary and secondary meanings as an illusory one and not necessarily a real one. On these above points, I would like to submit that there are some constraints if we derive the meaning of the *tat* as *Brahman* through primary signification.

Text and Context — The Analysis of Purport

From here, I go on to discuss how the *tātparya* (purport) becomes significant as far as Advaitin's hermeneutics is concerned. The type of analysis on the relation between word and meaning shows the depth of Indian hermeneutic tradition and the penetrating insights given for understanding the texts. The text at times poses a problem for a reader as the meaning of the text deludes the reader not directly suggesting whatever they have been intended for. The fundamental issue of the theory of interpretation is to acquire the real and entire purport of the text. Both the schools of *Mīmāṁsā* take up this issue and there are certain formulations to derive the meaning of the texts. In the context of the dialogue between Uddālaka and Śvetaketu in the *Chāndogya Upaniṣad*, we come across the statement *tat tvaṁ asi*, which is regarded as a statement giving the sense of self in the tradition of Advaita. The father cum teacher Uddālaka starts his teaching with the statement "the

6. *Na ca śudhe saṁbandhābhāvanā lakṣaṇāpitivācyaṁ, atāttvika saṁbandhenaiva lakṣaṇopāpattenaḥ*, *Advaita Siddhi*, Nirnaya Sagar Press, p. 674.

real alone was in the beginning" and ends it with the conclusion that "all this is the nature of the self." This proves that there is co-ordination between beginning and the end, *upakrama-upasaṁhāra-aikya*. The repetition (*abhyāsa*) of this statement *Tat tvaṁ asi* shows the importance and pervasive nature of the theme in that text. The conclusion derived is something new as the knowledge gained through *Tat tvaṁ asi* cannot be derived from any other means except from the scriptures. The passage preceding *Tat tvaṁ asi* goes to say that by knowing this truth all that is worth knowing is known. This satisfies the criterion of eulogy (*arthāvāda*). The final result (*phala*) of the understanding of this *mahā-vākya* is liberation. This *mahā-vākya* is preceded by an elaborate philosophical discussion satisfying the criteria of reasoning (*upapatti*). The reasoning is based on the tools of interpretation so that one is not distracted from the topic treated through the elucidation of the meaning of a sentence known as *vākyārtha*. This meaning derivation is in accordance with the tradition of Advaita; and other schools have their own hermeneutic tools to disprove this theory of identity.[7]

In post-Śaṅkara tradition, it was Sureśvara who dealt with this problem of text and context at length. His idea is that the sentence like *Tat tvaṁ asi* gives a non-sentential sense. In his *Naiṣkarmya-siddhi*, he refers to the hermeneutic treatment of this sentence which makes the reader/hearer to go beyond the meaning of the terms *tat* and *tvaṁ* and grasp the non-sentential sense.[8] He says that every sentence, whether scriptural or secular gives only a relational sense as its meaning. He prefaces his argument by saying that after attaining the

---

7. Recently Joel P. Brereton in his article entitled "*Tat tvaṁ asi* in Context," argues that the traditional meaning of identity is untenable since it is not in tune with the grammatical formations.
8. *Naiṣkarmya-siddhi*, 3. 3.

sentential sense of "I am *Brahman*" one must meditate on that relational knowledge till one attains liberation.[9] He answers that non-sentential sense comes directly from the sentence with the removal of the incompatible determinants in the meanings of the words like *tat* and *tvaṁ* by three ways *samānādhikāraṇyaṁ* (equal competence), the relation between *viśeṣaṇa-viśeṣyata* (the qualifier and the qualified), and *lakṣya-lakṣyaṇa* (implier and implied or end and means). The crux of the discussion is that *viseṣaṇa-viśeṣya-bhāva* has to be transcended from *samānādhikāraṇya-jñāna* and since the primary meaning of the words cannot be related as qualifier and qualified, we need to resort to *lakṣya-lakṣyaṇa-saṁbandha-jñāna*. This is the third stage in which the two sets of determinants like remoteness, omniscience in case of *tat* and immediacy in case of *tvaṁ* — which are incompatible — are to be removed and we retain the consciousness as the implied meaning of the word.[10] Sureśvara tries out all the possibilities to derive the non-sentential sense and uses *anvaya-vyatireka* (anti-thesis) method as the one of the major techniques for understanding the purport. In and through the analysis of the terms, he has tried to derive the purport of self in both these terms. In order to substantiate this point, he says that discriminative cognition is the cognition of difference; whereas in the witness-self there is no difference. This perception of difference is due to ignorance and the function of the sentence is to remove the difference through the knowledge of non-dual consciousness. His very attempt is to bring home the idea that it is not the mere sentential sense, which is useful, but something more

9. *tattvaṁasyādi vākyebhyaḥ saṁsargātmakaṁ ahaṁ brahma iti vijñāya tāvat nididhyāsita yāvat avākyārthātmakaḥ pratyagātmaviṣayo avabodhaḥ ahaṁ brahma iti samabhijayate.* Vide: *Naiṣkarmya-siddhi of Sureśvara* by R. Balasubramanian, p. 236.

10. *samānādhikāraṇyaṁ ca viśeṣaṇa viśeṣyata lakṣya-lakṣaṇa-saṁbandhaḥ padārthaḥ pratyagātmāni, Naiṣkarmya-siddhi,* 3. 3.

than that. To me, both the components of the sentence are meaningful only in a different level of spiritual attainment, and not through the hermeneutic surgery as analyzed by Lipner. His analysis can be best fitted to a context where we have to understand an empirical or objective world-view. But Advaitin relates the knowledge of identity to the holistic knowledge where the ethics and metaphysics merge and hence incising the meaning of the *tvaṁ* is not sufficient to get the sense. One more problem as I have indicated is that if the word *that* stands for *Brahman,* would that not be another word having the connotation of the former, which is beyond the range of the *śabda-prapañca,* the realm of illusion. This is an exercise, which relates *Brahman* to the *Jīva* through either *mithyatva* or *ananyatva.*

Sarvajñātman in his *Saṁkṣepa-śarīraka* points out that the statement *ahaṁ brahmāsmi,* can be interpreted by resorting to *jahallakṣaṇa* alone. This is the extension of the view proposed by Sureśvara as *a-bhāsa-vāda* as far as the nature of the *jīva* is concerned. In *Prati-biṁba-vāda,* the reflected image is identical with the original and hence it is real. What is illusory is the limiting adjunct by which the reflected image is created. In the *a-bhāsa-vāda* the reflected image is not identical with the original and it is illusory. The primary meanings of the words *tat* and *tvaṁ* are *Īśvara* and *jīva* respectively, which are illusory in character. These two are the reflected images of the self in *a-vidyā* and intellect respectively. The primary meanings of the terms *tat* and *tvaṁ* are indeterminable entities; the two words give up their primary sense completely and secondarily signify pure-consciousness, *Brahman* which is the basis of the two entities.[11]

---

11. Sarvajñātman says: Just as the sentence "The boat makes noise, The iron burns, In front of you there is the rope bearing poison," the words convey the multitude of men, fire and the serpent →

Dharmarāja, the author of the *Vedānta-paribhāṣa*, suggests that there is no need to have *lakṣaṇa* at all since we can get the meaning affirming identity through *Śakti* or *abhidhā*, as the intention (*tātparya*) of the *Śruti* is only consciousness, which is the purport of the statement *Tat tvaṁ asi*. It is not very clear why Dharmarāja discards the generally accepted view that *lakṣaṇa* is necessary for getting the meaning of the sentence *Tat tvaṁ asi*. If a predication is made, then we take the predication as true of the bare subject without resorting to secondary implication. For example, "pot-ness" is part of the significance of "pot" and that is also a qualification of the "pot." In this, when non-eternality is predicated of pot, it is understood to be related to the "pot" alone, not "pot-ness." For that we do not say that "the pot is non-eternal" should be interpreted secondarily. We treat the qualification "pot-ness" as irrelevant and hold the statement to be true in its primary sense. The rejection of the irrelevant does not thus come because of the secondary signification. If that is the case, then any sentence which uses the words like pot, say "Bring the pot" should be interpreted through *lakṣaṇa* (character), since "pot-ness" which cannot be brought has to be discarded. In the sentence "the pot is eternal," the eternality is significant only with regard to "pot-ness," and not with regard to the primary sense (actuality) of the subject. Here we may accept the secondary (character) signification.[12]

→ respectively, so also (in the sentence *ahaṁ brahmāsmi*) what objection can there be if the words *Brahman* and *ahaṁ*, which primarily signify respectively *a-vidyā* and the intellect inspired by the reflection of the self, should convey the supreme self through exclusive secondary signification." Vide: *Saṁkṣepa-śarīraka of Sarvajñātman* by N. Veezhinathan, University of Madras, 1972, Verse 1. 169.

12. *Tasmāt Tat tvaṁ asi iti vākye ācāryanāṁ lakṣaṇoktiḥ abhyupagamavadena bodhya, Vedānta-paribhāṣa*, p. 73; Dharmarāja →

Anantakrishna Sastri has pointed out one more difficulty in the understanding of the sentence, *Tat tvaṁ asi*. He says that only the previously known things can be secondarily implied, like riverbank by the word river. If *tat* and *tvaṁ* are secondarily known, then how is this consciousness known? If it is known, then there is no possibility of *saṁsāra* (life in the world or bondage). He suggests that one may understand this at the state of *asaṁprajñata-samādhi* (the deepest-extraordinary wisdom). So how does one get the knowledge when he has not attained such a state? Hence, he suggests that we need not have to have secondary signification, i.e., *lakṣaṇa* for getting the import.[13] S. Suryanarayana Sastri says that the problem still continues because we do not know what to remove and how much to remove and where to stop.[14] Another argument is raised in *Advaita-siddhi* where it is said that the relation between the two words being opposed to perception, needs to be tackled by perception. The reply given is that the interpretation through *lakṣaṇa* is necessitated not by perception, but by the need to sustain the appositional relation revealed by the six-fold criteria as the purport of the texts.

Madhusūdana says:

anyārthatātparyakatvāt ca amukhyātvaṁ na lakṣaṇikamātraṁ.

It may be said that Dharmarāja takes to the methodology of *Naiyāyikas* to prove that primary sense is sufficient to get us the meaning of the *mahā-vākya, Tat tvaṁ asi*. It is because when we say "you are the king's son" or "tenth man," we need not

---

→ says that the *lakṣaṇa* can be resorted to in the examples like "Let the curds be protected from crows, where crow also includes others which are non-crows."

13. Anantakrishna Sastri, *Vedānta-paribhāṣa*, pp. 206-07.
14. S.S. Suryanarayana Sastri, *Vedānta-paribhāṣa*, p. 197.

take the process of dropping the meanings and taking something else. It happens automatically and the barriers between the secondary and primary significations fall off.

Conclusion

In Advaita, which gives such a lot of importance to *aparokṣa-jñāna*, we need to see that the relation between knowledge and the sentence does not suffer mediation as proposed by the traditional scholars even. The whole purpose of the *mahā-vākya* is to bring home the idea of such a state of identity in which the mortal man loses his identity of mortality. In Vedānta, this knowledge of identity is not the beginning of the spiritual journey, but the ultimate phenomenon. The tradition is open to the idea that even without the knowledge of and indulging in *mahā-vākya*, a person can be liberated like that of Vamadeva of the Upaniṣadic days and Ramaṇa, Ramakrishna of yester years. This seems to be the exclusive trait of the Advaita Vedānta tradition where the so-called scripture, an instrument of self-knowledge, goes back to the oblivion for a person who has attained such a state of fulfilment, *Jīvan-mukti*.

7

Ahaṁ Brahmāsmi
Its Logical Foundation and Value Implication

Ganesh Prasad Das

I HAVE chosen for deliberation here a topic that many profound scholars before have done so with the hope to create an ambience of novelty and clarity.

I have set myself the task of assembling some of my thoughts that I articulated on *Vedānta-paribhāṣā* of Dharmarajadhvarindra in the idiom of Anglo-American philosophy of logico-linguistic analysis following the lead of Ganeswar Misra. The views of Misra, and quite naturally the views of those who more or less followed his line like me, were judged to be contra-tradition and vehemently criticized. The views that emerge out of such exercise are critic-constructive and quite in keeping with the tradition. I do not stand here to affirm what Prof. Misra meant to say by making a survey of the whole philosophy of Advaita. However, I have instead chosen to limit myself to the import of the *mahā-vākya* (great logia) *"Ahaṁ Brahmāsmi"* that constitutes the quintessence of Advaita. I shall first speak on the logical foundation of the *"Ahaṁ Brahmāsmi"* and then speak about its value implications.

I

Ahaṁ Brahmāsmi is one of the four/five great sentences (*mahāvākyas*) enshrined in the Upaniṣads.[1] This great sentence *mahāvākya* that occurs in the *Bṛhadāraṇyaka Upaniṣad* is regarded as an experiential statement of the pupil.

R. Puligandla seeks to muster phenomenological justification for *ātman-Brahman* identification. In a paper entitled, "Is the Central Upaniṣadic Teaching a Reductionist Thesis?" he argues that "*ātman* is *Brahman*" cannot be a reductionist thesis in the sense in which this is conceived in the Western philosophical tradition. There the physical and the mental both are regarded as phenomena and one of them is regarded as being ultimate. According to Puligandla, "Nothing could be more absurd than to think of consciousness as a phenomenon."[2] Consciousness is transcendental. In short, it is formless and nameless which cannot be raised and erased, expanded or contracted. There is no lower consciousness or higher consciousness, as it is impartial and unitary. He concludes by saying that the Upaniṣadic teaching is nonetheless a reductionist thesis, but it is better to call it as Upaniṣadic reductionism. Elsewhere, he characterized the Upaniṣadic ultimate reality as being at once immanent and transcendent. According to him, *Brahman* is the power whose varieties of manifestation are the phenomena of the world without as well

---

1. *Prajñānaṁ Brahma* (*Aitareya Upaniṣad*)/*Sarvaṁkhalu Idaṁ Brahma* (*Chāndogya Upaniṣad*), *Ayamātmā Brahma* (*Māṇḍūkya Upaniṣad*), *tat tvaṁ asi* (*Chāndogya Upaniṣad*), *Ahaṁ Brahmāsmi* (*Bṛhadāraṇyaka Upaniṣad*), Vide, P.T. Raju, *Structural Depths of Indian Thought*, New Delhi: South Asian Publishers, 1985; and Indu Lata Das, *Mysticism and the Upaniṣads*, New Delhi: Nag Publishers, 2002.
2. *Asian Philosophy*, vol. I, no. 1, 1991, p. 17.

as within man. It is unborn, uncreated, undying and eternal which the senses and the mind cannot perceive. *Brahman* is not a he, nor a she, but that, *tat*. *Ātman* like *Brahman* is unborn, uncreated, undying and eternal. It is pure, objectless consciousness not to be identified with the empirical ego or the metaphysical self. *Ātman* is also formless and nameless and it transcends space and time and is therefore unperceivable, inconceivable and inexpressible. *Ātman* and *Brahman* are not, however, two numerically different realities. They are two different labels for the one and the same non-dual reality. Whatever is experienced in the three states, waking, dreaming and sound sleeping is only a manifestation of *Brahman*, which Puligandla labels as "power." By the practice of *Yoga*, mental modifications could be halted and there could be consciousness without any object. This objectless consciousness is the *ātman* and is none other than the un-manifested *Brahman*. *Brahman* is immanent when it gets manifested into varieties of worldly phenomena. It is transcendent because it cannot be experienced as a phenomenon that is the object of consciousness. "*Ātman* is *Brahman*" is, according to Puligandla, a profound phenomenological-analytical truth.

I shall devote my time to offer my understanding of the identity statement, *Tat tvaṁ asi* and thereby hope to dispel the confusions that I think are involved in the views of scholars. For this purpose I shall make reference to Dharmarajādvarīndra's text, the accredited Vedānta-*paribhāṣa*.

The thrust of all the *mahā-vākya* is that *ātman* is *Brahman*. In the sentence, *ātman* is *Brahman*, *ātman* stands for "this" as well as "I" which function as the subjects of knowledge in the propositional symbolism, whereas "*Brahman*" that stands for Existence as such (*sat-ghana*) and Knowledge/Consciousness as such (*cit-ghana*) functions as the subject of the whole of intelligible discourse.[3] There are different ways of expressing the sentence like "This is that," "Everything is *Brahman*," "You are that," and "I am that," These are known as extraordinary statements or great logia (*mahā-vākyas*) as already stated. All such statements have the same import, that is, the ultimate limit of the actual language is the maximum approximation of the ultimate limit of any possible language. Surely, "*ātman* is *Brahman*" is an extraordinary statement, because it is not a statement that can be found in our work-a-day use of language. Yet there are sentences in the work-a-day use of language, which are similar to this sentence in respect of grammatical structure. We have to apprehend how the statement "*ātman* is *Brahman*" is different from others in respect of logical behavior. In the sentence, "This is that Devadatta," which is admitted to be an approximation to its inner structure, the identity that it portrays cannot be an identity of substance. It cannot be an identity of some necessary attributes either, because that would presuppose a mitigated form of essentialism. The identity of two things or two persons or two events of the world, as the case might be, is not established on the basis of their substances or their attributes. Their identity is established on the basis of general characteristics, which are not necessarily abiding, but which constitute what Hospers calls, "a quorum." A thing or a person or an event in one appearance is, in the strict logical sense, similar to itself in another appearance to an appreciable degree. But they can sometimes be similar to such a low degree that doubts can be entertained about their similarity. When an appearance of a thing or a person or an event is similar to another appearance of a thing or a person or an event to an appreciable degree, we regard the two appearances as being appearances of the self-same thing or person or event. And

3. For a detailed discussion, vide, my *Vedānta-paribhāṣa: An Analytical Study*, Meerut: Anu Books, 1986.

we say that the particular having the first appearance and the particular having the second appearance are not two but one.

Ātman and *Brahman* are not entities according to the Vedāntin.[4] As such, they cannot be said to be identical in the sense that their substances are the same. Again, *ātman* and *Brahman* cannot be characterized as they are bereft of characteristics (*nirguṇa*). As such, they cannot be said to be identical in the sense that their attributes are the same. Because of this, it is improper too to say that *ātman* and *Brahman* are similar to each other. According to the Vedāntin, they are identical in a different sense. The identity of *ātman* and *Brahman* is to be understood in the sense that they are terms of identical or approximately identical significance. They stand for the selfsame feature of language and discourse. The term *ātman* stands for the limit of factual discourse and the term *Brahman* stands for the limit of any possible discourse. The former points to or shows the latter. What is shown is that the former is the maximum possible approximation of the latter.

According to Śaṅkara, *apnoteḥ atteḥ atāteḥ va ātma.*[5] *Ātma* is that which gets, eats up and goes or grows. *Brahman* comes from the root *Bṛha* that means "to grow," "to expand." The two terms are highly potent in their significance and used in philosophical, religious and cultural discourses as well. When they are used in the philosophical discourse, their meanings must not be got mixed up with that which they have in non-philosophical discourses. It pays to increase our clarity in understanding the rules in language games and roles in forms of life if we explain them in the philosophical logical idiom.

---

4. *Vedānta-paribhāṣa*, II-25 and VIII-66.
5. *Aitareya Upaniṣad Bhāṣya*, 1. 1. 1.

The sense in which *ātman* and *Brahman* are said to be identical is different from the sense in which an empirical particular is said to be identical with itself or rather with different appearances of itself. We can distinguish the two by labelling the *ātman-Brahman* identity as conceptual identity and the identity of empirical particulars as factual identity. Accordingly, the statement made by the use of the sentence "This is that Devadatta" expresses factual identity of terms whereas the statement made by the use of the sentence "*ātman* is *Brahman*," or any of its variants expresses conceptual identity of terms. In order to avoid a possible confusion, however, the Advaita Vedāntin says that *ātman* and *Brahman* are non-different. This is the maximum that the philosopher can say using language in order to clarify possible confusions of language use. Wittgenstein's observation with regard to the paradox generated by the use of the word "identical" is quite enlightening: "Roughly speaking, to say of two things that they are identical is nonsense, and to say of one thing that it is identical with itself is to say nothing at all."[6]

It is important to show, in this connection, the distinctive characters of a statement of conceptual identity. The structure of such a statement is different from that of a non-identity statement. We know that the basic structure of a statement symbolism that seeks to state something about the empirical world is that a particular is described under a universal. That is, the statement involves a distinction between two parts, namely, the particular (*viṣayī*) and the universal (*viṣaya*), or the support (*adhi-sthāna*) and the ascription supported by it (*adhyastha*). The two are sought to be related by means of an assertive tie. The subject term of the statement stands for the support and the predicate term of the statement stands for the ascription. These two terms are related by such words as

6. *Tractatus Logico-Philosophicus*, 5. 5303.

"is" or "am." So a statement of the form, "This is thus and so" or "I am such and so," involves a relation that is fundamental for human thought and discourse about the empirical world. It is called a *samsarga-vagahi* (involving relation) statement.

In contradistinction with this sort of statement, an identity statement like "*ātman* is *Brahman*" or any or its variants does not involve a distinction between a subject term and a predicate term. They are not really bound by a relational tie. It is called a *saṁsarga-na-vagaḥi* (not involving relation) statement. Such a statement appears to establish a relation between two terms because the device indicating the relation "is" is there. But it is only the semblance of a relation. The reason is that there is no distinction between the subject term and the predicate term, strictly speaking. We must make it clear that the distinction between a subject and a predicate, that is in question, is not the grammatical distinction between a subject and predicate but a categorical distinction between the two. According to the categorical distinction, we know, a subject cannot function as a predicate and a predicate cannot function as a subject. Their functions are absolutely demarcated. The statement "*ātman* is *Brahman*" seeks to point beyond the distinction between the two. Yet, to speak within the bounds of the distinction, both the terms that appear as being related are subject terms. The statement in question is not an exact statement because *ātman* and *Brahman* are not strictly subject terms. There cannot be, however, a more exact statement to convey what it intends to convey. It intends to convey that *ātman* that constitutes the limit of the actual language or the factual discourse is the maximum approximation of *Brahman* that constitutes the ultimate limit of any possible language and discourse in respect of logical status. This is a statement of extraordinary structure belonging not to language and discourse, but to their limits. An ordinary identity statement like "This is that Devadatta" comes in between a non-identity statement at the one extreme and a necessary identity statement at the other. It can be regarded as an "intermediary case" in the words of Wittgenstein.[7]

The meaning that a conceptual identity statement carries is said to be infinite. That is, knowledge conveyed by such a statement is not differentiated into subject and object that is inevitable in case of knowledge conveyed by a statement like "This is pot" or "I am happy." Hence the statement "*ātman* is *Brahman*" is said to express infinite meaning (*akhaṇḍ-artha*). Knowledge conveyed by a non-identity statement like "This is a pot" or "I am happy" is differentiated into subject and object. Hence, such statements are said to express partite meaning (*khaṇḍ-artha*).

Most of the criticisms that are leveled against philosophical logical analysis or critical-constructive analysis of the Advaitin's view that *ātman* is *Brahman* are rooted in certain presuppositions two of which I intend to put forward here. The first one is that 'linguistic philosophy and philosophies of language are one and the same.' This is not correct, as the former is a philosophical method whereas the latter is an area of philosophical pursuit. I shall not dilate on this except saying that Śaṅkara whose views are reconstructed linguistically has a philosophy of language to his credit. The second is that the *mahā-vākyas* like *Tat tvaṁ asi* or "*ātman* is *Brahman*" are not meant to be intellect-deep, but further and farthest deep. By the attempt to understand and construct the traditional doctrines and arguments in the current philosophical idiom, one does not intend to fix it at intellect-deep. We intend to put it there where it should properly be. But one cannot neglect and bypass the domain of the intellect. One has to pass through the domain of the intellect, not to get stuck there but to go beyond. (In the Vedāntic terminology "go" and "know"

7. *Philosophical Investigations*, Sec. 122.

logically mean the same.) In the West, philosopher F.H. Bradley came to the conclusion that the intellect must commit suicide to apprehend Reality. But there is no question and scope of suicide in Advaita. The Advaitin wants to transcend the intellect with the help of the intellect, as there is no bypass or short cut. The *Bhagavad-Gītā* is clear in this regard:

> *evaṁ buddheḥ paraṁ buddhva saṁstabhyātmānam ātmana. . .*
> (Knowing That, which is superior to intellect and disciplining the lower with the higher intellect. . .)[8]

One must expatiate in detail the reasons provided by the faculty of reason only to find that they are not adequate to render knowledge of the ultimate reality. The idea of ultimate reality, it might be clarified, is not foisted from outside by, nor is a figment of the imagination of, the philosopher. The present way of understanding the idea is neither an imposition nor grafting made by the present writer. There are some scholars who appear to think that when they use the current logico-linguistic idiom, they are not imposing or grafting, but when others use the same, they are imposing or grafting distorting the philosophical view under reappraisal.[9]

II

I think that those who are more or less averse to the logico-linguistic study of the doctrines and arguments of Advaita Vedānta, perhaps feel that the sap of the philosophy is destroyed. It bears important messages for philosophy of life and that is lost by this conceptual-critical study. I am fully convinced that this is not so. The metaphysical-epistemological

8. III-43.
9. Vide, for example, G.C. Nayak, "Śaṅkara's Formulation of Vedānta," in R. Balasubramanian and Sibajiban Bhattacharyya (ed.), *Perspectives of Śaṅkara*, 1989, pp. 11-23.

or the ontological-epistemological (such are the varied forms of description the differences among which are not easy to grasp) of the Advaitin does not imply any philosophy of life. In one of my published papers entitled *Brahman* as *sat-chit-ānanda*, I said that the philosophy of Vedānta could be employed in ways that might be opposed to one another.[10] For example, some commentators interpret the Vedāntin as propounding an illusionist philosophy that denounces the world as illusion.[11] Consequently people might become indifferent to worldly affairs and averse to all social actions, because the world is unreal without trying to appreciate that the world is said to be an illusion from a different standpoint altogether. On the other hand, one could employ the same philosophy in the opposite direction. One might argue that the philosophy of Vedānta is not antagonistic to the present day materialistic society. It is rather congenial to it. The modern man in the process of making money has lost the higher values of life and has moved away from his human nature. He looks upon his fellow men as so many contenders in the race for making money rather than so many selfs very much like him whose dreams and desires, attempts and achievements, are, in no way, different from his own. All are at bottom one. There should not therefore be any strife between region and region, and man and man. All must live in mutual peace and harmony instead of living in perpetual tension and terror, insecurity and uncertainty. There must be universal brotherhood of man.[12] R. Balasubramanian in the second volume on Advaita Vedānta, asserts:

---

10. *The Humanist Vision*, Bhubaneswar: The Humanist Philosophical Circle, p. 1981.
11. Cf. S.N. Dasgupta, *Indian Idealism*, Cambridge University Press, 1962, p. 163.
12. Cf. S. Radhakrishnan, *History of Philosophy: Eastern and Western*, vol. II, George Allen and Unwin Ltd., 1967, pp. 447-48.

> The message, which Śaṅkara wants to convey in his *Adhyāsa-bhāṣya* is simple, but profound. A life un-examined is not worth living. We are engaged in the *loka-vyavahāra* without a deeper reflection on the meaning and purpose of life. Śaṅkara expects human beings, who have the special competence for the pursuit of knowledge and the practice of religious duty (*karma-jñāna-adhikāra*), to reflect on their nature, deeds, and destiny. One who fails to understand the problem of *Adhyāsa* cannot understand the philosophy of Advaita.[13]

He further writes:

> Śaṅkara offers a solution to the problem of role-identification. We are called upon to play different roles in our day-to-day life. . . . The roles are both relative and temporary. . . . According to Śaṅkara, the problem of role-identification is a case of *Adhyāsa*. . . . A person who is sensitive to the fact of role-identification will be humble in his life, responsible in his conduct, and detached and self-controlled in his attitude and outlook.[14]

Swami Atmasthananda draws a message for the people of today's world from the Advaita philosophy thus:

> Today we are living in a shrinking world and what happens in one corner of the globe affect people thousand miles away. At the social, political and economic levels we have to appreciate the other man's point of view and realize the oneness of existence. For this, the recognition of the inner spirit of man, which binds all humanity by a single bond, is an inevitable necessity.[15]

---

13. P. 70.
14. P. 120.
15. *Vedānta: Concepts and Application*, Calcutta: The Ramakrishna Mission Institute of Culture, 1997, p. 11.

There are business *gurus* who claim to draw conclusions conducive to business from the Advaitic point of view. They think that, stress management, anger management and overall personality management can be done efficiently well by the concepts and principles provided by Advaita Vedānta. They have coined new expressions like "Spiritual empiricism" and "Vedāntic Spirinomy" (that is, economy Vedāntically spiritualized!) for this emerging state of affairs. They think that "Spirinomics" built on ideas of Vedāntic spiritualism stands a better chance of providing balanced fulfilment. Whereas, Hedonism (neo-classical economics of the Capitalists) transforms the individual into a consumerist automaton out of rapacious greed, and "Communomics" (economics of the Communists) rides roughshod over the individual self in the name of the party.[16]

Which message concerning life and world is evidenced by the doctrine of Advaita? I would like to reserve my response on this. Let us now look at some of the modern attempts to link the findings of Advaita Vedānta with those of modern science and to draw matters of fact conclusions therefrom. But we must not forget what Śaṅkara says about the necessity of the whole exercise of the philosophy of Advaita, that is, *atyantika duḥkha nivṛtti* (total elimination of suffering) and *akhaṇḍa sukha prāpti* (begetting total bliss).

There are attempts of some modern thinkers to bring in the findings of particle physics to justify the identity of *ātman* and *Brahman*. According to them, all the things and beings of the world including the psychophysical organism are manifestations of energy. What is known as matter of diverse names and forms are merely packets of energy, and energy, in its turn, is but a conscious principle. The whole world

---

16. S.K. Chakraborty, *Ethics in Management*, New Delhi: Oxford University Press, 1995, p. 21.

evolves out of it and devolves into it. But it needs to be appreciated that philosophical perspectives are not hypotheses or theories about the world requiring support from facts. They are independent of whatever there is or whatever happens in the world.

Swami Vivekananda once remarked that science is nothing but the finding of unity and that as soon as science would reach perfect unity, it would stop from further progress because it would reach the goal. He contended that the science of religion would become perfect when it would discover Him, who is the one life in the universe of death, one who is the constant basis of the ever-changing world, one who is the only Self of which all selfs are but delusive manifestations.[17] *Tat tvaṁ asi* is regarded as the principle, which asserts that the microcosm contains the macrocosm. Certain scientific findings are cited in order to buttress this point of view. Ferris asserts that the history and the fate of the universe are written in every atom.[18] The scientists claim that in the sub-atomic level no particle is an independent entity. These entities are interconnected with each other. A particle is "a dynamic pattern of interconnected energy," says Capra. Moreover, "consciousness may be an essential aspect of the universe." We may fail to understand natural phenomena if we do not take this into account.[19] According to Max Planck, "consciousness is fundamental and the matter is derived from consciousness." And Joad adds: "Everything we talk about, everything we regard as existing postulates consciousness." In the similar vein, the Nobel physicist Schrödinger contends that the

---

17. *The Complete Works of Swami Vivekananda*, vol. I, pp. 14-15. Religion, according to Vivekananda, is the science that learns the transcendence of nature through the transcendence of man.
18. *The New York Times Magazine*, 26. 9. 1982, p. 87.
19. *The Turning Point*, p. 95.

dualism of mind and matter can never be resolved in the material plane, but only in the psychic plane. Thus, both Planck and Schrödinger seek to accept the Vedāntic principle that consciousness creates matter, not vice versa. Consciousness is the singular of which the plural is unknown. Consciousness in the plural is a deception or *māyā*, says Schrödinger. This appears to be an echo of Vivekānanda's claim that although an atom is invisible, unthinkable, yet in it are the whole power and potency of the universe. This is exactly what the Vedāntin says of atoms.

H.P. Blavatsky, a theosophist, brings out a novel thesis in her book entitled *The Secret Doctrine of the East* that the Reality is Be-ness rather than Being. This reality is absolute consciousness, which is free from and symbolized by finite and conditioned intelligence. This is *Para-Brahma* whose two aspects are spirit and matter. It is the force of all individual consciousness and is the pre-cosmic substance, which is the substratum of matters of various grades. The secret doctrine (the Upaniṣads) teaches fundamentals of all selfs with the universal self. Again, J. Feys, a Vedāntic scholar of the West, in his little book, *A=B: An Enquiry into the Upaniṣad*'s *Basic Insight* tries to explode the mystery about *ātman-Brahman* identity. He approaches the Upaniṣad not as a revealed word, which the *ācārya*s do, but as a philosophic-religious document. From this "restricted but legitimate point of view," the Upaniṣads appear to substitute *ātman* for *Brahman*, the immanent self for the transcendental or the sacred. *Brahman*, according to him, "never is something quite definite. It is the sacred, the noun, the highest or supreme, the last ground of all reality or absolute. *Ātman*, on the contrary, is very clearly defined; it is the objectless consciousness of the pure self, the intuitive subject, term of the process of exteriorization."[20]

---

20. *The Complete Works of Swami Vivekananda*, vol. I, p. 38.

Ātman-Brahman equation, that is A=B, is according to him, not an assimilation of the sacred and the profane, or the noumenon and phenomena. The amalgamation is fatal to philosophy as well as to religiosity. The distinction between the two, human and the divine, is essential for the progress of man's understanding of reality.[21]

K. Satchidananda Murty in his Sarada Pitha address of September 1985 said that scientists and popularizers of semi-scientific and semi-mystic ideas have written a number of books, which try to prove that contemporary science supports some form of Eastern philosophy or mysticism. He rejects this view with detailed arguments, according to whom, no science can or need to confirm the truth that reality is non-dual, *sat-chit-ānanda,* nor is it ever opposed to or reject this. This truth, according to Satchidananda Murty, has been and can be confirmed in one way only, that is, by one's own experience. I wish to submit here that philosophy and science are the pursuits of two different orders. The putative truths of science are verified in sense experience in the respective segment. But the truths of philosophy are not verified in this way. One could say that they are not at all verified in sense-experience; or one can say equally, nay more cogently, that they are verified in any and every sense-experience. The sense of reality, which logic postulates — never arbitrarily, to be sure — is the sense that is critical and logical. It provides the basis for deciding what is real and what is not.

The truths of Advaita Vedānta could be approached in three ways. The approaches are: (1) scriptural, (2) rational, and (3) experiential as Arvind Sharma has sought to show clearly in his recent book — *Advaita Vedānta: An Introduction.*[22]

---

21. *The Complete Works of Swami Vivekananda,* vol. I, p. 44.
22. Arvind Sharma, *Advaita Vedānta: An Introduction,* Delhi: Motilal Banarsidass Publishers Private Limited, 2003.

The Vedāntic truths can be approached, assessed and appreciated in any of the ways that are by no means exclusive. They are comple-mentary to one another for, all dualities like that between fact and value, religion and philosophy, faith and logic are overridden by the supervening truths of Vedānta.

I would like to close with a couple of sentences. In Vedānta, there is no aversion to any view, there is only delightful toleration; no rejection of any view, only harmonizing accommodation and the Vedāntin leaves everything as it is; there is no question of reduction as some scholars allege. The method of philosophy is logical analysis and hence a *dārśanika* (philosopher) is regarded as a *pramāṇika* (standard) in India long before this was seen as a landmark in philosophic progress in the West.[23]

---

23. Hiriyanna, *Outlines of Indian Philosophy*, p. 178 n and *Wittgenstein, op. cit.*, Sec. 124.

8

Some Thoughts on Vedānta Ethics
An Analysis of the Vedānta-sāra

Maya Das

THE *Vedānta-sāra* is usually considered as a treatise on Vedānta metaphysics, centering round the explanation of the Advaita doctrine of super-imposition (*adhyāsa*) of the non-real upon the Real, *Brahman*. As per the oft-heard interpretation, for attaining the highest knowledge of reality, it is necessary to turn away from the world of experience, the creation of *ajñāna*, and the morality associated with it. According to many philosophers of Vedānta, liberation is a world-and-life negating process.

This in itself is a debatable issue. It can be argued that if life-negation had been the only attitude of Vedānta, then Vedānta would not have dominated the Indian cultural tradition across the ages. Actually, Vedānta has always been considered as "an art of right living." In its pragmatic aspect, Vedānta has given full recognition to the irresistible power and attraction of the visible world. The apparent contradiction of the life-affirming and the life-negating traditions of the philosophy never posited any obstacle to cultural advancement.

If it is accepted that cultural advancement is spiritual in nature, then all human actions are meant for self-refinement (*ātma-saṁskāra*). Here refinement implies disciplining, cleaning, and purifying of the present mental state. It can also be stated that so long as impulses and passions confine man, man cannot discern his right path, and cannot choose his *puruṣārtha*, the meaning of life: *Parava śīkṛta cittasya asāmarthyaṁ puruṣārtha sādhana prati pattou*. Thus, man needs to go beyond the life of worldliness and ritual-centered action. Vedānta philosophy does not advocate a radical renunciation of the entire life of action.

According to Vedānta, man is the universal self, only hidden behind a finite guise. The very fact that man aspires and acts for something beyond, something better, something higher, indicates that he is not ready to accept his limitation, his finite state. It is characteristic of him to think in terms of vastness, *bhūma*. The idea of the immortality of the self makes man spiritual. For grasping the wider and higher significance of the self, man needs to realize his fundamental identity with *Brahman*, the final truth through his personal experience. It is not mere intellectual acceptance.

If we accept that the final aim of Vedānta is to transform man into a wholly spiritual being, then emphasis should be given to the steps prescribed for that transformation. The Advaita dictum, *Brahma satyaṁ, jagat mithyā, jivo brahmaiva nāparaḥ*, makes it evident that man's life or existence is centripetal in nature. The belief in one supreme reality, *Brahman* is the base for the whole process of life-experience that leads to the ultimate realization of *Brahman*. Being one with *Brahman* means to return to the basic assumption that it is not a new achievement, but a re-achievement. In Advaita terminology, it is the *prāpta prāpti*, achievement of the already achieved. If the process of regaining the truth is termed as *apavāda* or withdrawal, then this withdrawal is not a negative attitude to life. It is more affirmative than the attitudes dominated by ignorance or ego-sense. Man's entire life process is considered as a preparation for attaining the final goal gradually. Each step leads to a larger and positive dimension, transcending not negating the previous one. Hence, the present situation is accepted as partial and imperfect manifestation of the infinite, whose very presence constitutes the possibility for future progress.

The "present-situation" and the "would-be-situation" paves the ground to construct moral thinking; motion, conviction, faith or belief sustains the moral codes. Conviction for truth and the immortal is "being;" and deep conviction, having bearing on actual life generates the process of "becoming." The Vedic concepts of *satya* (truth) and *ṛta* (pre-established law of nature) convey the aspects of being and becoming respectively. The acceptance of *ṛta*, a regulative purpose present behind all movements and activities, makes man more disciplined, more fruitful. It sets his aims and objectives, and provides the real meaning to his life. A close study of the *Vedānta-sāra* indicates that action-oriented process of liberation incorporates the ritual-centric, socio-centric, liberation-centric traditions of morality. The individual, social and spiritual dimensions of life are inseparable and structured hierarchically for the culmination in the spiritual end, *niśreyasa*.

The *Vedānta-sāra* begins with a prayer for *abhīṣṭa-siddhi*, the fulfilment of the desired goal. The word *abhīṣṭa* means desired aim, which is the result of knowing facts of value; it leads to action with a positive aim of securing something or a negative aim of avoiding something. The emphasis here is on the actualization of the desired goal. One's own experience rather than mere theoretical knowledge is necessary in this regard. *Siddhi* or fulfilment, in this context, indicates disciplining of the mind. On par with the classical texts of

Vedānta, the *Vedānta-sāra* recommends social morality as the first stage of disciplining of the mind. In fact, Sadānanda has not offered the prayer of *abhīṣṭa-siddhi* for his own sake, but for the sake of others. Evidently, his intention has been to help people to overcome their suffering and attain their goal worthy of realization. The prayer acknowledges the responsibility of the professional philosophers to the society. Vacaspati also says the same — *lokavyutpādanarthatvāt śāstrasya tasaivātradhikārāt*. For the sake of the people, philosophical treatises are expounded. In Indian philosophical thought the very foundation of social morality has been laid on the acknowledgement of the three debts (*ṛna*s): debt to the gods (*deva-ṛna*), debt to the father (*pitṛ-ṛna*), and debt to the sages (*ṛṣi-ṛna*). Sadānanda's declaration of indebtedness to his revered preceptor and his mode of describing the essence of Vedānta to the other members of society is an instance that he repaid his debt to his teacher and affirmed solidarity with all his fellow beings.

Sadānanda supported the view that until and unless the Vedānta ideas are spread to the ordinary people, as to the intellectuals and the seekers of higher truth, the integration of social morality is not possible. In explaining the term Vedānta as signifying the Upaniṣads — the *Śruti-prasthāna*; the *Brahma-Sūtra* — the *yukti-prasthāna;* and other, i.e., the *Bhagavad-Gītā* — the *Smṛti-prasthāna*, he acknowledges three dimensions in the teaching of Vedānta for *loka-saṁgraha*, the well-being of the whole society.

In describing the *anu-bandha*s, the preliminary considerations in Vedānta, Sadānanda emphasizes on three major phases,

(1) the primary training required to begin the study of Vedānta,

(2) the discipline necessary for the realization of the Vedāntic teaching, and

(3) *jīvan-mukti.*

The first phase is partly moral and partly intellectual. It is often said that the Advaita Vedāntins categorically deny the path of action for a seeker of liberation. Liberation being an individual-centric process, there is no need to adhere to socio-moral obligations. Perhaps the opposite is true. As it has been pointed out from the very beginning, the *Vedānta-sāra* has significantly paid attention to socio-centric morality. Since the very process of liberation has been viewed in terms of the individual self, realizing its identity with the supreme Self, the separate identity of the individual self and its distinctiveness from the other selves have not been given importance. The Advaita concept of liberation cannot be conceived in individual-centric terms.

Moral or ethical discipline has a vital role in the context of liberation. Moral training includes *sādhāraṇa-dharma*s, *varnāśrama-dharma*s and *kāmya-karma*s. The *sādhāraṇa-dharma*s are obligatory to all and their observance is the prime moral training. The *kāmya-karma*s have an indirect value. The *varṇāśrama-dharma*s are the most significant in ethical discipline. The activities of a *varṇa,* social class and the activities at the specific stages of life (*āśrama*) have been recommended as *nitya-karma*s, obligatory social duties to be performed by all the communities. The binding character of these activities restricts individual activity in certain courses. This implies that individual man must submit his will to the will of others. The emphasis given to self-restraint and self-denial in Vedānta is related to the social obligations.

According to *Vedānta-sāra,* the *adhikāri,* the inquirer of Vedānta, needs to have knowledge of the Vedas and the *Vedāṅga*s. His study should be *vidhivat,* as per rule and should be carried on under proper guidance. Before beginning the study of Vedānta, one is not required to have an acquaintance with the rituals of the Vedas and the *Vedāṅgas*. Vedic rituals have a significant role in shaping man's life-process. Vedic sacrifices (*yajña*) have been performed symbolically. Renunciation of one's sole proprietary claim towards anything in the world — is the basic import of *yajña*. This gives rise to the feeling of sharing one's own possession with the others, not as giving away something out of pity, but as a part of social duty. Ultimately, nothing belongs to the sacrificer. *Yajña* presents the unity of universal life and promotes dedication towards betterment and upliftment of all. As a natural corollary to this, *yajña* also represents the universal Self (*Puruṣa*), the all-pervading consciousness, *Brahman*, and the ever expanding, ever growing knowledge. *Yajña* is equated with the creator itself.

The Vedas have been considered the only source of all human thoughts and actions. The Veda and the *yajña* being the two fundamental integrals of Indian culture, the study of the Vedas has been declared as the most significant duty of an inquirer. This study is to be done in the present life, which implies observation of ritual-centric morality.

Sadānanda's elaborate discussion of the Vedic *karmas* highlights liberation as an action-oriented process. The desired (*kāmya*) and the prohibitory (*niṣiddha*) acts are self-centric. They are undertaken to secure personal benefit here or hereafter and accordingly vary from person to person. Their value in ethical training is only preparatory; a reason why the regular practices are restricted. Other Vedic acts like regular (*nitya*) and occasional (*naimittika*) rites; purificatory (*prāyaścitta*) ceremonies and meditation (*upāsanā*) are considered essential for the purification of the mind, since they eliminate selfish impulses. These rites have been recommended to perform throughout the life-process, which includes previous lives as well. The rites remove all sins (*kalmaṣa*), promote concentration of the mind and the purification of the heart. All these imply moral and intellectual upliftment of the inquirer.

Through the performance of these acts, the inquirer should possess the following four-fold means to study Vedānta:

(i) the discrimination between the eternal and the non-eternal (*nityānitya vastu viveka*),

(ii) the absence of desire for securing happiness or avoiding pain here or elsewhere (*ihamūtra phala bhoga virāga*),

(iii) the control of mind and senses, etc., (*samādhi ṣat saṁpatti*) and

(iv) the desire for liberation (*mumukṣatva*)

None of the four-fold means indicate any life-negation. Self-restraint is not life-negation, but restrainment of the narrow self for the attainment of the wider one. Desire for self-realization makes the whole process affirmative of life. The process is often criticized as too individualistic, implying a neglect of social morality. Actually social morality is not neglected in the process. The individual's own training has its obvious impact on the society.

The second phase of the ethical training centers round the disciplines required for the realization of the Vedānta teaching. The methods of *adhyāropa* and *apavāda* adopted in the *Vedānta-sāra* to explain the metaphysics of Vedānta first show the diversity of the world-experience and then proceed to explain the ultimate unity of all. Since in these methods the world of unity-in-diversity is presented as mere appearance, the obvious conclusion is that reality exists beyond the world of appearance. In this context, the ascertainment of the true nature of the self, both cosmic and individual, is interpreted as a negative process of rejection of all appearance. The method of *apavāda*, however, points out that although the false appearance (*vivarta*) negates everything that falsely appears as another, it actually establishes the real. The negation is not actual world and life negation. It is rather the negation of the falsity.

After the correct apprehension of the Vedāntic teaching what is needed is a rigorous self-discipline to reject all the false and thereby misleading notions and theories. The three-fold discipline of study — hearing (*śravaṇa*), repetition (*manana*) and profound reflection (*nidhi-dhyāsana*), recommended at this phase, are mutually connected. Although these disciplines aim at directing the mind away from the world and even from one's own inner thoughts, the distance is not unwelcome. Sadānanda explains that these disciplines awaken the mind and calm the mind during distractions. The mind should be made like a lamp-flame in a windless place so that it does not flicker. The implication is the mind should not be kept away from the world, but from the worldly distractions. Without concentration, nothing can be achieved. The concentration makes the ethical life.

The third phase of the ethical life is the outcome of the previous discipline. When a person actually realizes the truth, he is known as *jīvana-mukta,* the liberated-while-living. The liberated-man is the paradigm of human perfection. His practice of morality and moral values make the norms for the liberation. The description of *a jīvana-mukta* in the *Vedānta-sāra* never creates an impression that a *jīvan-mukta* ceases to act. Only selfish activities are excluded in his case. The common laws of social life or relative morality lose their relevance as far as a *jīvan-mukta* is concerned. For, he has already attained perfection, has realized his own nature as the part-less *Brahman*.

Though the scriptural text says that all the *karma*s of a *jīvan-mukta* perish, because he has seen both cause and effect

— *kṣīyante asya karmāṇi tasmin dṛṣṭe parāvare* — it does not imply that all *karmas* are destroyed. The *prārabdha-karmas* that regulate the present life continue to be effective. When not in trance, the liberated one stands witness to all activities. The result of the *karmas* does not affect him. His habits and tendencies continue, but do not influence him. Virtues and moral good become natural to him. Whatever he does is right, he discovers his own self everywhere. The liberated self exists for the others. All his activities are geared to setting examples to the people at large what a perfect man is like. In this regard, it can be said that if the first phase of Vedāntic discipline is socio-centric and the second phase individual-centric, the third phase is once again socio-centric.

The three phases of moral disciplines highlighted in *Vedānta-sāra* make evident that in no phase Vedānta has acclaimed life-negation. All the phases are action oriented, only the attitude to action changes in different phases. The activity of a beginner, the activity of one who is in process of realization of truth and the activity of a liberated self are different in keeping with the change in the situation. The change, however, does not imply the rejection of the previous one. The ritual-centric, socio-centric and liberation or self-centric moralities make an all-comprehensive, universal morality. The very catholicity and receptivity of the Vedānta ethics, across the ages, have been nourished by the universal morality.

Bibliography

Barlingay, S.S., *A Modem Introduction to Indian Ethics*, Penman Publishers, Delhi, 1998.

Hiriyanna, M., ed. *Sadānanda Vedānta-sāra*, Oriental Book Agency, Poona, 1929.

Jhingram, Saral, *Aspects of Hindu Morality*, Motilal Banarsidass Pvt. Ltd., Delhi, 1999.

Section - III
Schools of Vedānta, and Compositions

9

Concept of Consciousness in Rāmānuja's Viśiṣṭādvaita Vedānta

Abha Singh

RĀMĀNUJA is the chief exponent of Viśiṣṭādvaita Vedānta. The following pages contain his thesis on consciousness. Viśiṣṭādvaita is a school of Vedānta, which although affirms the ultimate unity of self and supreme Self, recognizes and affirms the specific attributes of the supreme Self, i.e., *Īśvara*. Thus, endowed with attributes, the supreme Self possesses *Viśiṣṭa* (qualified), and is not a *nir-viśeṣa-chaitanya* (undifferentiated consciousness). As Radhakrishnan writes:

> Rāmānujas philosophy is called Viśiṣṭādvaitam for the reason, among others, that it insists on the non-duality of two different objects, *Viśiṣṭayor Advaitam*.[1]

Rāmānuja's Vedānta recognizes three entities as ultimate and real (*tattva-traya*): matter (*a-cit*), individual self (*cit*) and God (*Īśvara*). Bringing out the perception of duality and the conception of non-duality in Rāmānuja's Vedānta, T.M.P. Mahadevan remarks that God is qualified (*viśiṣṭa*), and the

1. S. Radhakrishnan, *Indian Philosophy*, vol. II, London: George Allen and Unwin Ltd., 1951, p. 686 footnote.

world of souls and matter are non-dual (Advaita).[2] Though all the three entities are equally real, Rāmānuja says that matter and individual soul depend on God (Īśvara) for their existence. They are substances in themselves, yet in relation to God, they become His attributes. They are the body of God who is their soul. Hence, the matter and soul are supported and controlled by Him for his own purpose. Matter and souls are called attributes (*prākāra*) of God; and they are the controlled (*niyamyā*), the supported (*dhārya*), the parts (*aṁśa*) and the accessory means (*śeṣa*), while God is their substance (*prākari*), controller (*niyanta*), support (*ādhāra*), the whole (*aṁsi*) and the principal end (*śeṣī*). They are eternal with God, but are not external to Him. God is free from all external differences homogeneous (*sa-jātīya*), as well as heterogeneous (*vi-jātīya*), since there is nothing either similar or dissimilar which is external to or other than Him. But He possesses internal differences (*svagata bheda*), as His organic body is made of real and diverse elements like matter and souls. His relation with them is natural and eternal.[3] Thus Rāmānuja's Vedānta is called Viśiṣṭādvaita because the attributive elements, i.e., matter and soul and the substantive elements, i.e., *Īśvara* form a synthetic unity.

What is Consciousness?

Consciousness, which is the ultimate principal of human experience, is the opposite of unconscious. Consciousness implies the awareness of situation characterized by the relationship of subject and object in an act of cognition. It also implies the consciousness of selfhood, an *ahaṁ-pratyaya* as no

2. T.M.P. Mahadevan, *Outlines of Hinduism*, Bombay: Chetana Ltd., 1971, p. 151.
3. C.D. Sharma, *A Critical Survey of Indian Philosophy*, Varanasi: Motilal Banarsidass, 1976, p. 347.

one is even empirically conscious without being implicitly conscious also of one's own self. A reflective self-feeling sharply divides the world of consciousness from the world of unconscious. The "I" as the distinguishing feature of the realm of consciousness, is absent from the realm of unconscious. A stone in the heap of stones, or a flower in a bed of flowers is not aware of cognate object by its side. It does not appear in any cognitive relation with its neighbour as it does not cognize itself. But the moment we imagine that one knows the other, then it is, at once, raised to the status of a subject with reference to the one which is for the moment the object of its awareness. And then if the other also is in its turn a subject, the unconscious heap of stones becomes a society of subjects with introspective relations. Consciousness or *saṁvit*, is therefore a capacity to be a subject, and implies the presence of a cognitive relation (*grahaṇa*) between a known (*grāhya*) and the knower (*grāhaka*). It is a peculiar illumination of *jñāna* (awareness), which reveals the subject, the object and the soul.

Thinkers beginning with the Upaniṣadic sages, together with Gautama, Kapila and Bādarāyaṇa, down to Śaṅkara and Rāmānuja, Śrīdhara and Jayanta, responded to the problem of consciousness, but there is hardly any answer, which is not so unsatisfactory as not to give rise to a fresh problem in turn.

Meaning of Consciousness

Rāmānuja interprets consciousness as attributive consciousness (*dharma-bhūta-jñāna*) as opposed to unconscious (*a-vidyā*) which is action (*karma*) and related to *prakṛti* (Primeval Nature). He talks of two kinds of consciousness the inward (*pratyak*) and the outward (*parak*) in relation to mind and senses. A distinction between *svarūpa-jñāna* (existential consciousness) and *dharma-bhūta-jñāna* (phenomenological consciousness) is also drawn by Rāmānuja to have a clear vision of knowledge, which, on deeper analysis, remains not easily explainable.

The distinctive feature of consciousness (*jñāna*) is that it is neither material nor spiritual, but immaterial (*a-jaḍa*). It illumines itself and other objects. It always exists for another and never for itself. That is, it cannot know itself but illumines objects for the conscious subject of whom it is the attribute. Consciousness is the attribute of both *Īśvara* and *jīva* as well. Therefore, it is known as attributive consciousness (*dharma-bhūta-jñāna*) which suggests there is substantive intelligence as well. *Īśvara* and *jīva*s, while possessing knowledge, are conscious in the substantive sense. As attributive knowledge, consciousness is eternal and all pervasive in respect of *Īśvara*, eternal-divine (*nityasuris*) and liberated self. In mundane life, consciousness (*jñāna*) is subject to contraction and expansion, though it endures in all the three states of waking, dream and deep sleep. Consciousness in its perfect expanded state reveals reality without any blemish. But in *saṁsāra*, consciousness reveals partial visions, and incomplete knowledge of things.

For Rāmānuja, there is no difficulty in maintaining that consciousness is the substratum, as well as the attribute of the self as it is the essence as well as the property of self. This point has been clarified with the help of the illustration of a lamp. The light of a lamp constitutes the essence of a lamp, and its property; similarly, consciousness is also both a substance and a property, consciousness is a substance, as it constitutes the essence of the *jīva*s (self) and *Īśvara* (God). In this sense, *jīva* is of the nature of consciousness (*jñāna*) and is not the *āśraya* (substratum) of consciousness. However, knowledge or consciousness in the shape of *dharma-bhūta-jñāna* exists as a property of the *ātman*; and since there is the relation of *aprithak-siddhi* (inseparableness) between substance and its property, the soul is regarded as the substratum of *chaitanya* (consciousness).[4] Soul is ever qualified by *dharma-bhūta-jñāna*, therefore it is always the knower and not merely knowledge.

Dharma-bhūta-jñāna is eternal and all pervasive in respect of *Īśvara* and *jīvas*. It is not only self-illumined but is also of the nature of both *dravya* and *guṇa* (substance and attribute). *Dravya* is that which is the substratum of states, and *guṇa* depends upon *dravya*. Therefore, *dharma-bhūta-jñāna* is conceived as a *dravya*, since it is the substratum of change through its states of expansion and contraction; and as a *guṇa*, since it inheres in a substance like *jīva* or *Īśvara*. Regarding the concept of *Dharma-bhūta-jñāna* M. Hiriyanna opines:

> It characterizes *jīvas* or *Īśvara* and is always, as its name indicates, secondary to them, the relation between them being inseparable. It is conceived as both a *dravya* and a *guṇa* — a *dravya* in as much as it is necessarily dependent upon a *dravya*, viz. *jīva* or *Īśvara* and cannot by itself.[5]

Distinctive Features of Consciousness

According to Rāmānuja, Self is eternal and its natural quality, consciousness is also eternal. The eternal consciousness is *cid-rūpa* and *chaitanya-guṇaka*: *eva-mātma cidrūpa eva caitanya-guṇaka*.[6] In other words, the self is made up of consciousness, which is both the *svarūpa* as well as *guṇa* of it. The self is not mere knowledge but the subject of it. Knowledge is as distinct from the knowing-subject, of which it is a quality, similar to the smell of the earth, which is a quality of earth: *ātman jñāta*

---

4. *Tattvatraya*, Vara Vara's Commentary, Varanasi: Chowkhamba Sanskrit Series Office, 1938, p. 14.
5. M. Hiriyanna, *Outlines of Indian Philosophy*, Blackie and Son, India Ltd., 1979, p. 404.
6. *Śrī-bhāṣya*, 1. 1. 1. p. 30.

eva na prakāśa-mātraṁ.[7] Thus, the self is not of the nature of pure consciousness because consciousness always relates itself to objects, and in the form of this or that and distinctive.

Consciousness is Determinate

Rāmānuja holds that the self is an eternal self-conscious subject of which consciousness is the essence of it. But he demurs in identifying self with pure consciousness for there is nothing like pure consciousness, as consciousness is always qualified and possesses specific attributes. It always belongs to a subject and points to an object; and there is no way to prove the existence of an unqualified consciousness. Even if one accepts consciousness itself as a proof (*siddhiḥ*), then the question arises as to what and to whom to be proved? Even if one tries to prove that one's own experience, which is qualified in nature, is unqualified, then one has to ascribe some special trait to it. Because of these special traits, one may try to establish the unqualifiedness of consciousness. Nevertheless, by that very fact the attempt is defeated since that special trait makes it qualified. S.M. Srinivasachari presents this paradox in a lucid way:

> The term proof is a relative notion like that of "son" and therefore these two questions arise. The Advaitin may say that consciousness is the proof of itself. If it were further questioned as to what the self is, the Advaitin would reply that it is consciousness, as the two are regarded identical by him. The argument thus involves a vicious circle, Vedānta Desika therefore urges that because of self-proof it is impossible to prove the existence of an undifferentiated consciousness.[8]

---

7. Cf: S.K. Saksena, *Nature of Consciousness in Hindu Philosophy*, Delhi: Motilal Banarsidass, 1971, p. 63.
8. S.M. Srinivasachari, *Advaita and Viśiṣṭādvaita*, Delhi: Motilal Banarsidass, pp. 44-45.

Further, the essential and inseparable feature of consciousness according to Rāmānuja, is self-consciousness. Self is a conscious subject, which never loses selfhood *ahaṁ-pratyayā*: "*ahaṁ pratyayā skidoo hi asmād-arthaḥ*."[9] The *ahaṁ-pratyayā* is present even in deep sleep, though in a dim degree.

The Object of Consciousness

According to Rāmānuja, consciousness is "self-luminous" but this self-luminosity (*svayaṁ-prakāśātva*) is conditional. Although consciousness does not require to be manifested by knowledge at the time of revealing an object (*viṣaya-prakāśan-velayam*), yet it manifests itself through its own being to its own substrate: *vartmāna dasayāṁ sva sattaiva svāśrayāṁ prati prakāśamānaṁ*.[10]

As for Rāmānuja, manifestation of consciousness itself is conditional, i.e., it manifests itself under certain conditions. Hence Rāmānuja has been designated as *ardha svaprakāśa vādi*. Rāmānuja further holds that consciousness reveals an object and is also revealed as an object. For him the contention that consciousness is not an object holds good for the knowing self at the time it illumines other things. Moreover, our daily experience goes against the contention that consciousness is always self-luminous as the knowledge of one person may become the content of cognition for another. Non-belief in the possibility of knowledge of thoughts and experience of other persons as object of knowledge would make our practical life standstill. Because, the experience of one individual becomes the object of inferential knowledge for another based on the individual's appearance. Rāmānuja, in his commentary on *Brahma-Sūtra*, points out that "unless it were admitted that there is the inferential knowledge of thought of others there

---

9. Cited in S.K. Saksena, *op. cit.*, p. 118.
10. *Ibid.*, p. 95.

would be no connection between the words and their meanings and this would imply the termination of all empirical usage depending on speech."[11] Even in the case of one's own experience, past states become the object of cognition, as expressed in the judgment "at one time I knew, etc."

Again, in the strict sense of the term, it is not possible to prove that consciousness is not an object of knowledge. The term "consciousness," in the statement "consciousness is self luminous," refers to "something." If the referendum is *Brahman*, then that becomes manifested as far as it is the object of knowledge, conveyed by the term. In that case it may be contended that the nature of *Brahman* is itself illuminating, and so the predicate is only a restatement even then the manifestation of it is inevitable in as much as it is the object of that cognition conveyed by the restatement. Above all, it cannot be said that the term does not denote anything as it would make the proposition meaningless. Hence consciousness, for Rāmānuja, is always an object of knowledge even though it is self-luminous in character.

Consciousness is Temporal

In favor of the temporal character of consciousness, Rāmānuja says that when knowledge flows through the channel of sense organs to the object, knowledge is produced. When the knowledge of an object ceases to exist, it is destroyed. Moreover, consciousness does not reveal only that which is experienced in the present moment as in that case the connection between past and future would cease. Had knowledge been eternal memory, inference, scriptures and intuitive mystic cognition of sages could not communicate events, which occurred in the past or is supposed to happen

---

11. *Śrī-bhāṣya*, p. 30.

in future. In other words, there would have been an end to all empirical usage depending on speech.

Even the other sources of knowledge, i.e., perception and inference favor the temporal character of knowledge. Rāmānuja is of the view that the consciousness of ordinary objects such as a table or a blackboard, etc. is revealed at a particular time. Perception does not reveal its existence for all times. It means that the revelation by consciousness is limited in time. Inference also strengthens the temporal feature of consciousness. The presupposition of the absence of knowledge of a particular thing makes one proceed to instruct the other on it: *tasmāt na pragabhāvādi asiddhya samidaḥ anupattiḥ upapatti mati.*[12] S.N. Dasgupta had this content in mind when he writes:

> If revelation of knowledge were not itself limited in time, then the objects revealed by it would also not be limited in time, which would be the same thing as to say that these objects such as jug, etc. are all eternal in nature, but they are not. This sort of argument may also be applied to the revelation of knowledge in inference, and it may well be argued that, since the objects must be of the same type as the knowledge, which reveals them, then if the knowledge is not limited in time and is eternal the objects also will be eternal. For there can be no knowledge without an object.[13]

Consciousness is Changeable and Manifold

The basic content of Viśiṣṭādvaita-Vedānta is that Reality is a qualified entity. Reality, i.e., *Īśvara* is associated with *cit* (sentient individual selfs) and *acit* (non-sentient matter). The changes, such as origination and destruction, belong to the

12. *Ibid.*, I. I. I., p. 33.
13. S.N. Dasgupta, *A History of Indian Philosophy*, Delhi: Motilal Banarsidass, 1975, vol. III, p. 338.

latter, and these do not affect *Īśvara* in any way. *Īśvara* is no doubt omniscient, but His knowledge is not subject to contraction and expansion. It is the knowledge of individual self, which undergoes various transmutations. This in nutshell is the explanation of *nirvikāratva* or immutability of Reality in Viśiṣṭādvaita-Vedānta.

The changeable character of consciousness implies its difference. Rāmānuja argues that since the experience varies differently with different spaces and time, i.e., we perceive here a jug, there a table and then again at another moment here a toy and there a horse. We do not have one continuous experience of one entity in every space and time. For Rāmānuja, the difference in knowledge is proved through the difference in the cognition of objects, which is established by valid knowledge in the same way as the difference of acts of cutting is proved by the difference of the objects cut: *Abadhita pratipatti siddha dṛsyabheda-samarthāneva darśana bhedopi; saṁśarthi to eva chedya-bhedat, chedana-bhedāvat.*[14]

Now the question is, how can knowledge, which is eternal, admits difference? Rāmānuja sorts out this difficulty by admitting that although knowledge is eternal, it also undergoes contraction and expansion in respect of its objects in accordance with the *karma* of the individual: *nityapi saṁvit tattat karmanirūpaṁ tesu viṣayesu saṁkocam vikāsaca bhaejate.*[15] With reference to these adaptations due to the senses Rāmānuja asserts that consciousness never ceases to be. It functions throughout the life of an individual in a more or less restricted manner. Therefore, in a view of the changes in respective objects, which become content of experience in accordance with the *karma* of the individual the difference in knowledge

---

14. *Śrī-bhāṣya*, I. I. I., p. 34.
15. S.M. Srinivasachari, *op. cit.*, p. 27.

as well as the relationship of knowledge to respective objects (*pratiniyata viṣayata*) is established.

Consciousness is Qualified

Manifold character of consciousness strengthens the contention that it is not possible to apprehend an unqualified Being. Neither any source of knowledge, nor any proof, is able to establish the unqualified character of Being. All proofs in this regard are based on the assumption of some qualified character. Unqualifiedness is beyond the reach of direct experience. Even if one tries to prove that one's own experience, which is really qualified in nature, is unqualified one ascribes some special trait on it. Based on these ascribed traits one tries to prove the unqualified character of consciousness. But the very ascription of that special trait makes it qualified. Highlighting this position of Viśiṣṭādvaita, S.M. Srinivasachari observes:

> In the statement "Consciousness is *nir-viśeṣa*," the term *nir-viśeṣa* denotes anything more than what is implied by the term "consciousness" or not. If it were the latter it would amount to saying that consciousness is consciousness, which is tautologous. If it were the former, then the predicate adds something to the subject in which case consciousness becomes determinate. It may be argued that the term "indeterminate" implies that consciousness is devoid of all characteristics including indeterminateness itself as a quality of consciousness. In a judgment the predicate should be admitted to be related to the subject in the same way or other. If it is not related in any way then the judgment has no meaning. According to Indian Logic, there would follow that fallacy of non-relationship between the subject and the probandum is admitted to be related to subject, it would inevitably follow that the subject is determinate. Hence it is

> not possible to assert that consciousness is devoid of all characteristics.[16]

As Rāmānuja recognizes two levels of consciousness — empirical and transcendental — if consciousness (*anubhūti*) refers to knowledge concerning empirical world, it is clearly qualified. On the other hand, if consciousness (*anubhūti*) refers to the nature of *Brahman* as depicted in scriptures, it does not testify to a characterless reality. Since inference is a collection of words arranged in order and relation, and each word is a whole, "comprising a stem and a suffix"[17] it is not possible for scriptures to yield any meaning which would signify the characterless or unqualified feature of *Brahman*.

Conclusion

The above analysis of the nature of consciousness in the Viśiṣṭādvaita of Rāmānuja reveals that it is based on his epistemological realism. Rāmānuja appears to be one with realists in objectifying consciousness or knowledge. He argues that consciousness refers to some object to which it is related. The distinctive feature of Rāmānuja's theory of consciousness is that it is two-way relational. It is related to an object on the one hand, and to a subject on the other. In other words, consciousness as an attribute requires a locus for its support. The self, which has consciousness as its attribute is itself of the nature of consciousness. Self, which is *chid-rūpa*, is self-luminous. Thus, it appears that there are two levels of consciousness in Rāmānuja's thesis — one is substance (*dharmi*) and the other is its attribute (*dharma*). The two are although physically inseparable but logically distinct. To make the distinction clear one is called substantive consciousness

---

16. *Ibid.*, p. 56.
17. S.N. Dasgupta, *op. cit.*, p. 166.

(*dharmi-bhūta-jñāna*) and the other is called attributive consciousness (*dharma-bhūta-jñāna*). Attributive consciousness is related to worldly object in the state of bondage, but in the state of release it has *Brahman* as it object. Further, consciousness is not only an attribute but also the essence of self. Attributive consciousness undergoes contraction and expansion, but consciousness as the essence remains unaffected by the changing contents of attributive consciousness. Hence, it can be regarded as transcendental. These observations help us in noticing that Rāmānuja's analysis of the concept of consciousness is "consciousness in its essence." In Viśiṣṭādvaita the "consciousness in its essence," besides being a phenomenological presupposition, enjoys the status of being "an individual metaphysical reality."

10

Doctrine of Sākṣī in Madhvācārya's Darśana

V.V.S. Saibaba

ŚRĪ Madhvācārya (1238-1317 AD) who was admitted into the religious order under the name of Pūrnaprajña is the historical founder of the Dvaita Vedānta. He is a rare integrated blend of a creative thinker, a prolific writer, and a scholar endowed with inexorable logic. A Saint-philosopher and a mystic, he is the celebrated author of thirty-seven works which include the great commentaries on the *Prasthāna-trayī*, the *Anuvyākhyāna*, the *Bhāgavata-Tātparya-Nirṇaya*, the *Mahābhārata-Tātparya-Nirṇaya*, the *Viṣṇu-Tatva-Nirṇaya*, the *Tattvodyota*, the *Tattva-Saṁkhyāna*, the *Karma-Nirṇaya*, the *Upādhi-Khaṇḍana*, the *Mayāvāda-Khaṇḍana*, the *Pramāṇa-Lakṣaṇa*, etc. which reflect his wide range of penetrative knowledge of ancient Indian literature. Also known as Ānandatīrtha in many of his works, Madhvācārya is regarded as *Samanvayācārya* (the great reconciler) of Hindu scriptural tradition.

Madhvācārya is perhaps the first medieval commentator who interpreted the Vedas in the light of Upaniṣadic and post-Upaniṣadic thought. He was also the foremost commentator on Vedānta who attempted to reconcile the existence of "eternal substances" (*nitya-padārthas*) like *jīvas*, *ākāśa*, *prakṛti*, etc. while accepting the universal causation of *Brahman*. Through his doctrine of "*Parādhīna-viśeṣapati*" he endeavored to bridge the gulf between eternals and non-eternals. In the interest of Hindu revivalism and upholding *Vaidika* Hinduism he integrated his new philosophical realism blending with the principles of Ancient Vaiṣṇavism. He made a significant contribution to Indian thought by his introduction of new metaphysical doctrines, concepts and categories, viz. *sākṣī*, *svatantra*, *sa-viśeṣa-bheda* and *parādhīna-viśeṣapti*.

Nature and Scope of Sākṣī

In the scheme of his epistemology, Madhva accepts three *pramāṇa*s or means of valid knowledge, viz. sense-perception, inference and scripture or verbal testimony defining their nature, scope and function in his own way, differing from others.

> Perception is the flawless contact of sense-organs with their appropriate objects. Flawless reasoning is inference. Flawless word, conveying valid sense, is *Āgama*.[1]

According to Madhva the word "flawless" indicates specific conditions which are to be fulfilled only when the *pramāṇa*s become the valid means of knowledge. These conditions are applicable to the object, the sense-organs and their contact. When all these conditions of flawlessness are fulfilled the valid knowledge *yadhārdhaṁ* (truth) arises. The entire system of Dvaita Vedānta may be summarized in the following verse of the *Mahābhārata-Tātparya-Nirṇaya*:

> *jagat-pravāhaḥ satyo'yaṁ pañca-bheda-samanvitaḥ,*
> *jīveśayor bhidā caiva jīva-bhedāḥ parasparaṁ,*

---

1. *nirdoṣardhendriya sannikarṣaḥ pratyakṣaṁ;*
nirdoṣopapattiranuman nirdoṣah śabdāhagamaḥ.
— *Pramāṇa-Lakṣaṇa.*

jaḍeśayor jaḍānañca jaḍajīva-bhidā tathā[2]

Herein, Madhva advocates the reality of five-fold differences between soul and God, between soul and soul, between soul and matter, between God and matter, and between matter and matter. Madhva gave a new connotation to his conception of *bheda* by using a new category called *viśeṣa*, while keeping in view the severe criticism levied against the concept of "difference" (*bheda*) by eminent dialecticians of Advaita School, i.e., Maṇḍana Miśra, Vimuktātman and Śrī Harṣa. According to his *Viṣṇu-Tattva-Nirṇaya* difference is of the nature of things (*dharmi*) in most cases, which are revealed in perception. In his view objects cannot be distinguished without there being different characteristics of phenomena in the world. The *viśeṣa*s are the basis of identity, which enable us to distinguish without introducing an actual difference, which was admitted by Advaitins while describing *Brahman* as *Neti Neti*.[3] Thus, difference is the nature of the thing (*dharmai-svarūpa*) and being "a fact of experience" cannot be denied as unaccountable and therefore "illusory."

The concept of *Sākṣī* is the key concept in Madhva's Dvaita Vedānta on whose foundation his whole Philosophical Realism is built. Madhva recognizes two kinds of cognitive senses, viz. (i) *Vṛtti-jñāna,* (i.e., cognitive state of the senses and the mind) (ii) *Sākṣī-jñāna* (The Intuitive faculty of the cognitive agent whose perception springs from one's pure consciousness). In his scientific and realistic temper, Madhva contends that all knowledge cannot be regarded as true, valid, and self-luminous. In his opinion, the sensory and other forms of *vṛtti-jñāna* are to be tested in order to become indubitably valid.

---

2. *Mahābhārata-tātparya-nirṇaya*, I, pp. 69-70.
3. *ekasminneva vastuni viśeṣa-stairapyaṅgīkṛta eva;*
   neti neti tyatra sarva-vailakṣyaṅgīkaṛat.
   —*Viṣṇu-Tattva-Nirṇaya*, p. 21.

His *Anu-vyākhyāna* emphasizes the distinction of these two forms of knowledge. According to him, every kind of knowledge derived from sensory and mental channels, is sometimes liable to error. Unlike the former *Sākṣī* is the inner sense-organ of the self (*svarūpendrim*) which is both *jñāna-grāhaka* and *jñāna-pramāṇa-grāhaka* (intuiting knowledge and its validity). The perception and judgments of the *Sākṣī* are of the essence of *caitanya* or pure consciousness and therefore self-luminous concerning their nature and content of validity. In Madhva's perspective *Sākṣī* is not wholly distinct from *ātman*.[4] *Sākṣī* is the name of the spiritual sense-organ of the self through which it senses its experiences.

The Raison d'etre of the Concept of Sākṣī

The concept of *Sākṣī* is necessitated in Madhva Vedānta due to the limitations of other means of knowledge of the mind and senses. Further, knowledge derived through the sense-organs, inference, verbal testimony and interpreted by one's mind is subjected to doubt, misapprehension and is liable to correction by further evidence or by means of better perception, etc. Without tests, we cannot check their correctness; and these tests will need other tests and in turn others to ad infinitum. Since all *vṛtti-jñāna* (mental and sensory) is 'material' in essence and has no power to reveal its own existence, we need a non-material, ultimate and absolute principle of knowledge, whose judgments are infallible. Even the validity of sense-perception and other forms of *vṛtti-jñāna* is established ultimately by *Sākṣī* only after appropriate tests.

---

4. *sukhā-di viṣayaṁ svarūpa bhūtaṁ caitanyendriyaṁ hi sākṣī tyuchayate tad abhi vyaktaṁ jñānaṁ ceti.*

   Jayatīrtha's *Nyāya-Sudha*, p. 258. Cf. B.N.K. Sarma, *Madhva's Teachings in His Own Words*, Bombay: Bharatiya Vidya Bhavan, 1961, p. 44.

The raison d'etre of the doctrine of *Sākṣī* is mainly based on three principles: (i) *Sākṣī* is the ultimate guarantor of the validity of all other *Pramāṇas*. (ii) *Sākṣī* is the logical fulfilment and culmination of a real and perfect epistemology. (iii) *Sākṣī* is the only means of intuitive perception of certain super sensuous categories, viz. time, space, self and its attributes, the mind and its modes and all knowledge of pleasure and pain, etc. *Sākṣī* is an indispensable complement of sensory and other means of knowledge but in all cases, it is the true and highest principle of validation. In his *Anu-vyākhyāna* he asserts:

> The very validation of knowledge depends upon the *Sākṣī*, which is the ultimate principle that knows the knowledge.[5]

The decisions arrived at by the *Sākṣī* with regard to the tests are infallible[6] and their validity cannot be questioned because *Sākṣī* is competent to know its flawlessness and the validity of the tests applied, without recourse to further tests.[7]

Madhva holds that the criterion of *Sākṣī-pratyakṣa* backed by *parīkṣa* (tests) is the terminus of all tests and processes of reasoning by which belief could be converted to logical certainty. Owing its intuitive nature its approbation is the logical limit of all certainty, clarification and validation. According to his famous treatises[8] like the *Anu-vyākhyāna* and

---

5. *jñānasya grāhkeṇaiva māntatā mite* — *Anu-vyākhyāna*, 49.
6. *na parīkṣaṇavasthasyāt sākṣisiddhe tva saṁśayāt.*
   — *Ibid.*
7. *parīkṣadescha satyataṁ tena hyeva mataṁ bhavet.* — *Ibid.*, p. 14b.
8. *sukha dukkhādi viṣayaṁ suddhaṁ saṁsāragesvapi;*
   nirdoṣatvādinīya māt tadbaliṣṭataṁ mataṁ. — *Ibid.*, p. 15;
   atha ākāśakālādigātmamanāmsi sukha duḥkha dayasca sākṣā; sākṣīgocaraḥ; anyetu padārdhāḥ yathayathmindriyaliṅgāgamagamyā ityacārya Siddhāntaḥ. Vādavali, 426; Cf. P. Nagaraja Rao (ed. & tr.) *Vādavali by Jayatīrtha*, Madras: The Adyar Library, 1943, pp. 119-20.

Jayatīrtha's Vādāvali while elucidating the nature and function of *Sākṣī* Sri Madhva and Jayatīrtha, the greatest exponent of the former's works affirm that the validity of certain direct and immediate cognitions such as ether, time, space, self, mind, pleasure, pain, desire is established by *Sākṣī* or witness-consciousness. Jayatīrtha's *Vādavali* further adds that the rest of the objects are cognized by the appropriate means of valid knowledge, viz. the sense organs, inference and verbal testimony. Madhva as well as Jayatīrtha unanimously hold that the *svarūpendriya* of *Sākṣī* intuits pleasure, pain, desire, etc. not only in waking state but also in the state of *suṣupti* where the external senses and the mind do not function.[9] According to Jayatīrtha,[10] the validity of phenomena cognized in the past as well as present is established by witness-consciousness (*Sākṣī*).

According to Madhva, *Śruti* and its particular import have to be recognized by the *Sākṣī*, which in turn must be assured of its validity by the *Śruti*. According to Jayatīrtha[11] even the validity of cognitions from the scriptures by outsiders who have no faith in *āgama*s are established by Sākṣi or the witness-consciousness. In case by means of either scripture or some transcendental perception even the direct experiences of the *Sākṣī* are proved to have been illusory experiences, it roots out the very rationale of the conception of *Sākṣī*. When perception and inference come in conflict with *āgama* how to determine the truth? The Advaitins by drawing distinction between *vyavahārika* and *paramārthika* realities contend that the

---

9. *tasmātsusuptāvapi sukhānubhāvādiviśeṣenatayā; pratīyamānaḥ kālaḥ sākṣīnaivekṣanīyaḥ.* — *Ibid.* 458; p. 130.

10. *tadetaditi sarvañcha dṛsyaṁ vā smṛtigocaraṁ; sākṣīsiddena kālena khacitaṁ hyeva vartate.* — *Ibid.* 414; p. 114.

11. *tasmājñānagrāhakenaiva sākṣīṇa tatpramāṇyādhyāvasāyaḥ.* — *Ibid.*, 437; p. 123.

vyavahārika experiences are sublated and transcended by the experience of non-dual reality. Denying this contention, Madhva opines that the sanctity of scripture cannot brush away the validity of perception or inference.

Sākṣī and the God

In the philosophy of Madhva, God is the independent being who is endowed with infinite attributes[12] and unlimited powers. He is the controller of sentient (*cit*) and insentient (*acit*), which have limited powers and not all-knowing. *Prakṛti, puruṣa, kāla,* etc., metaphysically depend on one independent principle, God or *Brahman.*

While interpreting the truths of the scripture in accordance with the authority of *Sākṣī-pramāṇa* and *upajīvya-pramāṇa* Madhva's realistic metaphysics conceives God as *svatantra* who occupies the central position. In Dvaita Vedānta, God (Viṣṇu) is the independent, and conceived as supreme and perfect individual. Based on the scriptural authority of the second aphorism of the *Vedānta-Sūtra*s of Bādarāyaṇa, Madhva characterizes God (Viṣṇu) as the creator, sustainer, destroyer, giver of knowledge, and liberator, etc., of the universe. According to Madhva, Lord Viṣṇu is only the efficient cause of the universe but not its material cause, which is subject to transformation every moment. Lord Viṣṇu, is also the bestower of being (*satta*) to all souls. God's will is always true (*satya-saṅkalpa*) without whose grace liberation is impossible. Madhva's *Viṣṇu-Tattva-Nirṇaya* refers to the five-fold distinction of reality between *jīva*s, *jaḍa*s and *Brahman* on the one hand, and mutually among *jīva*s and *jaḍa*s themselves on the other. According to this treatise, since the above scheme

12. See: P. Nagaraja Rao, *The Epistemology of Dvaita Vedānta*, Madras: The Adyar Library & Research Centre, 1976, p. 118.

of five-fold difference is cognized, maintained and controlled by God, there can be no illusions for him.[13]

Sākṣī and the World

Madhva's doctrine of the reality of world-experience is a natural corollary from his doctrine of *Sākṣī*. According to Madhva, despite being imperfect, finite and its ever-changing nature, the world is a fact of experience. Its diversity, its dispersal in space and time are also true. Madhva examines the doctrine of *vyavahārika-pramāṇya* and remarks that the validity of sense-perception concerning the reality of world-experience cannot be restricted only to the present moment of perception or to the time of perception, endorsed by *pratyakṣa* including *Sākṣī-pratyakṣa*. In such case, *Śruti* will also lose its absolute validity. Madhva asserts that the *vyavahārika-pramāṇya* does not deny the sublation of world-experience. It would be a contradiction to regard *pratyakṣa* as valid at the time (*tatkālikaṁ*) and on the other hand maintain that it is sublated. Based on scriptural evidence[14] Madhva contends that the reality of world-experience as a fact is proved on the logic that God is the eternal perceiver/percipient of the world in which we dwell.

Sākṣī and Jīvas, Bondage and Release

Sākṣi is the eternal aspect of the non-substantive *manas* which is the real nature (*svarūpa*) of the *jīva*. Madhva contends that his doctrine of plurality of souls is based on the presupposition of the theory of *karma*. According to him, inequalities of all kinds between individuals are based on the hypothesis of the

---

13. *parameśvarena jñātvāt rakshitatvāccha na; dvaitaṁ bhrānti kalpitaṁ; na īśvarasya bhrāntiḥ.* — *Viṣṇu-Tattva-Nirṇaya*, p. 27.
14. *Śvetāśvatara Upaniṣad*, 1.3; 3.12; 5.5.

beginningless peculiarity (*anādi-viśeṣa*) which distinguishes one soul from another. He further asserts that the absence of direct experience (*anusandhāna*) of another's experiences as one's own is the ultimate basis of *jīva-svarūpa-bheda-vāda*. Since the origin of *karma* of an individual *jīva* is not traceable, Madhva is of the view that the conception of plurality of souls is without beginning. Madhva conceives *jīva*s as "*sa-viśeṣa*" (having aspects) because some aspects of the *jīva*s are obscured and some are un-obscured.

As a realist, Madhva holds that bondage and release are equally real. With reference to "bondage" Madhva admits the "doership" (*kartṛtva*) and "enjoyership" (*bhoktṛtva*) of *jīva*s, who out of ignorance think that these capabilities are their own. According to Madhva, the senses and intellect, etc. and their objects of enjoyment despite being real are not the possessions of *jīva*s, whose bondage is not due to *karma, ajñāna, kāla, guṇa*s, etc., but controlled by God.[15] Since the power of *prakṛti* is controlled by the inscrutable and mysterious will of God (*acintya-adbhūta-Śakti*), he is the cause of the bondage of the souls (*jīva*s). Owing to the dependence of all finite reality on God, even the power of doership of the *jīva*s is subjected to the divine will for its existence and functioning.

Since the soul's bondage is ultimately due to divine will, which obscures the intrinsic self-luminosity of *jīva*s, the removal of their bondage by means of the illumination of the souls is also due to divine will. Hence, in his *Anu-vyākhyāna*, Madhva affirms that without God's grace even the power of knowledge cannot serve as the means of release of souls. Madhva emphasizes the role of God's grace by enunciating that the highest form of devotion (*bhakti*) moves God to shower

---

15. *na ca karmavimāmakālāguṇapṛbhrtīsamacittanu taddhi yataḥ.*
— *Dvādaśa-stotra*, iii. 6.

His grace on the *jīva*, which releases the latter from bondage and even nullifies the soul's *prārabdha-karma* when an individual attains *aparokṣa-jñāna*.[16] Madhva contends that it is not one's *karma* or *a-vidyā* but God's own power (*paramacchadika*), which ultimately prevents the *jīva*s from realizing their own blissful nature and its intrinsic relation to God. In Madhva's opinion even after by true knowledge *jīva*'s *a-vidyā* is dispelled, they enjoy the innate bliss of selfhood only after the removal of the last veil of obscuration by God as the *biṁba*. Thus, Madhva lays stress on the new synthesis between spiritual enlightenment of the *jīva*s and the divine grace.

In the philosophical framework of Madhva, *mokṣa* is essentially a state of positive bliss, which presupposes the survival of an experienced. By definition, it is free from all imperfections and passions, evils of embodied existence. According to him, the freed souls experience unalloyed blessedness in blissful mutual fellowship and communion with God. From the theory of *svarūpa-bheda* of souls he deduces the hierarchic gradation in the nature, range, equality, intensity, etc., of *svarūpānanda* or innate bliss (*ānanda-tāra-tamya*) of released souls. He points out the natural gradation among the released souls as well as disparity in their *sādhana*, and also refers to the distinctive enjoyment of their own selfhood and *svarūpānanda*.

Thus, in Madhva's Dvaita Vedānta, *Sākṣī* is a distinctive feature of epistemology. It is the basis, prop and support of this whole theory of knowledge. He earned great recognition by discovering and postulating such an apriori criterion of epistemological reference on whose solid foundation his Philosophical Realism is built.

---

16. *ityaderna na harim vinā jñāna svabhāvatopi syānmuktiḥ kasyāpi hi kvacit.*

— *Anu-vyākhyāna*, p. 1.

11

Vallabha's Interpretation of Vedānta

K.A.P. Lakshmi

VALLABHA (1401 AD) is a Telugu Brāhmin of South India, who migrated to the north, and developed the views of Viṣṇusvāmin, who belonged to the thirteenth century. He accepts not only the authority of the Upaniṣads, the *Bhagavad-Gītā* and the *Brahma-Sūtra*, but also of the *Bhāgavata-purāṇa*. In his works, *Anu-bhāṣya*, *Siddhānta-rahasya* and *Bhāgavata-ṭīkā-subodhini*, he offers theistic interpretation of Vedānta, which differs from those of Śaṅkara and Rāmānuja. His view is called *Suddhādvaita*, or Pure Non-Dualism, and declares that the whole world is real and is subtly *Brahman*. The individual souls and inanimate world are in essence one with *Brahman*. Vallabha admits that soul (*jīva*), time (*kāla*), nature (*prakṛti*) and power/illusion (*māyā*) exist eternally; and are referred to the being of *Brahman* and have no separate existence. For him, those who accept the force of *māyā* to explain the world are not pure Advaitins, since they admit a second to *Brahman*. While Śaṅkara traces the world to *Brahman* through the force of *māyā*, Vallabha holds that *Brahman* can create the world without any connection with such a principle as *māyā*. In his view, the *śāstra* is the final authority, and our reason cannot protest against its dictates. God is *sat-cit-ānanda*, and has qualities; the *Śruti* passages, which declare that God has no qualities, mean merely that God has not the ordinary qualities.

God and Soul

God is personified as Kṛṣṇa, for Vallabha, when he is endowed with the qualities of wisdom (*jñāna*) and action (*kriyā*). He is the creator of the world, and we need not suppose that he should possess a physical body as worldly objects have, since what applies to us need not apply to the transcendent God. By the mere force of his will, God creates the whole world. Not only God is agent (*kartā*), but also enjoyer (*bhoktā*). Though God has no need to assume a body, he appears in various forms to please his devotees. The highest, when associated with wisdom, it is *Brahman*, and can be approached through knowledge (*jñāna*), as stated in the Upaniṣads. Kṛṣṇa is the supreme God, and has to be worshipped according to the principles of the *Bhagavad-Gītā* and the *Bhāgavata*.

Vallabha says that *Brahman* becomes whatever It wills by the evolution (*āvirbhāva*) and involution (*tirobhāva*) of Its qualities. The soul (*jīva*) is atomic in size, and is one with *Brahman*, and constitutes a part of it. When the *ānanda* of *Brahman* is obscured, we have the soul. Though soul is produced, it is a manifestation, and as real and eternal as *Brahman*. Vallabha distinguishes three kinds of souls. The pure souls (*suddha-jīva*s) are those whose lordly qualities (*aiśvarya*) are not obscured by the force of ignorance (*a-vidyā*). The mundane souls (*saṁsāra-jīva*s) are those, which are caught in the meshes of *a-vidyā* by experiencing birth and death because of their connection with gross and subtle bodies. The liberated souls (*mukta-jīva*s) are those, which are freed from the bonds of *saṁsāra* through insight into truth (*vidyā*). When the soul attains liberation, it recovers its suppressed qualities and becomes one with God.

The inanimate world is also "filled with *Brahman*" (*brahmātmaka*). In it the two qualities of *Brahman* — knowledge and bliss, are obscured, and what remains is *suddha-satta* or pure existence. Since it is *Brahman* that is manifested in the form of the world, the latter is regarded as the "work of *Brahman*" (*brahma-kārya*). Creation and destruction of the world are only the manifestation and non-manifestation of the supreme, who puts on these forms. *Brahman* becomes a product and is apprehended in the state of creation, while in destruction the world returns to its original form, and ceases to be an object of perception. The world, therefore, is as eternal and real as *Brahman* himself, and its creation and destruction are due to the power (*Śakti*) of *Brahman*. The world cannot be regarded as an illusory appearance; nor is it essentially different from *Brahman*. The relation of cause and effect is of absolute identity. The world in truth is *Brahman*. *Brahman* manifests himself of his own will as the individual souls and the world, without undergoing any change in his essential nature. He is the material as well as the efficient cause of the world. The charges of partiality and cruelty cannot be attributed to *Brahman*, since the difference of *jīva*s from *Brahman* is admitted by Vallabha. He holds that *jīva*, after freed from the fetters of *māyā*, becomes one with *Brahman*.

Vallabha looks upon God as the whole; and asserts that an individual is identical with God, and there is no real difference between these two. The analogy of sparks to fire is employed to this purpose. The individual soul is not a supreme Soul being clouded by ignorance (*a-vidyā*), but the soul is itself *Brahman*, with one attribute rendered imperceptible. The soul is both doer and enjoyer. It is atomic in size, though pervades the whole body by its quality of intelligence, as sandalwood makes its presence felt by its scent. For Rāmānuja, who accepts one ultimate substantive reality, the difference between the God and self is never destroyed. Rāmānuja relates the God and souls as whole and parts, where the parts are really different from the whole. His view of *samānādhi-kāraṇya* or *viśeṣa-naviśeṣya-bhāva* points out the co-existence of many parts in the same whole. Vallabha, on the other hand gives us something, where the differences are abolished.

The world of *māyā* is not regarded as unreal, since *māyā* is nothing else than a power which *Īśvara* of his free will produces. Vallabha asserts, "*Brahman* is the efficient and the material cause of the universe. He is not only the creator of the universe but is the universe itself." He accepts the account in the *Bṛhadāraṇyaka Upaniṣad*, which says that *Brahman* desired to become many, and himself became the multitude of individual souls and the world. A desire for self-expression is innate in *Brahman*. *Māyā* according to Vallabha, is the power of *Īśvara*, through which he brings about the evolution and the dissolution of the world. *Māyā* is different from ignorance (*a-vidyā*), which is responsible for the obscuration of the unity of things and the production of consciousness of difference. Vallabha does not admit an inert nature (*prakṛti*) which is energized by *Brahman*. Though *Brahman* in itself is not known, it is known when it manifests itself through the world.

Saṁsāra and Mokṣa

According to Vallabha, *saṁsāra* is unreal, and the world is real. However, he says that to ascribe plurality to the world is wrong. Though we do not realize that the world is a form of *Brahman*, yet it is true. The soul (*jīva*) is infected with a wrong view of the nature of the world. To those who have attained the truth, the world appears as *Brahman*. To those who have learnt the truth from the scriptures, it appears as both *Brahman* and *māyā*, i.e., something other than *Brahman*, though they know that the former is real and the latter is not. The ignorant make no distinction between the reality of *Brahman* and the unreality of the plural appearances, which set themselves forth as objective and independent. Ignorance (*a-vidyā*) is located in the mind of man. Vallabha thus does not accept the view of the unreality of the world as such. If the world is unreal, we cannot even say that it is one with *Brahman,* since a relation of identity cannot exist between a real entity and an unreal appearance. There is a possibility of deception, though it is not divinely conditioned.

The soul (*jīva*) bound by *māyā* cannot attain liberation except through the grace of God. Devotion (*bhakti*) is the chief means of liberation, though knowledge (*jñāna*) is also useful. All sins are put away if we have true faith in God, a principle that was much exaggerated in practice. Vallabha deprecated all kinds of self-mortification. The body is the temple of God, and there is no meaning in attempting to destroy it. *Karma*s precede knowledge of the supreme, and present even when this knowledge is gained. The liberated perform all actions (*karma*s). The highest goal is not liberation (*mukti*), but rather eternal service of Kṛṣṇa and participation in his sports in the celestial Bṛndāvana. Vallabha distinguishes the transcendent consciousness of *Brahman* from *Puruṣottama.* The souls, delivered from the trammels of life, are of different kinds. There are those who have freed themselves from previous subjection, like Śaṅkara, and those who dwell in the city of God, where they attain freedom through the grace of God. There are others, who resort to devotion (*bhakti*) and develop perfect love and become the associates of God. Vallabha lays great stress on a life of unqualified love of God.

The relation between *Brahman* on one side, and the individual souls (*jīva*s) and the inanimate nature (*jaḍa*) on the other, is one of pure identity, similar to the relation of whole (*aṁsin*) and part (*aṁsa*). While the difference is subordinated by Vallabha, non-difference alone is said to be real. He interprets the great sentence, *tat tvaṁ asi* (That thou art) as literally true, while Rāmānuja and Nimbārka take it in a figurative sense. When the self attains bliss, and the inanimate world, consciousness and bliss, the difference between *Brahman* and these will lapse a position, which Rāmānuja does not accept.

Means of Liberation

The temperamental difference in the world are responsible for the different ways of approaching God, as the *śāstra*s mention the three paths of action (*karma*), knowledge (*jñāna*) and devotion (*bhakti*) as the means of liberation. The emphasis on one of these three factors has resulted in difference among the different Schools of the Vedānta.

Vallabha has divided the souls into three classes in the descending order: *puṣṭi*, *maryādā*, and *pravāha*. Souls, which are aimlessly moving and completely engrossed in the world, and which never think of God belong to the class of *pravāha*. Those souls, which study the *śāstra*s, understand the real nature of God and worship Him accordingly form the second class of souls, *maryādā*. The *puṣṭi* souls are, however, the chosen people of God, who worship Him most ardently out of their boundless love for Him. The souls are called *puṣṭi* (strength/potential) as they are blessed enough to enjoy the divine grace, which enables them to realize the highest ideal.

Persons who live an objectionable life have to suffer and to move in the cycle of the world. Those who perform sacrifices for the fulfilment of desires get their reward accordingly and go to heaven by the "path of manes," and have to return to the world of mortals when their merit is exhausted. When a person performs Vedic sacrifices without any desire, he enjoys spiritual happiness, and later on when his life is over, assumes a new body according to the procedure laid down by the doctrine of five fires. In the new birth, he gets the knowledge of God, and ultimately qualifies himself for union with Him by passing through the different stages of the "path of gods." In the Vedic sacrifices, God manifests himself in the form of rituals (*agni-hotra, daśa-pūrṇa-māsa, pasu, chāturmāśya* and *soma*). Those who follow the ritual power (*kriyā-śakti*) of God by performing the sacrifices and possessing the knowledge of God enjoy liberation in the form of divine joy. The liberation in the *maryāda-mārga* is gradual, as one is required to move spiritually through the "path of gods." But, immediate liberation is possible only through the grace of God.

Devotion to the Lord is of many different forms, and there are nine stages such as (1) hearing, (2) reciting, (3) remembering, (4) falling at the feet, (5) worship, (6) salutation, (7) service, (8) friendship, and (9) self-dedication. These stages are in the ascending order, and show the progress of the devotee to love God. One who studies the *śāstra*s realizes the greatness of God, and considers Him as his own soul, and consequently bows down to God out of strong boundless affection. This kind of devotion, which has been enjoined in the *śāstra*s and which is, therefore practised accordingly, is known as *maryādā-bhakti*, and corresponds to the *vaidhi-bhakti* of other Vaiṣṇava Schools. The *maryādā* devotees generally enjoy union with *Puruṣottama*. Sometimes they enjoy the status of the Lord and dwell in his vicinity, or remain in His place.

In the case of *puṣṭi*, the devotees are further divided into four categories according to their special qualities. The four types are (1) *pravāha*, (2) *maryādā*, (3) *puṣṭi*, and (4) *suddha*. The *puṣṭi* devotees, in general, are first united with *Puruṣottama* without going through the stages of the "path of gods," and the Lord, out of sheer grace, then brings them out, gives them a new divine form, and allows them to participate in His eternal sport (*rāsa-līlā*). The devotees of the highest order, like the *gopika*s, immediately enter into the Lord's arena of sports, and enjoy the very bliss of the Lord for all time. In the eternal *līlā*, the devotee enjoys all sorts of pleasure in the company of the Lord who entirely places Himself at the disposal of the former. This is, according to Vallabha, the highest stage of liberation, the *summum bonum*.

Vallabha taught the philosophy of *Suddhādvaita* and the religion of *puṣṭi* on the authority of the *śāstras*, which are to him the final court of appeal. Some of his doctrines such as *Brahman* possessing attributes, transformation of *Brahman* into the world, the reality of the world, and combination of action with knowledge, were known even before Śaṅkara. The ideas of devotion, self-surrender and divine grace were current before Vallabha. However, the assertion of the coexistence of contradictory attributes in *Brahman*, the theory of the creation of the world from the very form (*sva-rūpa*) of *Brahman*, the transformation of *Brahman* into the world, self-dedication to the Lord, emphasis on God's grace, the aesthetic and emotional form of devotion are special features in Vallabha's teaching.

12

The Echo of Vedānta in Tyāgarāja's Musical Compositions

Prabala Janaki

PHILOSOPHY is a subject of subtle intellect and cannot be conceived by the minds associated with mundane affairs; and at the same time, philosophy without practice cannot yield the required results. In this context, Tyāgarāja has made it possible to understand the philosophical values by the common man in the society through his melodious style of writing in an attractive form of music. In the world of music, Tyāgarāja is a stalwart in the Karnatik (Carnatic) Style, who had thousands of compositions to his credit. Since he was a staunch devotee of Lord Śrī Rāma, all his *kīrtana*s (psalms) were dedicated to Him.

Every composition of Tyāgarāja overflows with the sentiment of devotion (*bhakti*) and arrests the attention of connoisseurs, the under standers of the music-taste (*rasajñas*) with the qualities of *sāhitya* or literature wedded to the attractive *saṅgīta* or music. Of the four-fold ways of knowledge (*jñāna*), action (*karma*), devotion (*bhakti*) and discipline of meditation (*yoga*) by which a person gets liberation (*mukti*) according to the Indian philosophy, devotion (*bhakti*) is the approachable way, which is within the reach of a commoner. *Bhakti* is of nine types as stated in the following *śloka*, according to *Bhāgavatam*:

> *śravaṇaṁ, kīrtanaṁ, viśnoḥ, smaraṇaṁ, pāda-sevanaṁ;*
> *arcanaṁ, vandanaṁ, dāsyaṁ, sakhya-mātma-nivedanaṁ*
>
> (Listening, singing to God, remembering, worshipping the feet; offering, praising, serving, closeness, self-surrender to God).

In addition, according to Nārada's *Bhakti-Sūtra*s they are eleven types of devotion. As *kīrtana* is treated as *bhakti*, Tyāgarāja took up this path of devotion; and he can be considered as second to none in expressing it through psalms. In the famous psalm, *endaro mahānubhāvulu; aṅdariki nā vandanāmu* (Numerous are the great multitude of thinkers; to all of them I salute), which is on the tongue of every music-lover, is filled with high emotion; the author salutes to everybody who enjoys the exquisite beauty of the Lord in his lotus heart.

> *candurin varṇintu yanda-candamuna;*
> *hr̥dayāra vindamuna jūci,*
> *brahm-ānandaṁ anubha viñcu varendaro.*
> (Moon is described in extraordinary beauty; but by seeing in the inner depths of heart, how many do enjoy the divine-great-joy).

The Upaniṣads differentiate the levels of joy (*ānanda*) in relation to the worlds of *manuṣya*, *paitrus*, *yakṣas*, *gandharvas*, *devatās* and *Indra*, etc. each 100 times greater than its predecessor. Finally, the highest bliss is *Brahmānanda*, being the highest goal of human endeavour according to the Upaniṣadic philosophy. Tyāgarāja says that those who can delight in music, i.e., the *samvedana* have the realization of God:

> *sāmagānalola manasija lāvanya dhanyamūrdhanyulu*
> (Blessed and benefited are those minds that enjoy music).

In the multifarious ways to the realization of the Lord, *sāmagāna* (singing of songs/psalms) is one aspect of music. Tyāgarāja indirectly paves the way to make music as the instrument for realization of *Brahman*, but not for earning money. He compares the mind that roams in the garden, which says, *mānasa vana chara vara sañcāramu nilipi*. . . reminds the song of Śaṅkara's *Śivānandalahari*. Like this in every composition of Tyāgarāja the highest philosophical truths are imbibed, if one can ponder over the inner meaning of the psalms through application of one's own mind; thus there is no need of studying any advanced texts in the philosophy. The intellect (*citta*) is compared to lotus, which is to be offered at the feet of the Almighty. The knowledge of sound (*svara*), diction (*laya*), and note (*rāga*) can lead one to the divine path according to Tyāgarāja. In the next stanza (*caraṇa*) it is said that divine wisdom is the only path to reach God; and overflowing love is said to be the devotion, that echoes with that of Nārada's *Bhakti-Sūtras*. In the sixth stanza *hoyalu meera*, Tyāgarāja says that the fulfilment of life lies in getting the direct "vision of the Self" (*Ātmā-sākṣātkāra*), which is transcendental bliss.

Tyāgarāja says that singing the glory of God, is the real devotion. The great musician teaches at large the way by which people can get lost in the path of devotion. He says briefly that the essence of great epics like the *Rāmāyaṇa*, the Vedas, and Śāstras, etc. is to inculcate faith in God, which is like experiencing Śiva in the music itself. He says that he who meditates with overflowing devotion on Rāma can only be the real servants of Śrī Rāma.

Keeping the time factor with reference to devotion, Tyāgarāja addresses the mind, by stating that it should not waste time, but contemplate upon God:

proddu poyyeni śrī rāmuni bhajiṁpa ve manasā;
niddura ceta konnāḷḷu, viṣaya buddhula ceta konnāḷḷu.

Until the sun sets, worship Śrī Rāma Oh, Mind !
Don't stop days for sleep; subjective intellect for days

This echoes the traditional Sanskrit *śloka*:

āyurvarṣa sataṁ nṛuṇaṁ parimitaṁ rātraṁ tadardhaṁ gataḥ;
paścārdhaḥ sva parasya cārdhama paraṁ bālatva vṛddhatva yo;
seṣaṁ vyādhi viyoga duḥkha bharitaṁ sevādhi bhirniyate;
jīve vaṛ taraṅga cāñcala tire saukhyaṁ kutaḥ prāṇi nāṁ.

The philosophical point is that the almighty pervades in all creation from ant to *Brahman*, *pīpilakādi brahma paryantaṁ* was brought out by Tyāgarāja beautifully in some other lines:

cīmallo brahmallo śiva keśavādulalo
prema meera melagu cu nunde . . .

(In ants, in brāhmaṇas, in Śiva and Keśava, with love you are moving, thoroughly existing)

Again he says:

anni nīvanuchu antaraṅgamuna,
thinnaga vedaki telesikontinaya. . . .

(All you are, believing in inner-heart after straight search, I came to know).

In other words, Tyāgarāja says that after a thorough search, he came to know in his inner self that the almighty is all.

The *Karma* theory, according to Indian tradition implies that one would surely get the result according to his or her previous deeds — either good or bad. Further, it is said that praying to God for incentives is a futile exercise, and God cannot grant the boons for requests, rather bestows his blessing out of his grace. Tyāgarāja in his verse, *adigi sukhamu levara-anubha viñciri rā* (By demanding comforts who has enjoyed), says that it is impossible to get liberation by one's effort, rather possible through God's abundant grace. The Vedāntic notion of devotion is that through grace of the *Īśvara*, one could get liberation. Similarly, Vedāntic notion of ultimate reality of life is reiterated in another line:

> *rānidi rādu surāśurula kaina ponidi podu bhū-surula kaina*
>
> (Un-attainable can not be acquired for lords or demons even that which cannot be left will not be lost by landlords even).

Self-contentment is another good virtue that a person should cultivate. Tyāgarāja in one his compositions says that though a man amasses huge wealth, he needs a fist of grain to satisfy his hunger; and though one has pairs of clothes, but only one is to wear. Similarly, the psalm continues to reveal the truth that though a river flows full one gets water as per the measure of his jug.

> *rūkalu padivelunna cāredu nūkalu gatigāni,*
> *o! manasā,*
> *kokal veyunna kattukonuta kokata gāni;*
> *eru nindi parina pātra ku thagu neeru vacchu gāni. . .*
>
> (Rupees ten thousand one may have, only a handful grains one needs O! self; though thousand *saries* one may have, only one to wrap the body; though a river overflows, we get water as per our jug only).

Tyāgarāja sings that even though one is an Emperor, one needs only six feet for funeral at the end of his life. His composition infuses the quality of generosity in the rich, so that they can share wealth with the poor and experience the highest state of joy in helping the needy. This view of Tyāgarāja echoes with the Upaniṣadic saying: *na karmaṇā na praja yatha nena; tyāgenekaina mr̥tattva māna suḥ*, which implies immortality cannot be obtained by *karma* and desires, neither by progeny nor by wealth but by *tyāga* (renunciation) only.

In *jñāna mosaga rādha* (give us knowledge) another composition Tyāgarāja hints at the *Advaita* doctrine that revelation leads to liberation. Here the word *jñāna* does not imply just knowledge but *jñāna-mārga* or *jñāna-yoga*. Śaṅkara says in his work, *Ātma-bodha*: *pākasya vahnivat jñānaṁ vinā mokṣa nasiddhati*, which means that without fire cooking is impossible and without revelation, one cannot be free from the cycle of birth and death. To put it in Telugu idiom,

> *manta lekundā vanta ela kādo,*
> *jñānaṁ lekundā mokṣamu rādu*
>
> (Without fire cooking is impossible, similarly without knowledge liberation is impossible)

The Upaniṣadic saying *satyaṁ jñānam anantaṁ brahma* can be remembered in this connection. The realization of the Almighty and Infinite *Brahman* is possible, not by mere intellect but by the illumination of knowledge. Moreover, here it refers to the necessity of knowledge (*jñāna*) to attain liberation (*mokṣa*) depicting the Upaniṣadic perspective. The Upaniṣadic sentence says *Brahman* is real, knowledge, and infinite; and similarly Tyāgarāja asserts the knowledge to be a pre-requisite. Further in accordance with the Upaniṣadic spirit of the *mahā-vākya* — *tat tvaṁ asi*, Tyāgarāja prays to Lord Śrī Rāma to grant revelation (*darśana*).

In his psalms, Tyāgarāja describes and emphasizes the Upaniṣadic and Advaitic virtues for liberation and at the same time brings out the role of devotion through singing (praise). For him *śāntaṁ* the quiet or peace is the most valuable, without which there is no happiness. One should control his senses. Tyāgarāja says, in one of his *kīrtanas* (psalms): *sāntamu leka soukhyamu ledu* (Without peace no comfort). In this psalm he remarks and asserts that one's expertise in all the Vedas, Sūtras and performance of *yajñas* (sacrifices), and even renunciation of other such *karmas* (rituals), and becoming a Bhāgavatār (performer of Vedic lore through singing) never bestow any happiness.

Thus, Tyāgarāja gives the whole essence of not only Indian philosophies but also the quintessence of Vedānta for the life of all, even for the followers of Vedānta; and he proclaims:

> *dāntula kaina vedāntula kaina,*
> *śāntamu lekha saukhyamu ledu.*
>
> (Either for ritualists or for Vedāntins, without peace, no comfort at all).

The peace, *śānta* is to be acquired by the individual with a gigantic effort, and to achieve that "worship through music" of the Almighty is the means according to Tyāgarāja, the "renounced king" who left everything for music.

Section - IV
Vedānta and other Systems

13

Meditation in Yoga and Vedānta
A Comparison

R. Venkata Reddy

PERHAPS it is true to say that meditation occupies an important place in Indian religious traditions and philosophy. However, some look upon meditation as a technique, some look upon it as "an insight into things as they really are" (*vipāsanā*), some as "intense mental worship" (*upāsanā*), and still others as the way to intense devotion (*bhakti*). Perhaps the most eloquent explication of meditation occurs in the two widely practised traditions — namely *yoga* and Vedānta. By *yoga* here, we understand Patañjali's eight-fold path of *Rāja-yoga*. The first comprehensive treatment of the subject of meditation is given in the system of *Yoga*. Its conclusions are based not only on theory but also on practice. Its approach to the problems of life is objective, its analysis is scientific, and its way of overcoming them is pragmatic. *Yoga* in the classical sense is the process through which the mind is silenced and transcended. *Yoga* does not merely mean a set of bodily postures or breathing practices; but its chief method is meditation. Of the eight aspects of *yoga*, physical postures (*āsanas*) bring calm and balance to the body and which lay stress upon the right bodily posture during meditation, etc., The fourth stage of *yoga* is breath-control (*prāṇāyāma*), and this brings harmony and energy to the vital force. The sixth stage is concentration (*dhāraṇā*), i.e., fixing the mind on a single object to the exclusion of all else. It requires withdrawal of the mind from other objects, and prepares it for meditation. These are of great value, and are the foundation for meditation.

Meditation in Yoga

Dhyāna (meditation) is the steady contemplation of the object without any break. In the stage of *dhāraṇā*, according to the system of *yoga*, the object is held continually before the mind (*citta*) with effort. When *dhāraṇā* matures, it becomes *dhyāna*, and when *dhyāna* matures, it becomes *samādhi*, (absorptive concentration). Mental techniques like *mantra* and visualization are additional important aids for meditation. They stabilize the thought process, which is necessary to allow it to rest. However, if we do not look beyond them to the Divine consciousness within ourselves, they can eventually become obstacles.

While many techniques have been introduced to facilitate the practice of *yoga*, the main process of it is very simple. Further *yoga* is not a process to find truth or happiness outward, but assures realization of the *puruṣa* or higher Self, which is free of all other considerations, in our real nature. This inner obedience requires inquiry and surrender, which are the two main aspects of *yoga*-practice. Inquiry in this context means tracing of our thought process back to its origin in consciousness, and surrender means faith in the inner reality, and relinquishing the outward seeking. Without practice of meditation, man cannot go beyond human problems. Not all other practices, however useful, will prove sufficient and bring a real change in human lives; and attention to the practice of *yoga* forms the basis of one's culture. It requires one's entire life be rooted in right consciousness and meditation. It is through meditation one enter into a new dimension of existence where fulfilment lies in perceiving. This state of perceiving allows one who practises meditation to merge into the entire universe and beyond. This is the real goal of meditation. While the goal remains the same, the kinds of meditation vary because of the different perceptions of the ultimate reality by different schools of thought. A spiritual seeker, depending upon his or her inner disposition, may choose one or another. In spite of the diversity in methods and techniques of meditation, three factors are common in the practice of meditation:

(1) The object of concentration in meditation,

(2) The centre of consciousness where the mind is held, and

(3) The method employed to invoke concentration.

The object chosen for the practice of meditation may be concrete or abstract: an image or a symbol, a word or an idea, a divine form or personality. According to Patañjali, the objects that are generally preferred for the practice of meditation are as stated below:[1]

1. The Radiant Light: The spiritual consciousness, which is beyond all sorrow, and shines in the inner recess of the heart, may be chosen. The seeker imagines in his heart a limitless, sky-like, transparent brilliance and thinks that the self is within that.

2. The illuminated Self: The heart of a holy person is always tranquil and free from all passion and attachment. By concentrating on such a heart, the mind absorbs that tranquility.

---

1. Patañjali, *Yoga-Sūtras* 1. 36-39; Cf: Swami Adeswarananda, *Meditation and Its Practices*, Wood Stocks, Vermont: Skylight Paths Publishing, 2003, p. 75.

3. Experiencing a Dream or Deep Sleep State: Dreaming about a holy personality or a divine symbol, or a blissful condition of sleep makes a deep impression on the mind.

4. Anything that is Spiritually Uplifting: A thing may be a place, some scenery, an idea, or any other thing that would evoke concentration of mind. If the mind can be concentrated on one subject, it also can be concentrated on any other object.

According to the system of *yoga,* meditation is more an objective technique than worship or subjective knowledge as conventionally understood. The goal of meditation is the cessation of all miseries through the realization of the indwelling Self or *puruṣa,* which is pure consciousness. According to *yoga,* ignorance causes all miseries; and cessation of ignorance is possible through the knowledge of reality, which is possible through meditation. The distinctive characteristics of meditation in *Yoga* may be summarized as follows:

(i) *Yoga* seeks to transform the subconscious by conscious effort.

(ii) It does not rely absolutely on reason to reach the state of concentration.

(iii) The object of meditation can be anything in the world.

(iv) The seeker of *yoga* need not have any pre-conceived idea about reality.

(v) *Yoga* considers meditation on God as an alternative method to reach the goal.

(vi) *Yoga* considers that control of the mind could be achieved through controlling physiological processes.

Meditation in Vedānta

According to the schools of Vedānta, the direct perception of the ultimate reality, the all pervading pure consciousness, *Brahman*, is possible through various paths such as knowledge (*jñāna*), and devotion (*bhakti*), etc. However, meditation is an indirect approach in Vedānta to the ultimate reality and is a form of intense mental worship (*upāsanā*). The Vedāntic concepts for direct path to self-knowledge are divided into two groups: Foundational and Structural. The seeker of self-knowledge must follow the four-fold discipline, which is said to be foundational: discrimination, dispassion, mastery over six virtues and intense longing for liberation. The three-fold steps of mediation — hearing (*śravaṇa*), repetition (*manana*) and profound reflection (*nidhi-dhyāsana*) — are said to be structural. Success in structural practices is proportional to success in foundational practices. One who aspires to greater heights must first build a strong and deep foundation, which path is prescribed for those spiritual aspirants who are more qualified and fully established in the practice of the four-fold pre-requisites, etc. In this context, meditation is a process of knowledge for right apprehension of reality rather than a focusing of the mind on some definite object. Right apprehension depends more on the knower's mind, while meditation depends on the nature of the thing known.

Vedānta directs the practices of meditation toward *Saguṇa Brahman*, the Absolute with name, form, and attributes superimposed upon it. *Saguṇa Brahman* serves as a bridge between the finite mind and the infinite, all-pervading pure consciousness. Success in mediation on *Saguṇa Brahman* qualifies the seeker for the right apprehension of *Nirguṇa Brahman*. Śaṅkara, in his commentary on the *Bṛhadāraṇyaka Upaniṣad*, describes intense mental worship or meditation (*upāsanā*) as the method to approach the deity,[2] and stated this as applicable to the lower state.

Of the four stages of meditation, worship through symbols and images is the first stage. Higher than the first stage is repetition of a sacred word and a prayer. Still higher is meditation, and the highest form of worship is maintaining constant awareness of the fact "That art Thou" (*tat tvaṁ asi*). These four stages might also be characterized in terms of three levels of worship: dualistic, qualified non-dualistic and non-dualistic. At the dualistic meditative stage, the seeker feels that God is separate from himself; and at the qualified non-dualistic stage, the seeker thinks of God as a whole and himself as a part of that whole. At non-dualistic stage, the seeker meditates on *Brahman* as all pervading pure consciousness and he feels that God and he are one. Accordingly, the *Viṣṇu-Purāṇa* illustrates the following stages in meditation:[3]

> First, meditate by fixing the mind on a divine form or Viṣṇu.
>
> Second, fix the mind on the auspicious qualities than the form.
>
> Third, fixing the mind on the divine form as one's own self.

Meditation may be objective or subjective, according to non-dualistic Vedānta. In the object-oriented meditation, the object or ideal is considered to be outside the body. Objective meditation may be associated with, or conditioned by, a sound symbol or a form symbol. In subjective meditation, the ideal or form is placed within oneself, one who meditates, usually

---

2. *Bṛhadāraṇyaka Upaniṣad* 1. 3. 9; Cf: David Frawley, *Vedāntic Meditation*, Berkeley, California: North Atlantic Books, 2000, p. 11.
3. Cf: Swami Prabhavananda and Christopher Isher Wood, *How to Know God: The Yoga Aphorisms of Patañjali*, Oxford: Clarendon Press, 1980, pp. 123-24.

in the region of the heart. As the seeker progresses in meditation, he begins to feel that his heart is not just a physical organ, but also a part of his mind where the reflection of *Brahman* is perceived. At this stage, meditation is raised from the physical level to the mental level, then the seeker casts *Brahman* in the mold of his mind, forming a mental image of it. At the final stage, this image in his heart becomes one with *Brahman*, the all-pervading pure consciousness. Vedāntic meditation aims at the state of unity, in which all beings abide in the self within the heart.

Vedānta does not neglect the psychological aspect, either. Like most of the schools of Indian philosophy, its purpose is to show us how to permanently overcome all suffering. Vedānta regards ignorance of our true self as the cause of all our life problems. By returning to our true self, we can transcend psychological suffering and detach ourselves from any possible physical suffering as well. The pain of body and mind do not belong to the self, which is beyond time and space. Another important aspect of Vedāntic meditation is clearing our minds of the afflictions and residues that block the practice of meditation. This involves affirming our true self, which is the master of the universe beyond all fear and desire, birth and death.

Vedānta suggests the practice of regular meditation for everyone, particularly during the hour or two before dawn, which it calls *Brahma-muhūrta* or the hour of God. Sunrise and sunset are other important times for meditation because at these transitional periods in nature, energy can be more easily transformed. Meditation is part or the very rhythm of life and nature and its ongoing transformations. Another very important time for meditation is the period immediately before sleep in order to clear from the mind the day's results and effects of the actions that have been performed.

According to the schools of Vedānta, there are three distinctive aspects of meditation. The main purpose of meditation is to seek the union of the individual soul or consciousness (*jīvātma*) with the all-pervading supreme Self, the pure consciousness (*paramātma*). Meditation is a form of intense mental worship (*upāsanā*) of God as one's own self. According to Śaṅkara, *upāsanā* is concentration on a divine object. In Vedāntic meditation, the mind is brought to concentration by reasoning and persuasion. The objects for the practice of meditations in *Vedānta* are: (1) a divine form, (2) an incarnation of God, (3) *Virāṭa Puruṣa*, or the cosmic person, (4) the sacred word "Oṁ", (5) *Gāyatrī mantra* or the sacred prayer of the Vedas, (6) Four *mahāvākyas* (great sayings), and (7) the meaning of a sacred text, word, or mystic syllable.

The seeker may select any of these for the practice of meditation; and through such meditation, he or she is purified of all sins and attains self-realization. Meditation should be practised on any one object. To practise meditation on different objects leads to mental confusion and defeats the very purpose of meditation. Finally, it is very pertinent here to mention certain fundamental differences between the systems of *yoga* and Vedānta with regard to meditation. The concept of reality is not the same in *yoga* and Vedānta. The ultimate reality according to Vedānta, is one without a second, while in *yoga* the ultimate realities are two: *Puruṣa* and *Prakṛti*. Thus, Vedānta is non-dualistic, while *yoga* is dualistic. The *asamprajñata samādhi* of *yoga* and the *nirvikalpa samādhi* of Vedānta are not the same. In Vedāntic meditation, the seeker does not dissociate the self from the mind. He concentrates his mind on the innermost self and meditates on it as *Brahman*. The two schools, *yoga* and Vedānta stress the practice of meditation as the sole means of attaining self-realization. Vedānta accepts the practice of eight aspects of *yoga*, but differs from the *yoga* in its philosophical view.

14

Ultimate Reality in Advaita and Tantra

Sree Jahennatha Swami

THE present essay aims to study the *Tantra* cult and its relation to Vedānta with reference to the concept of ultimate Reality. *Tantra* generally accepts the basic concepts of Advaita Vedānta and suggests the ways and means to self-realization. Further, it introduces some modifications to the theories of Vedānta with reference to the concept of ultimate Reality, which is an interesting study.

All philosophic doctrines, related to religions contain their own ideology about the ultimate Reality. Advaita Vedānta upholds *Nirguṇa Brahman* as the ultimate Reality with its *māyā* theory. Its theoretical aspect is the conception of *mokṣa* to be attained by merging of *jīva* in *Brahman*, whereas the practical method is realization of *karma-saṁnyāsa* or complete renunciation. It is true that ultimate Reality is not a mere unity underlying the diversity of the universe. For the Advaitin the ultimate Reality is beyond unity and diversity; unity and diversity are relative to each other. The ultimate Reality could be explained as the infinite consciousness implied by empirical knowledge or as the infinite being presupposed in all finite existence. *Tantra* is closely associated with *Śakti* cult. The *Śākta* philosophy confirms that the world is the *līlā* (play) of the

Śakti. Using this "unreal" world as an instrument, the *jīva* should attain emancipation, which is the *sammum bonum* of life. The duality is the act of *māyā* in Advaita but *līlā* of *Śakti* in *tantra*, which is an equal and opposite form of energy to Śiva. Advaita advances its synthesis by its concepts of different levels of Reality but the *tantra* does it by its doctrine of unity in duality and duality in unity.

The beginning of *Śakti* cult as the worship of the divinity in the female form or "mother goddess" could be traced back from the pre-historic times. But unfortunately the philosophy of *tantra* cult had been hidden and commented as a dangerous ritual or magic; later, the influence of Vedānta has reformed the *tantra* cult from the level of offering life-sacrifices to the worship of "mother goddess," and to the stage of realization of the ultimate Reality. The *tantra* cult enters a new phase only in the beginning of the seventh century CE and after the emergence of the Tāntric literary works, viz. *Lalitā-Sahasranāma*, *Saundaryalaharī* and some *Śākta Upaniṣad*s. There is a strong misconception about *Tantra* cult regarding the adoption of certain rituals related to the usage of *māṁsa* (flesh), *matsya* (fish), *madya* (wine), *mudrā* (gestures), and *maithuna* (fornication). In the light of Vedāntic realization, the word *māṁsa* has been explained as the sacrifice of earthly attachments, the *matsya* denotes the unrest of mind and mastery over such senses, *madya* means the nectar emerging from the top of the head and coming down through the inner tongue, *mudra* means the meaningful communications and *maithuna* denotes the unification of the male and female concepts within oneself.

The worship of Śakti is seen in the *Ṛgveda* where "mother goddess" is praised as "the supporter of the earth" living in heaven. The *Kena Upaniṣad* praises her as the "great mother of universe." Śakti is the power of existence, knowledge and bliss of *Brahman* and is inseparable. Śakti according to *tantra* exists in male, female or neutral form. The *Saundaryalahari* says that when Śiva is united with Śakti, he is able to create, otherwise he is unable even to move. Śiva without Śakti is a corpse. Liberation in Tāntrism is the knowledge of Śakti, which leads to the culmination of the blissful effulgence of the supreme.

Tantra-Śāstra recognizes the four Vedas as treasures of knowledge, and asserts the ultimate spiritual experience and the unity of *cit*, or the realization of *cit*, which is nothing but knowing *Brahman*. In the early Vedic literature all the female forms like Rātri, Vāk, Pṛthivi, and Sarasvati were given only a subordinate position. But, before the end of the Vedic period, Śakti as a supreme Goddess emerged. The *Taittirīya Āraṇyaka* refers to the three different names Śakti, as Kātyāyanī, Kanayākumārī and Durgā. In the *Kena Upaniṣad* she is identified with Umā Haimavatī, who symbolizes *Brahma-vidyā*. Śakti is worshipped as mother of the Vedas as well. Historical references confirm that the scholars brought all the tribal deities, beliefs and faiths under the aegis of the *veda* (wisdom) by spiritualizing with the Vedānta philosophy, without erasing the inner core of their individuality. We find such notions from *Devī Mahātmya* and *Lalitā-Sahasranāma*. This is the background for the tribal deity who is fond of flesh and wine with sacrificial victims then hailed as the mother of the Vedas and the presiding deity of *Brahma-vidyā* with the identification of *Brahman*, and leads to direct realization produced by the famous sayings: *Tat tvaṁ asi* (That thou art), *so haṁ* (He I am), *Ahaṁ Brahmāsmi* (I am *Brahman*).

Tantra contains a remarkable philosophic presentation of religious teaching, profoundly applying to the ritual of psychological experience, which leads to emancipation. *Tantra* is a word, which has always been misunderstood and misinterpreted. The word *tantra* is derived from the root *tan*, which means "to spread," and the suffix *tra* forms "to save." The real meaning is "spreading the knowledge which saves." *Tantra* is a great boon to humanity and it is the message for real peace and happiness. It is a practical philosophy built upon the edifice of scientific reasoning, which is being affirmed by the modem scientists. It teaches the best practices of meditation (*yoga*) and proclaims the unity of all existence, promotes the happiness and welfare of all beings, to make them free from chaos and contradiction.

Tāntrism consists of *jñāna* (the concepts of wisdom), *yoga*, (the guidelines for meditation), *kriyā* (instructions for rituals) and *cārya* (the programmes of morality and social duties). The *jñāna* is the union with *Brahman*, the *yoga* is meditation on *Brahman*, the *kriyā* is praise of *Brahman* and *cārya* is the external worship. There are sixty-four *tantra* texts, which strictly observe this regulation. *Tantra* is essentially a *sādhana-śāstra* (a manual or scripture for achievement).

According to Tāntric philosophy, the ultimate Reality is both partless whole and with parts, or without stains and all-encompassing (*niskala* and *sakala*). It considers the world as a lesser reality in a sense for it owes its existence to the association of Śiva and *śakti*, in Vedānta terms *Brahman* and *māyā*. The concept of *māyā* in *Advaita* philosophy, remains unexplained as true or false. But the concept of Śakti in *tantra* possesses as much reality and importance as Śiva. For *Advaita* the ultimate Reality is changeless, the reality of the world is only an appearance. However, *Tantra* confirms that the ultimate Reality is immutable in one aspect and undergoes a real evolution in another aspect. The ultimate Reality in *tantra* is neither wholly static nor wholly dynamic. It is both. The doctrine of unity in duality is the unique feature of Tāntric philosophy. *Lalitā-Sahasranāma*, a Tāntric work of seventh century CE, expresses in its hymns through the names of the "Mother Goddess," Lalitāmbikā as Śiva-Śakti-aikya-rūpiṇī (united form of Śiva and Śakti), Cideka rasa rūpiṇī (essence form of everything), Śiva mūrtin (form of Śiva), Śivī (the consort of Śiva), Śva-prakāśanī (self-illumined) and Vimarśa rūpa (pure luminosity of illuminated self-awareness). Thus, there is no Śiva without Śakti, and no Śakti without Śiva; and without supreme Śakti, there is no all-pervasive knowledge of *Brahman*. The Śiva is Omnipotent, the cause of all becoming, the leader of everything to be adored by all, and the cause of all *puruṣārthas*, cannot manifest without this supreme Śakti.

All Śruti and Smṛti, Epic, Purāṇic and other texts testify that Parama-Śakti is the form (*svarūpa*) and quality (*guṇa*) of Śiva. She is the form of entire sentient and non-sentient beings of this world. She is the knower of everything and the embodiment of bliss, unbounded by time, space, etc. and is the inherent power of the Lord. According to the Tāntric expression of the Tamil *Siddha* cult, the ultimate Reality is the fact beyond three thresholds of man, viz. the world, time and the finite consciousness. In the *tantra* cult of Śāktism, the ultimate Reality is beyond the world, time and consciousness as explained clearly as beyond the sphere of multiplicity of the world (*nis-prapañca*), that which grips the time (*kāla-hantri*) and the form of a special consciousness (*pratyeka-cit-rūpa*).

The 667th epithet of the *Lalitā-Sahasranāma* praises Devī as *nir-dvaita* (non-dual) and 668th as *dvaita-varjita* (remover of the duality). The dual aspect of seeing the *jīva* as a different aspect from *Brahman* is due to *māyā*, the illusion. If the illusion disappears, the dual aspect ends and the realization is attained or *Brahma-jñāna* is achieved. *Lalitā-Sahasranāma* also calls Devī as Ekāginī to express the non-dual ultimate Reality. The Advaita affects its synthesis by the doctrine of different levels of Reality, but the *tantra* does it by its doctrine of unity in duality and duality in unity. This is the impact of Advaita philosophy on Tāntric cult.

According to Sāṁkhya philosophy, the *tatvas* are twenty-four in number as *prakṛti* emerges from *puruṣa*. But according to *tantra* cult, the above concepts are thirty-six in number. In other words, the Tantra cult added another twelve *tatvas* along with the twenty-four of Saṁkhya to result in thirty-six *tatvas*. There is no controversy between Advaita and *tantra* about the end, but it matters in the beginning. With reference to the beginning of the world, the argument of Advaita is *Vivarta-vāda* and that of *tantra* cult is *Pariṇāma-vāda*. The meaning of *vivarta* is changing or transformation beyond cognition, which shows the delusive appearance, which is explained by the example of rope and snake. The *Pariṇāma-vāda* argues to prove the evolution. The *tantra* cult defines that the reflection of the sun seen in a water pot is not the real sun and this illusion can be removed by the consciousness attained through Tāntric practices. This is something like the milk becoming curd. Of course, there are some criticisms towards this idea as the milk becomes curd but not the curd turns milk. It is true that the philosophy of Tāntric cult explains that the realization is something like the curd becoming butter, butter turning as *ghī* and finally the *ghī* being burnt into a fire ritual and spreads in the atmosphere. The Tāntric cult strongly advocates *sādhanā*, the spiritual practice for the realization of the ultimate Reality. The realization is that of the unity of *jīva* and *Brahman* with the help of a true *guru*, master-teacher. Man must transform himself through *sādhanā* to accomplish his responsibilities. *Gandharva-tantra* says:

> Having saluted the *Guru* as directed and thought *so haṁ* the wise *Sādhaka*, the performer of the rite should ponder the unity of *jīva* and *Brahman*.

Kālī Tantra says:

> Having meditated in this way, a *Sādhaka* should worship Devī as his own *ātma*, thinking I am *Brahman*.

Kubjika Tantra Says:

> A *Sādhaka* should meditate on his own self as one and the same with Her and so on.

The doctrine of the *tantra* cult postulates that our body consists of the same elements as those of the universe. What is in the universe is there in the body as well; and what is in the body is there in the universe. In other words, by correlating the *cakra*s found in our body to the countless stars and planets in the universe, it may be understood that the universe and the body are one and the same.

Tāntrics affirm that the *Kuṇḍalini* energy lies in the shape of a spiralled serpent. Tāntric practice of meditation is the arousing through the *chakra*s of the *Kuṇḍalini* energy dwelling at the base *chakra,* raising the energy to the confluence at the centre between the eyebrows and to allow it to pervade its own expanse with the unification of Śiva. *Tantra* is the practical way to attain the ultimate Reality as mentioned by Vedānta. Thus *Śākta-darśana* or Tāntric cult is not a new one, but is the amalgamation of various cults, especially that of Vedānta doctrines, leading to a monistic realization through practice of Tantra.

Bibliography

Anna, *Sri Vidya,* Chennai: Sri Ramakrishna Mutt, 1998.

Hiriyanna, M., *Outlines of Indian Philosophy,* Delhi: Motilal Banarsidass Publishers Private Limited, 1993.

Nagaswami, *The Tantra Cult of South India,* New Delhi: Ahamkala Prakashan.

Namboodri, K.N. Krishnan, *Message of the Vedas,* Kodungallur: Vivekananda Kendra Vedic Vision Foundation, 2002.

Ramachandra Dikshitar, V.R., *The Lalitā Cult*, Delhi: Motilal Banarsidass, 1999.

Sharma, Chandradhar, *A Critical Survey of Indian Philosophy*, Delhi: Motilal Banarsidass Publishers Private Limited, 1960.

Subramanian, N.V., *Śrī Lalitā Śrī Rudra Triśatī*, Madras: Vaidhika Dharma Vardhini, 1943.

Subramanian, N.V., *Śrī Lalitā-Upakhyāna*, Madras: Vaidhika Dharma Vardhini, 1943.

Tapsyānanda, Swami, *Śrī Lalitā-Sahasranāma*, Chennai: Sri Ramakrishna Muth, 1996.

Vireswarānanda, Swami, *Brahma-Sūtras*, Calcutta: Advaita Ashrama, 1996.

Woodroffe, Sir John, *Śakti and Śākta*, Madras: Ganesh & Co. Private Ltd., Reprint, 2001.

15

Householders and Renouncers
The Holistic Combination in Indian Thought

Pankaj Jain

Deliverance is not for me in renunciation. I feel the embrace of freedom in a thousand bond of delight.

— Rabindranath Tagore[1]

In the presidential address delivered before the American Oriental Society in 1926, Walter Eugene Clark noted:[2]

> It is a widespread idea that Indian civilization has been completely dominated by mysticism and asceticism, by world-renouncing religions. The Indians are depicted as dreamy lotus-eaters who have been so engrossed with spiritual things, with questions of God, their souls, and their liberation, that they have paid a minimum of attention to worldly things. The facts of the matter are in sharp contradiction to the point of view just stated.

---

1. T.N. Madan, 1987, *Non-renunciation: Themes and interpretations of Indian culture*, India: Oxford University Press, p. 17.
2. Walter Eugene Clark, 1926, "Some misunderstandings about India," in *Journal of the American Oriental Society*, vol. 46. pp. 193-201.

Indeed, one of the most studied subjects within Indic traditions has been renunciation. Whereas the ascetic invited the imagination of scholars with his individualistic spirit rebelling against the maligned caste hierarchy, the householder has been seen as a poor creature living one's routine life according to one's caste-rules. For the rational and progressive West, asceticism seemed to epitomize the spiritual, mystic and exotic East. This Oriental Romanticism of the East, as world-denying mysticism was criticized in detail by scholars such as Edward Said,[3] Ronald Inden[4] and Richard King.[5]

In this paper, in order to counter-balance this overwhelming scholarly emphasis[6] on ascetics, I am attempting to focus on householders and on the tension, obvious and subtle, between the two, sometimes referred to as the "snake-mongoose conflict."[7] In addition, I speculate that the great

3. Edward Said, 1978, *Orientalism*, New York: Pantheon Books.
4. Ronald Inden, 2001, *Imagining India*, Bloomfield: Indiana University Press.
5. Richard King, 1999, *Orientalism and Religion: Postcolonial Theory, India and the mystic East*, London: Routledge.
6. Frederick M. Smith, Forthcoming, *Friendly Acquisitions, Hostile Takeovers: Deity and Spirit Possession in Indian Literature and Civilization*, p. 6. This is one of rare places where the author actually lists the subjects of interest to both the Indologists and the Indian orthodox elites: ". . . the Vedas, Sanskrit Grammar (*vyākaraṇa*), the "six systems" of Indian philosophy (*shad-darśana*), Buddhism and Jainism, law (*dharma-śāstra*), Epic poetry (*kāvya*), and to a lesser extent poetic theory (*alaṁkāra-śāstra*). Among the subjects neglected by respectable scholars were, for example, *Tantra*, *bhakti*, and astrology (*jyotīṣa*). . ." To the list of neglected subjects, I am suggesting we add the householder tradition and the philosophy of action, the *Karma-mārga*, or the *Pravṛtti-mārga*.
7. Romila Thapar, 1982, "The householder and the renouncer in Brāhmaṇical and Buddhist traditions," in T.N. Madan, ed. *Way of Life: King, Householder, Renouncer*, New Delhi: Vikas, p. 276.

Indian philosophers such as the Buddha, Mahāvīra and Śaṅkara[8] have influenced both emic and etic perspectives about Indic traditions largely. However, another unique dimension of Indic philosophy, *karma-yoga*, laid out in the *Bhagavad-Gītā*, has been ignored largely. Often Indic spiritual ideals have been equated with world-denying spirit. It is this stereotype about Indians that led to the dichotomy that the East is mystic and the West is scientific. I start with some of the earliest texts ranging from the Vedas, Brāhmaṇas, and the Upaniṣads and Dharma-Śāstras, to later texts such as *Rāmāyaṇa*, *Mahābhārata*, *Bhagavad-Gītā* and *Manu Smṛti*.

Vedic Āryans: Dominance of Householders

The Vedas, the first Indian texts, were composed several thousand years ago and yet they remain influential on the Indic traditions to this day. Although Indic theologians and philosophers historically had to somehow link their new doctrines with the Vedas to gain authenticity,[9] the new doctrines were often mutually contradictory. Especially in medieval (and even in modern) times, heated debates have resulted due to these different interpretations of renunciation and house-holdership.[10]

In the Vedic period, couple of millennia before the advent of Buddha and Mahāvīra, Āryan society was dominated by active householders as suggested by these exhortations from

---

8. Klaus K. Klostermaier, 1989, *A* Survey *of Hinduism*, SUNY Press, p. 334.

9. *Manu Smṛti* says: *Vedokhilo dharma mūlam*, literally, all the roots of religion and morality are to be traced to the Vedas.

10. Patrick Olivelle, 1986-87, *Renunciation in Hinduism: A Medieval Debate*, Vienna: Institute of Indology, University of Vienna Press.

the *Ṛgveda*: *krnvanto viśvaṁ āryaṁ* (9.63.5),[11] literally, "let us make the world noble." Similarly, *Ṛgveda* (3.30.6) says, *viśvaṁ satyaṁ kṛṇuhi*, literally, "let us make the world truthful." Indeed, Āryans had a dynamic view towards life and society.[12] The Vedas are full of references of zealous pursuit of materialistic goals such as wealth, sons, land, etc.[13]

Various kinds of *yajñas*, a term often translated as sacrifices, were the main religious activity of Indian society in Vedic period. Some of these *yajñas* were performed with political and social motivations such as *Aśvamedha-yājña* and *Rājasūya-yājña*. Both of these were performed by kings to expand their territories. Just within a few centuries after the advent of Āryans from the west, we see the similar religious ideologies in remote areas of southern and eastern India.[14] Furthermore, all the sacrifices demanded that the *yajamāna*, the sponsor, must be a married man. Thus, celibacy of renouncers was rejected. At the same time, sacrifices put some restrictions, especially dietary, on the *yajamāna*, thus combining the ascetic elements within the socio-religious life.[15] One of the Vedic sages, Atri expressly tells the deity of fire: "Married pairs, worn out by devout rites, jointly offer abundant sacrificial food, *Agni*, to thee who art mighty." Another famous Vedic sage Yājñavalkya was not a celibate renouncer but had two wives: Maitreyī and Kātyāyanī. Maitreyī, his wife,

11. Michael Witzel, 1997, Introduction, in F.B.J. Kuiper: *Selected Writings on Indian Linguistics and Philology*, ed. A. Lubotsky, M.S., Oort, M. Witzel, Amsterdam-Atlanta: Rodopi Bv, pp. ix-xxvi.
12. Rajesh Kochhar, 2000, *The Vedic People: Their History and Geography*, India: Orient Longman Private Limited.
13. Wendy Doniger O, Flaherty, 1981, *The Ṛgveda*. UK: Penguin Books
14. William Spencer Davis, 2000, *Agastya the Southern Sage from the North*, Ph.D dissertation, University of Chicago Press.
15. *Ibid*, G.U. Thite, 1975, *Sacrifice in Brāhmaṇa Texts*, Poona: University of Poona Press.

and Gārgi, the *Brahma-vādinī*, women in the court of king Janaka are cited in the Upaniṣads participating in several scholarly debates with Yājñavalkya.[16]

Perhaps, it was this preference for active life, which culminated in the concept of the four *Puruṣārthas* (literally, pursuits or goals) of human life: *dharma* (duty), *artha* (finance), *kāma* (sexual pleasures), and *mokṣa* (liberation). While *dharma* encompasses the entire life, the *artha* and the *kāma* refer to *pravṛtti* (activity), and the last *mokṣa* refers to the life of *nivṛtti* (passivity).[17] This means that materialistic goals were given equal social emphasis with spiritual goals, incorporating both *pravṛtti* and *nivṛtti*. This gave rise to the traditional argument in the later classical era that someone rebelling against the socio-cultural norms, in fact, announces one's servitude to selfish impulses which result in the ungoverned senses being overcome by the passions and hence to suffering.[18]

In contrast to the later śrāmaṇic philosophies of rejecting the life and worldly affairs, Vedic texts are replete with references to desires of living for a hundred years and performing worldly duties. The *Yajurveda* (40.2) says: "let us live for a hundred years by performing our duties and actions." Elsewhere, *Ṛgveda* (7.66.16), *Yajurveda* (36.24), *Atharvaveda* (19.67) say: "let us live for a hundred years."[19] Both sayings

---

16. Patrick Olivelle, 1996, *Upaniṣads*, New York: Oxford University Press, pp. 28-30.
17. Arvind Sharma, 2000, *Classical Hindu Thought: An Introduction*, India: Oxford University Press, pp. 186-188.
18. T.N. Madan, 1987, *Non-renunciation: Themes and Interpretations of Indian Culture*, India: Oxford University Press, Chapter 3.
19. Sahebrao G. Nigal, 1986, *Axiological Approach to the Vedas*, New Delhi: Northern Book Center, Author quotes *Ṛgveda*: *na rte śrantasya sākhyāya devaḥ*, emphasizing the self-efforts-based active life of Āryaṇs rather than relying solely on God's grace.

demonstrate the desires for active life rather than passive world-denying tendencies.[20] Materialistic schools of ancient India such as Cārvāka, Kapila, Jāvāli, Kaṇāda, etc. also claim to have their predecessors in the Vedic sages. It is also thought that the background for the rise of Indian classical sciences such as astronomy, mathematics and medicine was prepared in the Vedic period.[21]

Clearly, the Indian society before the advent of Buddha and Mahāvīra did not have renunciation at the forefront. Ascetics were few, were concerned with their personal quests, and hence did not impinge on the mainstream society of householders.

Renunciatory Challenges from Buddha and Mahāvīra

Between the sixth and the fourth century BC, the Vedic view of pro-social life was challenged by intellectual development within Brāhmaṇic culture as well as by socio-economic upheavals in northern India. This period witnessed the development of urban society based on the new "surplus economy." This led to the new social classes of merchants and kings. In the new urban society, the rural kinships were replaced by smaller families, which led to more individualistic spirit in the society. Several scholars, such as Patrick Olivelle, T.N. Madan, Robert Thurman and Romila Thapar, note that these new social developments helped launch the monastic movements such as Buddhism and Jainism and the Brāhmaṇical Upaniṣads. These new social developments also gave rise to the *āśrama* system. The original *āśrama* system offered the choice

---

20. Motilal Joshi, 2002, *Yajña Culture and Science of Life*, Jaipur: Motilal and Sons.
21. Uma Gupta, 1987, *Materialism in the Vedas*. New Delhi: Classical Publishing Company.

of householder life or ascetic life, after one completes the student life. However, this flexibility soon gave way to the classical *āśrama* system in which ascetic life was allowed only at the final stages of one's life. The four stages of one's life were designated as studentship (*brahmacarya*), householdership (*gṛahastha*), retreat (*vānaprastha*) and renunciation (*saṁnyāsa*). After repaying one's debts towards gods (*deva*s), fathers (*pitṛ*s) and teachers (*guru*s) one could live independently as an ascetic in the final *saṁnyāsa āśrama*. Each of the stages (*āśrama*) was associated with definite *dharma*s (duties) to be performed. Buddhist and Jain traditions encouraged the dichotomous categories in the role of the householder and the renouncer, but Brāhmaṇical tradition sought to weaken it by weaving them into a single life cycle of four stages.

The concept of *āśrama* (life-stage) based duty was also complemented by the concept of *varṇa* (class) based duty. The four *varṇa*s — brāhmaṇas, kṣatriyas, vaiśyas, and śūdras, each had their designated duties to be performed. The duties enjoined by these two series of stages were integrated in the new coined term called as the *svadharma* (self-duty). This emphasis on the duties based on *varṇa* and *āśrama* is reflected by designating the Indian socio-cultural life by the *varṇa-āśrama-dharma*. Furthermore the Upaniṣads, being contemporary of Buddhism and hence influenced by monastic ideals, remained only as marginal texts for Indian society and gained wider Brāhmaṇical acceptance only after Vedānta system gained popularity in 8th century CE due to Śaṅkara's new doctrines.[22] Olivelle has shown that the Sanskrit term for renunciation, *Saṁnyāsa*, rarely occurred in the early Indic texts.[23]

22. *Ibid*.

23. Patrick Olivelle, 1981, "Contributions to the Semantic History of Saṁnyāsa," in *Journal of the American Oriental Society*, 101/3, pp. 265-74.

In *Āpastaṁba-Dharma-Sūtra* (2.9.23.10), there is a clear preference for householder (*gṛhastha*) stage of life. It clearly rejects other ways of life in which Vedic injunctions are not obeyed. Moreover in 2.9.21.15, way of life of ascetics is explicitly stated to be against the (Vedic) scriptures.[24] *Aitareya Brāhmaṇa* (7.13.33.1) and *Śatapatha Brāhmaṇa* (10.5.4.16) also criticize ascetics.[25] In *Baudhāyana-Dharma-Sūtra, Kaṇḍika*s (chapters) 2.10.17 and 2.10.18, there is a clear suggestion that renunciation is to be taken only after the age of 70. *Manu Smṛti* says[26] : "Because men of the three other orders are daily supported by the householder with (gifts of) sacred knowledge and food, Therefore (the order of) householder is the most excellent order" (3.78). Further, the importance of marriage and householder life is strongly recommended: "When, unswerving in his chastity, (the student) has learned the Vedas, or two Vedas, or even one Veda, in the proper order, he should enter the householder stage of life" (*Manu Smṛti* 3.2). In general, most classical Indian texts highlight the importance of the householder stage of life over other stages and even incorporate the ideals of other stages within the householder stage without abandoning the family.[27] Thus, even while the Upaniṣads were proclaiming *mokṣa* to be the highest ideal, we find kings like Janaka and Ajātaśatru, who acknowledge that *mokṣa* is the highest personal goal to strive for, but continue to rule their kingdoms.

---

24. Johannes Bronkhorst, 1993, *The Two Sources of Indian Asceticism*, Germany: Peter Lang.
25. *Ibid.*
26. G. Buhler, 1964, *The Laws of Manu*, Delhi: Motilal Banarsidass, p. 89.
27. T.N. Madan, 2002, "The Householder tradition in Hindu Society," in *The Blackwell Companion to Hinduism*, edited by Gavin Flood, UK: Blackwell Publishing.

One of the other classical Indian philosophies, the *Sāṁkhya*, is traditionally attributed to the sage Kapila. In the *Mahābhārata* (12.327.64-66),[28] Kapila was portrayed as an *asura*, a demon born as the son of Prahalād (another *asura*) who is in constant war with the gods. This can be interpreted as a polemic against Kapila and his philosophy Sāṁkhya, which was a threat to the *pravṛtti-mārga* or householdership.

There are other stories in the *Mahābhārata*, which denounce asceticism, notably the case of Jaratkaru (1.14.1-1.44.22) and Agastya (3.94.11). Both are ascetics initially but retreat back to produce offspring as householders to help their ancestors. The *Mahābhārata* also endorses "the superiority of the householder" and argues that renunciation is to be taken only in old age.[29] In the *Mahābhārata* and *Rāmāyaṇa*, we encounter two great celibate characters, Bhīṣma[30] and Hanumān[31] respectively. But both are depicted not as passive renouncers but as great warriors and wise in the worldly as well as in the affairs of *dharma*. Moreover, all the main characters in these famous Indic Epics remain householders for their entire lives. In exile they meet hermits in the forest but even the hermits are described as performing their usual sacrifices and rituals with their wives and not as celibate renouncers.

Let us see some more examples from other texts. The fifth chapter in the *Bhāgavat-Purāṇa* has a story of king Priyavrata.

---

28. Wendy Doniger, 1980, *Women, Androgynes, and Other Mythical Beasts*, Chicago: University of Chicago Press.
29. Patrick Olivelle, 1993, *The Āśrama System: The History and Hermeneutics of a Religious Institution*, New York: Oxford University Press.
30. Aditya Adarkar, 2001, *Karna in the Mahābhārata*, Ph.D dissertation, University of Chicago.
31. Philip Lutgendorf, 1994, "My Hanumān is Bigger than Yours: The Divine Monkey of Hindu Mythology and his Growing Cult in India Today," in *History of Religions* 33/3. pp. 211-45.

Kṛṣṇa asks him emphatically: "Why do you hesitate to accept householder life?"[32] In the same Purāṇa, the first Jain Tīrthaṅkara Ṛṣabhadeva is converted from being an ascetic to a householder[33] and he advises his son Bharata to follow the path of active householder as well. One of the most popular Indic texts, the *Bhagavad-Gītā* clearly proclaims the path of action, *karma-yoga* and rejects renunciation — in 5:2, Kṛṣṇa states: "Renunciation-path and action-path both lead to liberation but out of the two, the action-path is superior to the former."[34] This is the response given by Kṛṣṇa to Arjuna's question of which of the two is better. In the *Bhagavad-Gītā*, 3.8, we find another clear preference for action, "action is superior to non-action."

---

32. *gṛahastha āśramaḥ kiṁ avadhyaṁ karoti?*

33. Padmanābh S. Jaini, 1977, "Jīn Ṛṣabha as an Avatar to Viṣṇu," in *Bulletin of the School of Oriental and African Studies*, 40/2, 321-37, London: University of London Press.

34. *saṁnyāsaḥ karma yogaś ca nihśreyas akaravubhau, Tayos tu Karma saṁnyāsat karmayogo viśiṣyate*, B.G. Tilak in his commentary on the *Bhagavad-Gītā* cites several Western references in support of the path of action. Some noteworthy are Aristotle's statement in his book *Politics*, "And it is equally a mistake to place inactivity above action for happiness is activity, and the actions of the just and the wise are the realization of much that is noble." French philosopher Augustus Comte in his book *Material Philosophy* says: "It is misleading to say that it is better to spend one's life in the contemplation of philosophy and the philosopher who adopts such a course of life and abandons the doing of whatever public welfare it is possible for him to do must be said to misuse the material which is at his disposal." Nineteenth century philosophers Spencer, Mill and Nietzsche support the path of action. Nietzsche has severely criticized those who are for giving up action. Also *Bhagavad-Gītā* verses 2.47, 4.15, 3.4, 4.6, 8.7, 18.6, 7 are cited for *Karma-Yoga*.

Similarly, another major text on *yoga*, the Patañjali *Yoga-Sūtra* has been interpreted by some scholars such as Ian Whicher,[35] David Carpenter and Christopher Key Chapple[36] as expressing a world-affirming *yoga* rather than a world-denying one. This interpretation also supports the idea that the great *yogins* need not be understood as world-denying renouncers. Rather, they can engage actively with the society underscoring the path of action rather than renunciation.

According to P.V. Kane,[37] in the classical Indian texts, the overall tendency "is to glorify the status of a householder and push into the background the two *āśramas* of *vānaprastha* and *saṁnyāsa*, so much so that certain works say that these are forbidden in the Kali age."

Monasticism in Medieval Times

In the classical and medieval times, the growth of Hinduism, with its firm roots in Indian society and freedom from the costly institution of the monastery, offered a colossal challenge to Buddhism heavily dependent on continuous financial support from kings for its monasteries. The eventual triumph of Hinduism in India can be followed by a number of landmarks often associated with opposition to Buddhism. The great Vaiṣṇava and Śaiva saints of the south, the Āḷvārs and Nāyanārs helped spread Vaiṣṇavism and Śaivism to a great extent. Their Hindu patrons were openly hostile to Buddhism and Jainism. Similarly, Śaṅkara (788-820 CE) emerged as a major

---

35. Ian Whicher, 1998, *The Integrity of the Yoga Darśana: A Reconsideration of Classical Yoga*. SUNY Press.
36. Ian Whicher, and David Carpenter, 2003, *Yoga: The Indian Tradition*, Routledge.
37. P.V. Kane, 1941, *History of Dharma-Śāstras*, II/I, Poona: Bhandarkar Oriental Research Institute.

philosophical challenger to Buddhism.[38] In the course of 1700 years of co-existence, the Hindus had taken over a great deal from the Buddhists. In consequence, the division between Buddhism and Hinduism had increasingly diminished and it was no surprise that Buddhists were absorbed into the largely Buddhified Hindu-fold. The philosophy of Nāgārjuna had been absorbed into the Vedānta by Gauḍapāda, Śaṅkara's teacher, just as the Vaiṣṇavas of later times, were greatly indebted to the Buddhists (*Bhāgavat-Purāṇa* incorporated the Buddha as the ninth *avatāra* of Viṣṇu). Eventually, the separate existence of Buddhism slowly disappeared from India.[39] Hindu sects of renouncers became common after the initial organization established by Śaṅkara in the ninth century CE. In subsequent centuries virtually every sect irrespective of its position in the spectrum of beliefs and forms of renunciation, was characterized by an institutional base.[40]

After Śaṅkara, the individualistic monastic goals were challenged by new devotional theologies propounded by Rāmānuja, Madhva and Vallabha. In 1380 CE, the brāhmaṇa scholar Vidyāraṇya composed a new text, *Jīvana-Mukti-Viveka* about *jīvana-mukta* (liberated while embodied).[41] According to this, liberation is not just reserved for the world-renouncing religious elite but is attainable by everyone through devotion and *karma-yoga*. Whereas the Śrāmaṇic monasticism encouraged

---

38. Kitagawa and Cummings, *Buddhism and Asian History*, p. 95.

39. Noble Ross Reat, 1995, *Buddhism: A History*, Asian Humanities Press, p. 76.

40, Romila Thapar, 1982, "The householder and the renouncer in Brāhmaṇical and Buddhist traditions," in T.N. Madan, ed. *Way of Life: King, Householder, Renouncer*, New Delhi: Vikas, p. 292.

41. Robert Alan Goodding, 2002, *The Treatise on Liberation-in-Life: Critical edition and annotated translation of the Jīvana-Mukti-Viveka of Vidyāraṇya*, Ph.D dissertation, University of Texas at Austin.

a revolt against the prevalent social hierarchy, the new *bhakti* movements supported the existing social hierarchy. One could remain in any caste, class, gender, age in the existing social system and still could connect to spiritual goals based on new concepts of unconditional love and devotion. Therefore, the need for renouncing one's social status or family was obviated. Arguably, these new movements were much more conservative compared to the Śrāmaṇic ones.[42] T.N. Madan in his seminal study of householders[43] lists a number of medieval and contemporary movements with millions of followers. All of them have emphasized the virtues of disciplined domesticity as against renunciation. He writes:

> Basava (12 c. AD), the founder of Liṅgāyat sect in the south, Nānak (1469-1538), the first of the Sikh *gurus* in the north, Vallabha (1479-1531), the promulgator of the *puṣṭi mārga* (way of abundance) in the west, and Chaitanya (1485-1534), founder of a popular sect in the east based on an exultation in divine and conjugal love, extolled domesticity as the good life as long as it was an affirmation of the bliss of the union of the devotee and the deity, and not a contradiction of it.

Olivelle cites the fifteenth-century *bhakti* Saint Kabir deriding ascetics:

> Go naked if you want, put on animal skin; what does it matter till you see the inward Rāma? If the union yogis seek came from roaming about in the buff, every deer in the forest would have been saved. If shaving your head spelled spiritual success, heaven would be filled with sheep. And

---

42. Patrick Olivelle, 2002, "The Renouncer Tradition," in *The Blackwell Companion to Hinduism*, edited by Gavin Flood, UK: Blackwell Publishing.
43. T.N. Madan, 1987, *Non-renunciation: Themes and Interpretations of Indian Culture*, India: Oxford University Press.

> brother, if holding back your seed earned you a place in paradise, eunuchs would be the first to arrive.[44]

One of the most interesting studies of contemporary Indian society and its critique of renunciation has been done by T.N. Madan.[45] Madan spent many years doing ethnographic research with Kashmiri Puṇḍits. Based on his research as well as the evidences from Indological and ethnographical literature, he has concluded that the life of the householder is the most highly valued in lay Hindu society, especially among the Kashmiri Puṇḍits. His informants were cynical about the renouncers and one of them went into the details of the way of life of the mythological Janaka to emphasize that "Janaka was not only the king of Mithilā but also a great householder, and at the same time, the supreme renouncer (*sic*)." Madan also observed that one of the greatest ambitions of his group of informants was to become a householder along with his own wife and children. Children, particularly sons, are greatly desired in contemporary Indian society today, as has always been the case throughout Indian history. One of his informants summarized the life of householder in this way:

> The home is the place neither for the indulgence of one's physical appetites nor for the performance of austerities. It is the narrow middle ground, the razor's edge: Like the sharp edge of a razor is the path, narrow and difficult to tread
>
> — *Kaṭha Upaniṣad* 1. 3. 14.

---

44. J.S. Hawley, and J. Juergensmeyer, 1988, *Songs of the Saints of India*, New York: Oxford University Press.
45. T.N. Madan, 1987: *Non-renunciation: Themes and Interpretations of Indian Culture*, India: Oxford University Press.

Conclusion

Out of many Hindu theologies, world-denying philosophy of Advaita Vedānta was chosen by Orientalist scholars from some Brāhmaṇical sources as being the central feature of Hinduism. However, most of the other Indic world-views, including many Vedānta interpretations, Tāntrism, Śāktism, and many folk traditions, are not renunciatory as already noted by Louis Dumont.[46] The holistic combination of *pravṛtti* and *nivṛtti*, as evidenced in classical Indian texts and archeological records, demonstrates that these are symbiotic aspects rather than opposite poles. This serves to refute the common view that one must choose between the wisdom of the East and the technological progress of the West. India had been an advanced civilization not only in the realms of spirituality and religion but also in the social, economic and political areas. This is evidenced from materialistic, artistic and economic advancements in Harappan as well as pre-colonial times. Paul Kennedy cites Bairoch to demonstrate that India had 24.5% of the share of world manufacturing output in 1750 and U.K. had 1.9%. In 1900, these shares simply swapped with U.K. having 18.5% and India a mere 1.7%.[47] These statistics can be interpreted to show that India as poverty-stricken society is a result of British colonization rather than due to world-denying ideologies from its religious traditions.

To recapitulate the message of the *Bhagavad-Gītā* on this issue, Arjuna's renunciatory arguments are defeated in his dialogue with Kṛṣṇa and *karma-yoga* is preferred. A *karma-yogī*

---

46. Louis Dumont, 1960, "World Renunciation in Indian Religions," in *Contributions to Indian Sociology*, no. 4. Paris: Mouton & Co., pp. 33-62.

47. Paul Kennedy, 1987, *The Rise and Fall of the Great Powers*, New York: Random House, p. 149.

is one who can achieve the balance of *pravṛtti*, the worldly affairs by selfless duty and *nivṛtti*, renouncing the attachment towards the result for one's duty. T.N. Madan cites J.L. Austin: "This history of Western philosophy was littered with "tidy-looking dichotomies," with the student being required to embrace one half or the other." However, in this paper, I am suggesting that the Hindu householder is someone who transgresses the dichotomy of extreme pleasure and extreme penance. This classical tendency is underscored by the ethnographic research by Madan to a great extent. Recent critique of renunciation is captured by Olivelle[48] by citing these words of the then Vice-President of India, B.D. Jatti:

> Who is better — the householder or the *saṁnyāsi*? Of course, the householder. While the householder willingly renounces all that he earns to his wife and children for their love and affection, the *sanyasi* depends on others for his milk and fruits. Parasites, who are a mere burden on society, are sinners. If man has to progress, everybody has to work.
>
> — Indian Express, May 8, 1978

To conclude, let us note the definition of *dharma* from the *Mahābhārata*: In the Karṇa-Parva of the *Mahābhārata*, Kṛṣṇa explains *dharma* for upholding both this-worldly and the other-worldly affairs.[49] Implicit in this definition is the fine balance of action and non-action, *pravṛtti* and *nivṛtti*.

---

48. Patrick Olivelle, 2002, "The Renouncer Tradition," in *The Blackwell Companion to Hinduism*, edited by Gavin Flood, UK: Blackwell Publishing.

49. *dhāranād dharma nityāhur dharmo dhārayate prajāḥ, yat syād dhāraṇa sanyuktaṁ sa dharma iti niścayaḥ.*

16

Music, Oral Tradition and Transcendental Bliss

Sarada Purna Sonty

Music is found in all human societies, as its vehicle is human body itself. Especially music is a powerful form of expression; and one does not need a lot of technical knowledge to enjoy it. Virtually every one sings or enjoys others singing. Music has been enriching the world cultures since time immemorial; and is known to be a phenomenon that connects different realms of life beyond time and space. To understand and experience music one should have any of the following aspects to one's faculty:

— Sensation to the music
— Hearing ear for listening music
— Knowledge on the origin of music
— Various facets of music
— Instruments and other representations of music
— Sound and music in accordance with time and space
— The music traditions of the world

Following these arises the fundamental question; what is the source of music? There are innumerable answers to this question. The basic explanation is that music would be defined as the "series of sounds arranged in patterns that are expressed by humans to communicate feelings or thoughts or both." The next question would be; what is the source of sound? Sound could be of human voice, a bird, a rainstorm or an air conditioner. These are mundane answers. Furthermore in many cultures of the world sound is at the centre of creation and is regarded as the source of creation itself. Scientifically and metaphysically sound can be linked to the opposite of "silence."

One can illustrate the relationship between "human voice" and "sound of the instruments" by giving many examples. One such is by citing ancient Indian thought from Upaniṣads and the *Nātya-Śāstra* (*NS*.XXVIII.12.15). In India the fundamental ideology and assumption is that the origin of everything is associated with *Brahman*, and *Brahman* is the creator of music. It is generally said that the composers are known as *nāda-brahma* (sound-creator).

Nātya-Śāstra speaks of human voice as *śarīra-vīnā* or the "bodily-lute." The instruments of music made in the world are known as *daravee-vīnā* or "wooden-lute." Incidentally, it is notable that ancient Indian thinkers state human body as *daiva-vīnā* or divine-lute. The Sūfi tradition also states that human body is a flute. Thus with reference to music most of the traditions in the world accorded a primary place for human body.

The composer of the music treatise of ancient India, Bharata in his work *Nātya-Śāstra* states *śabda guṇaka ma ākāśam* or "sound has the nature of air," and it is two-fold: tone-related (*svaravan*), and meaning-related (*abhidānavan*). The tones are first born out of a bodily-lute and then transmitted to instruments: from the bodily-lute to drums to unravel the rhythms, and then to cymbals to bring "time-space" concept to human realms. Musicologists eulogized human body as a medium of primary manifestation of sound *nāda*. As the physical body is the field of experience and primary source of voice, it is considered primordial. The instrument represents the external. Bhartṛhari says that, by the will of *ātmā*, the *vāyu* or air moves upwards from the base of the tongue and is held on the wall of it to produce sound, *nāḍis* and in space to result in notes or delightful sounds. The process and production of sound in the body is described in four steps:

1. The rising of the will to produce sound,
2. Activation of mind,
3. Activating kinetic energy, and
4. Propelling the air upwards.

Silence being the vital element for the emergence of sound, it does need movement of the throat to produce sound to break the silence. This claims the vitality in the form of crescendo of pauses, punctuations, musical notes, time gaps, frequencies, rhythms, and so on by living the durations and subside into silence.

There have been variations of views about the process and production of sound in different traditions of the world. The sound in Chinese culture has two states: High culture and Low culture. The organized and manipulated sound was named as "High culture;" whereas the sounds experienced on other side of the realm of sound is named as "Low Culture."

Oral traditions, in fact, are the strongest links binding together all the types of music in the world. The very existence of this unwritten music depends entirely on the acquisitions and preservations of families and people of different tribes and groups, which are not the fruit of bookish intellectual speculations. The music of advanced cultures is no doubt the highly structured music and has original schematic notation; but it cannot be invalidated with the above presupposition. The music of ancient times of the oral traditions in many parts of the world shared a common characteristic; that it is essentially a utilitarian music with magical, symbolic and social functions. This music is more than entertainment. Indeed, in the oral tradition, singers, performers and players considered music as the spiritual manifestation of their efforts. Music holds revered positions in both advanced higher cultures and the so-called primitive cultures of the oral tradition. Music occupied a central place in the mythology and religious traditions of China; and a subject of semi mysticism in the school of Pythagorean philosophers of Greece. Music played a dominant role in the systems of Australian aboriginals, and in the ceremonial, religious and social practices of Africans. According to all these schools, music and musicians have immense power, which they believe is beyond mundane existence; they believe that sound itself is primeval force of creation.

For a long time it was believed that there is no formal structure to the ancient recitative chants but in fact, there were very rigid systems of melodic and rhythmic patterns. The development of Indian music indeed is a fascinating complex phenomenon. Indian music envisages the concepts of poetry, drama, aesthetics, art and principles of sciences. Scientific principles are at the bottom of melodic patterns of *svara* or sound evocation. All art and science rests on creative imagination. This imagination carries a rational basis in its own way. The musician tries to explore the interrelation between the cresses of tones, notes, semitones, intervals, rhythmic modulations, and metrical cycles to express or share his thoughts; and communicates his imagination to the listener. The process and production of sound starts internally where every thing is in unmanifest state. At this stage the individual is forced to build an edifice. Here a method and arrangement are necessary, from which different oral traditions emerge, from which again the modern or systematic music patterns evolved.

The study of the relation between nature and music, and the harmony that resulted can be traced back to antiquity. Not being limited to Vedic and Pre-Vedic times in India, during the sixth century BC, Pythagoras and his followers believed that both mathematics and music are the expressions of the harmony in nature. The findings of a scientist, attributed to Pythagoras can be expressed like this:

> Pluck a stretched string and observe the pitch. If only one-half the length of the string is allowed to vibrate, it will sound an octave higher. If one third of the string is allowed to vibrate, it will sound a perfect fourth higher. If two thirds of the string is allowed, it will sound a perfect fifth higher. The relationships are perceived as harmonious in its broadest sense.

English words that are used to describe the "tone" are — bright, dark, hollow, nasal, harsh, pure, golden, vibrant, rich, round, tinny, raspy, woody, reedy, mellow, fuzzy and so on. Expressing subjective quantities of music in objective terms is not an easy task. Let us see an example in Sanskrit; and how *dhvani* or sound is explained with sixteen words that are synonyms of the very word, they are: *nināda, svara, dhvāna, dhvani, rava, svana, svāna, nirghoṣa, nirhrāda, nāda, nisvana, nisvāna, ārava, ārāva, saṁrāva, virāva.*

The human mind can be compared to an ocean, which is active at its surface and more and more quiet and silent at its depth. A state of pure silence is said to be a state of pure wakefulness. When we are conscious of this consciousness we feel comfortably certain that this state is the basis for all our individual experiences. At the same time, we confirm to ourselves that this state is a state of all our experiences of the waking state-moods, thoughts, memories, attentions and volitions. Is there a mention of this consciousness in the Vedas? Would Veda differentiate the two states? This concept is yet to be understood. However seven basic elements or words can be seen in the *Veda-mantras*; they are: (1) *Jñāna* (2) *Manas*, (3) *Svaraṁ*, (4) *Matra*, (5) *Chandas*, (6) *Yajña*, and (7) *Devata*. According to the Veda, utterance of the *akṣara* (word) constitutes these seven elements:

> *vūha* (creativity and imagination),
>
> *vāñca* (desire) are the elements of *mano-vyāpāra* (activity of mind);
>
> *ardha* (meaning or) is the element of *jñāna-deha-vyāpāra* (activity of knowledge and body); and
>
> finally *svaraṁ, matra, chandas* are the *bhoutika-vyāpāra* (activity of the physical world).
>
> In totality this becomes *jñānaṁ* (wisdom).

In Indian Tradition, *svaraṁ* (sound) is a word seen often in the Vedas as well as in musicology. It is the sound that makes life communicable in this world. These sounds are centres for energy, of un-conscious, sub-conscious, conscious and beyond. Because of the inherent quality of modulations, oscillations, tones and microtones, *svaras* (sounds) gain the capacity to express various moods. A distinction can be drawn between physical and metaphysical sounds. The *svara* (sound) is the primordial nature (*lakṣaṇa*) of *sāma-gāna, stobha-gāna, stoma-gāna, vuhya-gāna* and many other aspects of the *Sāmaveda*. The three primordial *svaras* (sounds) of the *R̥gveda* are: *udāta, anudāta,* and *svarita*. Now it is to be remembered that the *R̥gveda* can also be chanted in:

1. *Ēka svara arcika gāyana* — chanted in one notes
2. *Gādhino gāyana* — chanted in two notes
3. *Sāmika gāyana* — chanted in three notes
4. *Sāma gāyana* — chanted in seven notes

The chanting of the Vedic *mantra*s (hymns) in such a way has given a scope for the evolution of Indian music today. The *Śruti* (microtones) involves seven notes of *Sāma Gāna Mūrcanā;* and the distribution of *Śruti* among the seven notes (*svara*s) is as follows:

Sā-4 Re-3 Gā-2 Mā-4 Pā-4 Dā-3 Nī-2.

This system of distribution suggests that the first scale is *Sāma Gāna*, which was named *Hara Priya* or *Khara Hara Priya* by later musicologists. This primordial scale, *Sāma Gāna* Scale gave raise to other six scales by the process of model shift or a small adjustment of *Śruti* or *gṛha bheda*, as stated below:

Hara Priya	-	Khara Hara Priya	-	S. RG. M. P. DN. S
Todi	-	Hanuma Todi	-	N. SR. G. M. PD. N
Kālyāṇī	-	Mecha Kalyāṇī	-	D. NS. R. G. M P. D
Kāmbhoji	-	Hari Kāmbhoji	-	P. DN. S. R. GM. P
Bhairavī	-	Nata Bhairavī	-	M. PD. N. S. RG. M
Chyuta Pañcama Todi - (Obsolete-Gāndhāra Grāma)				G. MP. D. N. SR. G
Śaṅkarābharaṇaṁ -				R. GM. P. D. NS. R

In Indian music the metrical *Chanda*s systems are important elements; the *Agni cayana mantra* of the *Kṛṣṇa Yajurveda* (4.3.7) says:

pṛthivī chando nantarīkṣaṁ chando dyous chandaḥ
samās chando nakṣatrāṇi chando manaschando
vāk chandaḥ kṛṣichando hīraṇyaṁ chando
gous chando ja chando svaschandaḥ.

According to Indian tradition *pṛthvī, antarīkṣam, dyouḥ, samaḥ, nakṣatra, manas, vāk, kṛṣ, hīraṇyaṁ, gouḥ, ajaḥ* — are said to be metres (*chanda*s). One cannot define these words or explain these words with Sanskrit etymology that are available today.

But one can only experience these in one's own self through tradition, experience of learning from teacher, because these are associated with inner spheres of a living being.

Today the scientists have defined the sound (*svara*) as the mechanical vibration transmitted in elastic medium. Moreover, the objective and subjective interpretations of sound can be otherwise explained as "measurable and perceptual" interpretations. Music or making sound elastically is one of the natural instincts of human being. "The art of music" and "the science of Music" are the two prominent concepts used in the study of sound in present times. Our present knowledge and treatment of sound is usually divided into three parts:

Sources - Transmissions - receptions

In a hymn of the *R̥gveda* (1.164.45), we can see the pulse of this theory:

chatvari vāk parimita padāni
tāni vidur brāhmaṇa ye maniṣinaḥ
guha triṇī nihita nengayanti
turīyaṁ vaco manuṣya vadaṅti
(Four are the limitations to the paths of speech,
Know the wise Brāhmaṇas among humans.
Un-knowable three of nature, of birds, of animals
Fourth is that phonetically expressed by humans).

The art of music is also developed from the causal state into the gross form of music through the medium of gradual progress. The *rāga* is the norm or matrix of Indian music. The ancient seers, musicologists, musicians and scholars laid the foundation for music and left vast knowledge in the realm of music. Nārada says:

sapta svara strayo grāma mūrcanā steka vimśatiḥ
tāna ekona pañca saḍiyettat svara maṇḍalaṁ

tāna rāga svara grāma mūrcananamtu lakṣaṇaṁ
pavitraṁ pāvanaṁ puṇyaṁ nāradena prakirtitaṁ

According to Nārada, *Tāna, Rāga, Svara, Grāma* and *Mūrcanā* are the "constituents of the sound," *svara-maṇḍala*. These constituents are sacred, and purifying; and bring permanent solace and tranquility to the mind of man. Fundamentally Bharata, Sāraṅga Deva and many others threw light on this subject and created a music system, which is different from the music of later years.

Oral traditions are strictly practised in India. All the musicologists of India of ancient times dealt with the study of tones and microtones, explained about the intricate positions, problems and difficulties. The names, positions and structures of these microtones are very significant, as they convey very intricate, complex aesthetic sentiments and moods (*rasa*s and *bhāva*s).

Based on five causal microtones expounded by Nārada, Bharata has expanded the theory into twenty-two microtones, which connote twenty-two different moods. Bharata's theory also contains the science and art of music, metres, phonetics, tones, microtones, tunes, modulations, accents, moods and sentiments and so on. The folk music may be the source of refined, structured, exalted music of present years. It is needless to say that Vedic music *Sāma gāna* is the inspiration to all the post-Vedic music. The main source of music being "sound," tones, microtones and philosophic concepts, music centers around the "sound theory." The seers of India understood this concept of "sound" much before the West dreamt of it. Helmholtz, the great scholar on music has discovered the mystery of sound (*nāda*), which forms the background of the grand structure of music. Philosophy is always concerned with the theory and value of the causal sound (*nāda*).

Music can be understood as a system of education, which imparts knowledge, comfort to the ears, elevates the levels of consciousness, consoles the mind and helps to experience universality, to involve oneself into deep bliss. Music conveys the idea of broadening the intellect. It is strength, a tool, a vehicle for human being to express and to communicate his or her feelings and thoughts. It is to be infused with our lives, vital and dynamic energies to visualize our intuitive visions.

According to Indian tradition, of all the human experiences *ānanda* (bliss) is the highest level, which can be attained through music. The Upaniṣads proclaim that *rasa* is essence of music, which is associated with devotional practices while singing the psalms and Vedic *sāma-gāna*s in the temples. The absolute joy of oneness of *Brahman* and *ātman* is presented in Śaṅkarācārya's *Saundaryalaharī* and in his other psalms. Some of the *stotra*s and songs composed by Śaiva tradition for recitation in devotional practices have been instrumental to experience the world of transcendental bliss. Music reflects the manifestation of human activity in ascending to the divine level with supreme delight, *ānanda* (bliss). Thus, since bygone times music has been enriching world cultures as oral tradition, especially in India, as the source and primeval force of creation, which serves not only as medium of communication by elevating our different levels of universal consciousness but also leads us towards the ultimate transcendental Bliss.

Section - V
Vedānta and Global Parallels

17

Vedānta Philosophy and Sartrean Existentialism

Namboodri R. Jeevan Babu

It is fashionable and also a matter of pride for Indians to remark that the Western philosophy has borrowed a great deal of ideas from Vedānta. Though there is no concrete and substantial evidence to prove this it is very common to draw, between the two, parallelisms or similarities and study the impact of Vedānta on Western philosophy. In fact, many eminent Western philosophers and thinkers acknowledge the overbearing influence of Vedānta on the West.

In this article, an attempt is made to examine some correspondences between Vedānta philosophy and Existentialism of Jean Paul Sartre. It tries to focus on the deviations of the one from the other, and touch upon only the quintessence of the Vedānta system. The highest Self (*Brahman*) is true, the world (*jagat*) is false and the self (self) is even *Brahman*. And we do not intend to go beyond the famous dictum of Sartre "Existence Precedes Essence." Here Sartre speaks of two kinds of beings; existence refers to the "being-in-itself" and essence to the "being-for-itself." The first one is that "which is" and the second that "which is not." Man takes off from his existential state of that "which is" through action to attain an essential state of quality or aim. But once he attains an essence another one crops up in its place and so on and forth until death puts an end to the ever-changing "being-for-itself." Thus, man is a synthesis of the two beings or man is always passionately pursuing transcending essences. In brief, man is a transcending being.

Let us see how Vedānta Philosophy has a bearing upon Sartre. We proceed on the premises that Sartrean existentialism may be regarded as Indian thought viewed from materialistic point of view. This position is understandable because, unlike in the East, Philosophy in the West, is independent of Religion.

The Two Selfs and the Two Beings

Vedānta also speaks of two beings; the real self and the true self. The real self corresponds to the "being-in-itself" and the true Self to the "being-for-itself." Just as the real self aspires to be in one with the true Self, the "being-in-itself" is in hot pursuit of the "being-for-itself." The difference is that while the real self is not different from the true Self in that the former is the manifestation of the latter, "being-in-itself" is very different from the "being-for-itself" but tends to attain it. While the true Self is absolute in Vedānta the "being-for-itself" is only relative; and while the true Self never ceases to be, "being-for-itself" no longer "is" after death.

Let us now take the process of thought and its complement action. The thought of the real self corresponds to the "why" of the contingent existence of the "being-in-itself." Thought, which is self itself, strives to embrace the absolute self or the Universal being, just as the "being-in-itself" seeks to dispel the thought or feeling of its contingency. The common means to these different ends is obviously action. But while Sartre envisages an action which consists in making use of personal freedom without antagonizing the society, or in other words, turning responsibility of choice to one's own and, thereby, others advantage, action in Vedānta philosophy is more or less a ritual aimed at liberation or eternal bliss and far from being socially committed. Nevertheless, let us say, in passing, that these two different kinds of action engage and benefit the society at large as both Sartre and the Vedāntins speak of altruistic love.

Māyā and the Absurd

Māyā is a certain power to which the deceptive appearance of the entire world is due. If *māyā* is "this" in ignorance and "not that" in knowledge, then it corresponds to the elusive "being-for-itself" and since *māyā* is neither being nor non-being, the concept of the absurd in existentialism, which is inability or powerlessness to find reason or explanation for being/ existence, may be considered to be the alter-ego of *māyā*. Thus, what the Vedantins call *māyā* Sartre calls the "absurd." Just as one encounters *māyā* on his way to be a better being as one realizes there is a higher being, it is akin to the elusiveness of the "being-for-itself" which, once materialized gets automatically replaced by an other being qualitatively still higher in its essence then that of its preceding one. Both *māyā* and the "being-for-itself" are the material causes of the phenomenal world, but while *māyā* evades comprehension and can be understood only by the principle of abstract reality, "being-in-itself" is realized by the principle of concrete reality, though, curiously enough, both are deeply founded on reason and experience. The non-enlightened is unable to look through and beyond *māyā* as it covers its true nature, as if it were, with a veil. On the contrary, layman can seize his "being-for-itself" consciously if he so wishes wilfully, unconsciously otherwise. Again, while *māyā* is deceptive and illusory, "being-for-itself" is the *raison d'etre* which projects man to a virgin future and keeps him sustained for a purposeful and meaningful existence.

Spiritualism and Humanism

The excellence of Vedānta is that it begins with and ends with the idea of God, while existentialism extolls man. Vedānta proclaims God in man and man in God. It is universally accepted by every religion. Even atheists are marvelled by its non-vulnerability to criticism, thus Vedānta philosophy is, at the same time, both a humanism and a spiritualism.

Sartrean existentialism is widely believed to be exclusively a humanism. God seems to be dead there. But we think otherwise: Sartre never denied the existence of God. What is important for him is not whether God exists or not; it is a matter best left untouched because man always finds himself on the plane of men, not on the plane of God or Gods. Thus in Vedānta, transcendence is vertical, that is towards God, while for Sartre, it is horizontal, that is towards and through men. While Vedānta philosophy, in this respect, is lofty, the philosophy of Sartre is loftier because of the fact that we all endorse that service to man is service to God. Therefore, in spite of the deviation, the horizontal transcendence of Sartre is as good as the vertical transcendence of Vedānta. But the vice versa is not so because spiritual pursuit with a religious perspective has sense only when it is complemented with the kind of humanism without frontiers that Sartre advocates. That is why it is said of people like Sartre that all good philanthropic and philosophic seekers in their best moments are Vedantins.

Realization of the Self

The aim of Vedānta is the realization of all human aspirations. Existentialism is also embedded in man's aspirations. But while

Vedānta speaks of liberation, which is supreme, bliss derived from realization of the absolute Self on which *māyā* has no effect, Sartre does not give any thought to ultimate liberation. For Sartre, liberation is action, which releases man from his metaphysical anguish and from his consciousness of the "absurd." While Vedānta takes man through action beyond the appearance of this phenomenal world, existentialist action is restricted to the temporality of this world. However, it does project man towards a better being.

The main objective of Śaṅkara's Vedānta is the reconciliation of religion with philosophy and of philosophy with religion. It delights to turn all things to the glory of God. The main objective of Sartre is the reconciliation of metaphysics with phenomenology. He prides in the power of man to be the master of his own destiny; the phenomenal world is all that matters as man is obliged to carry on with the business of living ethically. Spiritual way of life is to Vedānta as ethics is to existentialism. While spirituality embraces man in the form of organized religion, existentialist ethics relegates, if not negates, God and though individualistic, engages the society. Vedānta speaks of eternity attained by being one with the divine Self; Sartre does go beyond "here and now" in that the future is virgin and man seeks his being of tomorrow within the framework of temporality.

Conclusion

Modern philosophical thinking has led to conclusions identical not only in the spirit but with the letter of the Vedānta philosophy. Most of the ideas contained in the existentialism of Sartre approximate to the transcendental doctrine of the Vedānta, though they are derived at from a different point of view. The commonality is reason, action and experience, but while in Vedānta truth is attained by the way of reason, Sartre needs reason to do away with the contingency of being in order to be able to attain and experience authentic existence.

If philosophy is the understanding and the explanation of all things, then Vedānta, though speculative in its discussions and arguments in favor of the realization of the true self, scores over existentialism. While Sartre does not conclusively establish his understanding of existence nor does he convincingly explain the *raison d'etre*, Vedānta gives solution and has a profound respect for truth.

18

Advaita and Aletheia
An East-West Parallel

J.P. Johnson

THE present study is an attempt to look into an area of East-West parallel between two comprehensive notions in the philosophical thinking of two stalwarts in philosophy: Advaita in Śaṅkara[1] and Aletheia in Heidegger.[2] Śaṅkara and Heidegger are rightly regarded as two of the most prominent thinkers, respectively from the classical philosophy in the East

1. Śaṅkara (*c.* 788-820) is the most influential metaphysical theologian in the Hindu tradition, and the main exponent of Advaita Vedānta. He was born at Kaladi, Kerala state, India. Within his short span of life he travelled extensively in India, and gained remarkable achievements in his philosophico-theological thinking and writing.
2. Martin Heidegger (1889-1976) brought about a revolution in Western philosophy by his radical departure from the traditional way of philosophizing. Taking inspiration from the "question of Being" posed by Aristotle and the "method of phenomenology" developed by Husserl, Heidegger launched a primordial thinking of Being (*Seinsdenken*). His thinking has been so pivotal and seminal that most of the contemporary Western disciplines of knowledge and movements of philosophy have taken inspiration from his thought.

and the contemporary thinking in the West. Advaita and Aletheia, between which the paper tries to strike a parallel, are the central notions in the respective thinkers. Lest it be misunderstood, we would like to make it clear that we do not dare into a comparative study of these two thinkers and their philosophies;[3] we rather look into the notions of Advaita and Aletheia, focusing our attention on the similarity of the "word formation" by these two thinkers: the use of the negative prefix *ai* to bring out a meaning that transcends the either/or structure. We shall begin with a clarification of the notion of Advaita of Śaṅkara (I), followed by that of Aletheia of Heidegger (II).[4] In the final part we shall dwell on the close relation between these two notions, and on the primordiality of such an approach (III).

I

Classical orthodox Indian philosophy is traditionally discussed

---

3. Of late, there has been an increased interest in relating the Eastern and Western philosophy, especially that of Śaṅkara and Heidegger. A few of the comparative studies are the following: Vensus George, *Authentic Human destiny: The Paths of Śaṅkara and Heidegger* (Washington: The Council for Research in Values and Philosophy, 1998); G. Srinivasan, *Studies in East-West Philosophy* (New Delhi: Arnold Heinemann Publishers, 1974); Bosco Correya, *Heidegger and Śaṅkara: A Comparative Study of the Thinking of Being and Advaita*, Kalamassery: Jyothir Dharma Publications, 2003.
4. Although we are trying to clarify both the notions of Advaita and Aletheia, it must be noted at the very outset that the inspiration to look into their relation occurred to us, while doing research on Heidegger. Hence we will be focusing more on Heidegger's Aletheia. Besides the minimal competence of the present writer in the philosophy of Śaṅkara does not allow us to make an in-depth study of the philosophy of Śaṅkara.

in terms of six systems, the last of which is Vedānta, and Śaṅkara with his non-dualistic (advaitic) interpretation of reality is the chief exponent of Advaita Vedānta. He synthesizes and systematizes it on the triple foundations of Vedānta: Upaniṣads, *Bhagavad-Gītā*, and *Brahma-Sūtras*.[5] With sophisticated skill and subtility Śaṅkara worked out his Advaita philosophy, basing himself on the sacred writings. But he was not merely giving a commentary on the texts, but developed a non-dual vision. This vision may be summed up in three statements: *Brahman* is non-dual and unchanging reality; the world is illusion; *ātman* is not different from *Brahman*, the reality.[6]

The Upaniṣads repeat: "Verily, all this is *Brahman*."[7] This statement does not aim at establishing an identity between the phenomenal (*vyavahārika*) world of appearance and the ultimate reality (*paramārthika*) of *Brahman*. It rather aims at showing that the world, which appears to be real, is dependent on *Brahman* for its Being, whereas *Brahman* is not dependent on the world.[8] *Brahman*, which is really the real and the only real, is variously described in the Upaniṣads; but all these descriptions can be boiled down to the three constitutive characteristics: *sat-cit-ānanda*.[9] But it should not be taken as

---

5. William M. Indich, *Consciousness in Advaita Vedānta*, Delhi: Motilal Banarsidass, 1980, p. 2.
6. *Ibid*. Cf., also S. Sankaranarayanan, *Śrī Śaṅkara: His Life, Philosophy and Relevance to Man in Modern Times*, Madras: Adyar Libraray and Research Centre, 1995, p. 156.
7. *sarvaṁ idaṁ brahma eva. . . . Chāndogya Upaniṣad* 3. 14. I; *Maitrī Upaniṣad* 4. 6; *Bṛhadāraṇyaka Upaniṣad* 2. 4. 6; 3. 4. 1.
8. William M. Indich, *Consciousness in Advaita Vedānta*, p. 4.
9. P.T. Raju, *Structural Depths of Indian Thought*, New Delhi: South Asian Publishers, 1985, p. 393.

three attributes; *sat-cit-ānanda* is a single whole, which is *Brahman* itself.[10]

What we are interested in is the *advaitic* vision developed by Śaṅkara, as it is demanded by the purview of our study. The notion of Advaita refers to a relation, a special kind of relation, of *identity* and *difference* that transcends the strict mathematic-logical understanding of the West. Primarily it refers to the relation between *Brahman* and the self.[11] The nature of this relation is one of "difference-cum-non-difference" (*bhedā-bheda*).[12] Between *Brahman* and the self there is difference as well as non-difference (identity). They are not-one (*an-eka*), not-two (*advaita*); they are "non-dual" (*a-dvaita*).[13] Understanding of this non-duality is not by an intellectual cognition, but rather it is our becoming non-dual with *Brahman*.[14] Non-duality can be understood, on the one hand, as the absence of all differences in the state of *Brahmānubhava*, and on the other hand, as the realization of the ultimate unreality or illusory nature of all differences because of the realization of *Brahman*, which is everything, or besides which there is nothing.[15] Paul Deussen points out that

---

10. S. Sankaranarayanan, *Śrī Śaṅkara: His Life, Philosophy and Relevance to man in Modern Times*, p. 161.
11. We can also speak of a non-dual relation between *Brahman* and the world, and the humans and the world.
12. S.M. Srinivasachari, *The Philosophy of* Vedānta-*Sūtra*, New Delhi: Munshiram Manoharlal Publishers Pvt. Ltd., 1998, p. 79.
13. S.C. Mudgal, Advaita *of* Śaṅkara: *A Reappraisal*, Delhi: Motilal, 1975, p. 2.
14. Subash Anand, *Hindu Inspiration for Christian Reflection: Towards a Hindu-Christian Theology*, Anand: Gujarat Sahitya Prakash, 2004, p. 69.
15. A. Ramamurty, *Advaitic Mysticism of Śaṅkara*, Santiniketan: Viswa-Bharati, 1974, p. 182.

Vedānta, while maintaining the unity and non-duality of *Brahman* that permits no Being beyond itself, calls *Brahman* "the Lord" and sets him up as the ruler of the world.[16] This shows the impossibility of holding exclusively to an absolute *monism* without any difference between *Brahman* and the creation, or a *dualism* that points out that *Brahman* is totally other than the creation.

From what has been noted above, we are made to understand that Śaṅkara does not hold to one or the other extreme position of total *identity* (monism) or total *difference* (dualism). In his wisdom and philosophical acumen, Śaṅkara developed a philosophical vision: *a-dvaita* (non-dualism). Because of the novelty of this notion, it has been subjected to a variety of interpretations. Our contention is only this: by coining a term with the help of the negative prefix *a*, Śaṅkara takes us to a realm that transcends the logically precise realms of one-ness and two-ness of reality. Such a characterization of Advaita made many a Western mind consider Śaṅkara as logically "imprecise" and ambiguous, until perhaps a thinker from the West, Martin Heidegger, began to think non-logically in the twentieth century, just as Śaṅkara did in the ninth century.

II

Heideggerian philosophy has two clearly distinct phases: the *earlier* Heidegger and *later* Heidegger.[17] For our purpose here

---

16. Paul Deussen, *The System of* Vedānta, tr., C. Johnston, Chicago: The Open Court Publishing Co.,1912, p. 271.

17. For a detailed consideration of Heidegger's philosophy in its two phases, cf., Johnson J. Puthenpurackal, *Heidegger: Through Authentic Totality to Total Authenticity*, Louvain: Leuven University Press, 1987.

we are presently concerned about Heidegger's notion of *a-letheia* which finds itself in the context of his notion of truth in his later thought. Just as Heideggerian thought is marked by the distance he took from the traditional style of philosophizing, so also his understanding of truth as Aletheia is evidently different from the traditional conception of truth as *adaequatio*. This *distance/difference* becomes obviously present in his later thought, but is vaguely present in his earlier philosophy as well.

Later Heideggerian thinking is so richly and overlappingly stuffed with insightful sparks on "truth," that one is at a loss as to how to give a clear elucidation of this all-pervasive notion.[18] The earlier thought of Heidegger is a transcendental inquiry of Being from the perspective of *Dasein* or the human, whereas his later thought is characterized as the authentic thinking of Being as the happening of truth. Thus in later Heidegger "Being is not clarified in its relation to the human, on the contrary, the human is looked at in his relation to Being."[19] Being/truth that *Dasein* has been trying to disclose, un-cover, or un-conceal, shows itself now as the very *un-concealing,* rather than the *un-concealed*. In keeping with the thought-pattern of Heidegger-II, truth as *essencing* or *un-concealing* too has to be thought in terms of *Ere ignis* or "Event-

---

18. The difficulty of elucidating the later Heideggerian thought in clear and precise terms is a generally accepted fact, mainly because of the poetical style of his thinking and writing. It is much more true with regard to truth, since it is spoken of everywhere, at the same time nowhere in particular.

19. "Das Sein wird nicht gedeutet durch seine Beziehung rom Menschen, sondem umgekehrt der Mensch durch seine Beziehung zum Sein." Llambias de Azevedo, J., "Der Alte und der Neue Heidegger," *Philosophisches Jahrbuch* 60 (1950): 165.

ing."[20] It implies a two-fold relation: on the one hand, the "belonging-together" or "complimentarily" between Being as *giving* or *presenting* and the human as *receiving* or *responding*, and on the other hand, the "difference" or "un-concealing" between Being as *concealing* and entities as *revealing*.[21] The dual aspect of truth as revealing and concealing is very much central to Heidegger, and he spares no means to shed more light onto it.

In his lectures on Heraclitus,[22] Heidegger dwells at length on the pre-Socratic notion, *physis*, relating it to Aletheia. He sees the essence of *physis* in the unity of "emerging" (*Aufgehen*) and "submerging" (*Untergehen*), revealing and concealing.[23] In *Logos* too Heidegger finds the striking unity of its original meaning with that of *physis* and Aletheia:[24] "*Logos* is in itself and at the same time a revealing and a concealing. It is Aletheia."[25] Thus we have come to the climax of Heideggerian thinking on truth as Aletheia, wherein is contained its dual

---

20. Although the present author has rendered *Ereignis* as "Event of Appropriation" in his book, *Heidegger: Through Authentic Totality to Total Authenticity*, he is inclined to render it now as "Eventing."

21. For a detailed analysis of this structure of *Ereignis*, cf., J.J. Puthenpurackal, *Heidegger: Through Authentic Totality to Total Authenticity*, pp. 144-45, 175-225.

22. *Heraklit*, Gesamtausgabe, Abt., II, Bd., 55 (Frankfurt am Main: Vittorio Klostermann, 1979), These lectures were delivered during the summer-semesters of 1943-44.

23. *Ibid.*, p. 110.

24. For a more detailed consideration of these pre-Socratic notions, cf., J.J. Puthenpurackal, *Heidegger: Through Authentic Totality to Total Authenticity*, pp. 204-07.

25. "Der *Logos* ist *in sich zumal* ein Entbergen und Verbergen, Er ist die Aletheia." *Vortrage und Aufsatze*, 4. Aufl., (pfullingen: Neske, 1978), p. 213.

dimension: revealing and concealing.[26] Aletheia is expressive of the inseparable unity of concealment and revilement, of Being (*Sein*) and entities (*Seiendes*). Being never *presences* (*west*) without the entities, and entity never *is* without Being;[27] so also truth comes to pass only through an entity.[28]

Being and truth, according to Heidegger, are to be thought together; "thinking of Being" and "thinking of truth" refer to "the same" (*das Selbe*). Traditionally Being and truth have been considered merely in positive terms: Being as opposed to what is absent, truth as opposed to what is false. The *concealing* aspect has been forgotten, and so Heidegger takes pains to emphasize this dimension by various means, such as using the expression "the naughting of nothing" (*das Nichten des Nichts*) as equivalent to "the presencing of Being" (*das Wesen des Seins*),[29] or by the peculiar way of writing "Being" with a crossed marks:[30] Later-Heidegger's thinking of truth and Being is

---

26. Heidegger uses numerous images to speak of the dual aspect of the truth of Being, such as world and earth, giving and withholding, appropriation and expropriation, nearness and farness, emerging and submerging, presencing and absencing, waking and sleeping, etc. For a more complete list with the appropriate references, cf., J.J. Puthenpurackal, *Heidegger*, p. 209.
27. "... das Sein nie west ohne das Seiende, daB niemals ein Seiendes ist ohne das Sein." Heidegger, "Nachwort zu: Was ist Metaphysik?" *Wegmarken*, 2. Autl., Frankfurt am Main: Vittorio Klostermann, 1978, p. 304.
28. "... Wahrheit nur west, indem sie sich in ein Seiendes einrichtet," *Holzwege*, p. 57; *Poetry, Language, Thought*, p. 69.
29. *Vier Seminare*, Frankfurt am Main: Vittorio Klostermann, 1977, pp. 99-102.
30. *Zu Seinsfrage*, 3. Autl., (Frankfurt am Main: Vittorio Klostermann, 1967), pp. 34-35, *The Question of Being*, trans., W. Kluback and J.T. Wilde (New Haven: College and University Press, 1958), pp. 89-91, Following the example of Heidegger, Derrida too has made use of this Devīce.

directed to neither exclusively to concealing nor to revealing, but to the very *difference* between the concealing of Being and the revealing of entities. This dual aspect is well contained in the term "un-concealment" (*Un-Verborgenheit*),[31] which is the original meaning of *A-letheia*.

Our hitherto elucidation of truth as *a-letheia* can be crowned by taking the duality of revealing and concealing into a primordial realm of unity. In his Parmenides-lectures[32] Heidegger leads us into it. He speaks of four ways of translating the term, *a-letheia*. The first two ways correspond to the emphasis placed on one or the other part of the term: *un-concealment* and *un-concealment*: the former has an overtone on concealment, the latter on revilement.[33] The third way, that dominated the metaphysical period, takes *a-letheia* as truth in opposition to untruth, correctness to falsity. What we are interested in is the fourth way which consists in considering Aletheia as Aletheia, i.e., the very essence of Aletheia as un-concealment. "In the essence of the unconcealment reigns the

31. This vaguely touched upon distinction between revealment and un-concealment is of importance, in our view. Logically and metaphysically both the terms mean the same: double negative (un-concealment) is equal to positive (revealment). In Heidegger, "un-concealment" speaks of a realm somewhere between concealment and revealment — a realm characterized not by a structure of "*either/or*," but by that of "*neither/nor*" and "*both/and*." In the Indian tradition such a distinction does not appear anything strange. For instance, the most important Indian philosophical system developed by Śaṅkara is called *a-dvaita* (non-dualism): an approach to reality that falls between both dualism and monism.

32. Parmenides, Gesamtausgabe, Abt., II, Bd., 54, Frankfurt am Main: Vittorio Klostermann, 1982.

33. *Ibid.*, pp. 22-23.

Open (*das Offene*),[34] to which the Greeks never paid any attention. The Open as truth is the "Eventing" (*Ere ignis*) of truth, the clearing (*Lichtung*) from which the interplay of revealing and concealing (brightness and darkness) comes to pass, as authentic thinking (*Licht*, light) enters into it.[35] This indicates that the human has a special role in the eventing of truth.

In Heidegger's thought-structure, Being/truth presences itself to the receptive mortals: "Mortals are irrevocably bound to the revealing-concealing gathering which lights (opens, *lichtet*) everything present in its presencing."[36] Standing in the Open of the clearing, man looks into the Open; the human thus becomes the genuine "seer" (*Seher*)[37] of the revealing-concealing process. "He sees because the lighting-up (*Lichtung*) has been visited upon him."[38] The light of authentic thinking by the mortals lets the eventing of truth come about. Truth as un-concealing has the priority over the human response of authentic thinking. The role of the humans in the eventing of

---

34. *Ibid.*, pp. 27, 38-39 and 42. . . .
35. Heidegger, *Zur Sache des Denkens*, 2. Aufl., Tilbingen: Max Niemeyer, 1976, p. 72; *On Time and Being*, tr., J. Stambaugh, New York: Harper and Row, 1972, p. 65.
36. Heidegger, *Vortriige und Aufsiitze*, p. 273; *Early Greek Thinking*, tr., David F. Krell and F.A. Capuzzi, New York: Harper and Row, 1975, p. 12:2.
37. Heidegger introduces this notion in his "Der Spruch des Anaximander," *Holzwege*, p. 318; *Early Greek Thinking*, p. 33. The term "seer" goes well with the Indian thinking, according to which the philosopher is called a "seer" (*darśanika*), and philosophy is termed as "seeing" (*darśana*). For more on this, cf., J.J. Puthenpurackal, *Heidegger*, p. 201, note 226.
38. Richardson, *Heidegger: Through Phenomenology to Thought*, 3rd ed., The Hague: Martinus Nijhoff, 1974, p. 525.

truth is made clear by Heidegger by his use of the term "the shepherd" (*der Hirt*) as different from "the lord" (*der Herr*). Man is not the Lord that dictates, but the *shepherd* that cares and receives the happening of truth as *a-letheia.*

The term *aletheia* literally means "truth." But Heidegger does not take truth as opposed to "untruth" or falsity; he takes it as the revealing-concealing process. To bring out this meaning Heidegger exploits the etymological meaning of *a-letheia* (un-concealing) — "a" the negative prefix with "lethe" (concealing). Instead of using the familiar terms, concealing or revealing, Heidegger uses the unfamiliar expression, "un-concealing" (*Un-Verborgenheit*), *a-letheia.* Through this expression he wants to convey that Being/truth does not consist merely in "revealing" nor in "concealing;" he takes us rather to the realm of "un-concealing" that transcends the logically precise realms of "revealing" and "concealing."

III

Now that we have delineated the notions of *a-dvaita* and *a-letheia,* we can look into the parallel that we find between them. These terms do not have the same meaning; but they have the same structure of meaning because they are coined in the same manner: with the help of the negative prefix, *a-*. In the ordinary logical understanding, *a-dvaita* (non-dualism), as the negation of dualism, should have meant "monism." So also, *a-letheia* (un-concealment), as the negation of concealment, should normally mean "revilement." But both Śaṅkara and Heidegger have distanced themselves from such an ordinary logical meaning that goes in line with the *either/or structure* of thinking — monism as different from dualism, revealing as different from concealing. Perhaps shedding a little more light onto the either/or structure of thinking is in place.

Logical precision and definition goes with the "either/ or" style of thinking. When we define something, we place it within a boundary, differentiating it from what it is not, i.e., differentiating what is within the boundary from what is outside. Thus P is differentiated from non-P, truth from falsity, beauty from ugliness, etc. Western philosophy of last two millennia has been a philosophy of "either/or" or of binary opposites,[39] in which one is excluded from the other, as both cannot go together without violating the principle of contradiction. The above-referred two notions too have been subjected to mutual exclusion: monism from dualism, concealment from revealment.

What have Śaṅkara and Heidegger done with their binary opposites? Have they broken open the "boundary" that separates monism and dualism, concealing and revealing? Of course, they have removed the boundary of precision separating the opposites, and they are able to consider the opposites together: Advaita is both monism and dualism, and at the same time neither of them; Aletheia too is both revealing and concealing, but neither of them exclusively.[40] But it does not mean that the "opposites" are merely juxtaposed or mixed together, creating a logical vagueness and confusion! We need to look at Advaita and Aletheia not with the rigid logicality,

---

39. It is the post modem thought in the West that has brought out very clearly the rigidly metaphysical structure of "*either/or*" or binary opposites. Derrida tries to deconstruct this structure in his philosophy. For an introductory elucidation of post modem themes, cf., J.J. Puthenpurackal, ed., *The Postmodern: A Siege of the Citadel of Reason*, Delhi: Media House, 2002.

40. In the language of Heidegger revealing and concealing are "the same" (*das Selbe*) but not "the identical" (*das Gleiche*).

but with a supra-logicality that is able to "see" the *difference*[41] rather than merely "the different." The realm of the "difference" is a primordial realm, to which both Śaṅkara and Heidegger take us through the notions of Advaita and Aletheia. To take to this realm both these thinkers, belonging to two different traditions of philosophy, and to two historical periods, have used the same methodological device of coining a term with the negative prefix *a*-. Besides, both of them have transcended the "boundary of precision" — the "either/or" structure. By going beyond the "limitation of precision" ("this" as opposed to "that,")[42] Śaṅkara and Heidegger have not taken us to a philosophy of confusion, but rather to a primordial realm that is intensively deeper and extensively wider.

Finding a parallel between Advaita and Aletheia, the central notions in the two prominent thinkers from two philosophic-cultural worlds open the door for a philosophy of complementarity in the new millennium. Such an openness of thought will hopefully emerge by the merging of the apparently irreconcilable opposites.

---

41. We are using here an expression of Derrida, "difference" for which the inspiration was Heidegger. Contemporary Western Philosophy is increasingly becoming a philosophy of difference.

42. The present writer has made an attempt to look into the possibility of such a philosophizing that transcends the *either/or* structure. Cf. Johnson Puthenpurackal, "Philosophizing for the New Millennium," *Vijñānadīpti*, II, 2, (June 1999): 189-201.

19

Brahman and Dao

A Comparative Analysis of Hindu and Chinese Metaphysics

K.R. Sundara Rajan

BRAHMAN and the *Dao* are central metaphysical concepts in the Hindu and the Chinese philosophical traditions respectively; both designate supreme reality, *Brahman* meaning "the all pervasive," and the *Dao* meaning "the way." In the Vedānta of Śaṅkara known as Advaita Vedānta, *Brahman* is the only Real, which is unchanging in its nature, and hence the day-to-day world of multiplicity subject to change is not ultimately real, but a "phenomenal world" which is illusory (*māyā*). In the theistic Vedānta of Rāmānuja known as the *Viśiṣṭādvaita* (qualified monism), and in the dualist Vedānta of Madhva (1197-1278) known as Dvaita Vedānta, Śaṅkara's defining feature of what is Real is not accepted and *Brahman*, the highest being, is seen in formal relationship with other beings (*ātman/ jīvas*) and with the physical world (*prakṛti*). In addition, there is a school of *bhedābheda* (difference and non-difference) of Bhāskara (950), where *Brahman* as the supreme principle is also the underlying substance of all changing beings and material things. Similar to the different ways that *Brahman* is conceptualized in schools of Vedānta, we find that the *Dao* is conceptualized differently in Chinese metaphysics and refers to different things in the Chinese traditions. For instance, A.C. Graham, points out that in the *Analectes* of Confucius, *Dao* is used only in the sense "of the proper course of human conduct and the organization of government, which is the Way of "antiquity" of "the former kings," of "the gentleman," of "the good man" and of "Wen and Wu" the founders of Chou, or else of what someone teaches as the Way ("my Way," and "our master's Way"). Confucius does not use it as Confucians as well as the Taoists soon came to do, of the course of the natural world outside of man."[1] However, in *Daodejing*, according to Philip Ivanhoe, "The *dao* is the source, sustenance, and ideal pattern for all things in the world. It is "hidden" and difficult to grasp but not metaphysically transcendent. In the apt metaphor of the text, it is the "root" of all things."[2] For the purpose of this paper, I will confine myself to the *Daodejing* to explicate the concept of the *dao*, and to the Vedānta school of Rāmānuja for the concept of *Brahman*.

A comparative study requires points of commonality as well as difference. My choice of Rāmānuja's writings to be compared with Lao Tzu's *Daodejing* is based on the following factors: (1) On the concept of *Brahman*, Mādhva is not different from Rāmānuja; (2) I feel that both Rāmānuja's works, and *Daodejing* exhibit a similar metaphysical orientation with regard to the conceptualization of *Brahman* and the *Dao* respectively, especially on the question of the relationship between the One and many;[3] (3). However, there are also

---

1. *Disputers of the Tao*, 1998 sixth printing, Chicago and La Salle, Il: Oopen Court, p. 13.

2. *The Daodejing of Laozi*, 2002, New York and London: Seven Bridge Press. p. xxii.

3. Both Rāmānuja and Lao Tzu may be regarded as panentheists in terms of Charles Hartshorne's description of panentheism. Runes' *Dictionary of Philosophy* describes panentheism as follows. ". . . the →

significant differences between Rāmānuja and the *Daodejing* in the areas of metaphysics and ethics. These factors make this comparative study challenging as well as interesting. My paper will first present the concept of *Brahman* in the Vedānta schools with Rāmānuja's Vedānta as the main focus, and then refer selectively to some of themes on the nature of the *Dao* in *Daodejing* for purposes of comparison.

According to Rāmānuja's Vedānta, there are three eternal principles (*tattvas*), namely, *Brahman*, *ātman*, and *prakṛti*, that is, the supreme Self, individual self/selfs, and primordial matter, respectively. Unlike *Brahman* of Śaṅkara which is unqualified, One without a second, Rāmānuja's *Brahman* is qualified; *ātman* and *prakṛti* are its qualifying "modes." Rāmānuja describes the relationship of *Brahman* with Its modes as that of the self and body (*śarīri-śarīra*), with *Brahman* as the self (*śarīri*) and both *ātman* and *prakṛti* as its body (*śarīra*). It is the body-self relationship that accounts for the description of *Brahman* as one as well as many. Since the body serves the

---

→ view that God interpenetrates everything without cancelling the relative, independent existence of the world of entities; moreover, while God is immanent, the immanence is not absolute (as in pantheism); God is more than the world, transcendent, in the sense that though the created is dependent of the creator, the creator is not-dependent on the created. God is thus held to be the highest type of Unity, viz. a Unity in multiplicity. The term is employed to cover a mediating position between pantheism with extreme immanence and a theism of the type which tends to extreme transcendence." (cited in John G. Plott, "Rāmānuja as Panentheist," *The Journal of Annamalai University*, vol. xvii (1953). p. 65). Hartshorne, however, does not place Lao Tzu and Rāmānuja under the same group; Lao Tzu is grouped under "Ancient or Quasi-Panenentheism," and Rāmānuja, under "Classical Pantheism." (See Hartshorne and W.L. Reese, eds. *Philosophers Speak of God*, 2000, Amherst, New York: Humanity Books).

needs of self, the Self becomes the final point of reference for the body. Therefore, one could speak of Reality as one, as some of the scriptural passages describe *Brahman* to be. However, it is equally valid to say that "oneness" is qualified by "many-ness," since both *ātman* and *prakṛti* are eternal principles (*tattvas*) alongside of *Brahman*, and they are neither created by *Brahman* nor are they modifications of *Brahman*.

Śaṅkara on the other hand, builds up his philosophy of non-dual *Brahman* on two grounds: First on the basis of his understanding and interpretation of the scriptural passages, particularly the Upaniṣads, and second, on a definition of Reality. On the basis of the Upaniṣadic passages, he establishes the following: there is no distinction between the individual self (*ātman*) and the universal Self (*Brahman*). And they are totally identical; due to ignorance (*a-vidyā*) multiplicity is "superimposed" on the Real which is one only without a second. The removal of this superimposition is indeed the goal of all Upaniṣadic teachings according to Śaṅkara.[4]

Śaṅkara's definition of the Real as that which is not subject to change (*trikāla abhadyam*, existence at all times, past, present and future) is the metaphysical basis on which he brands all the changing phenomenal world as ultimately illusory (*māyā*). For Śaṅkara, the ontological status of *māyā* (*illusion*) is that it is neither real nor unreal; Since illusory objects appear, they are real, since unreality cannot appear; however, since they change they are not ultimately real.[5] For Śaṅkara, illusory appearances belong to the category of things that are "indescribable" (*anirvacanīya*).

---

4. See *The Hindu Tradition*. Ainslie T. Embree (ed.), New York: Vintage Books, p. 202.
5. S.N. Dasgupta, *A History of Indian Philosophy*, vol. II. Delhi: Motilal Banarsidass, 1988 reprint, p. 271.

This definition of reality on which Śaṅkara builds up the *māyā* theory is not accepted by Rāmānuja. Along several theories of cause-effect relationships in the Hindu metaphysics, Rāmānuja is committed to a theory known as *sat-kārya-vāda* which says that the effect is a "real" transformation of the cause, thus stressing the reality of both the "source" as well as its "transformations," like the ocean and its waves. This is different from Śaṅkara's theory of causality called *vivarta-vāda*. According to the *vivarta* view, there is no "real" transformation of cause into effect. The "transformation" is only "apparent" just as the *māyā* world is only an appearance.[6] This *vivarta* view can also be appropriately described as *sat-kāraṇa-vāda* instead of *sat-kārya-vāda*, according to which the cause alone is true and its effects are false impositions on it. It is interesting to note that Rāmānuja would agree with Śaṅkara on the point that *Brahman* is eternal and changeless. However, its "body" consisting of *ātman* and *prakṛti*, he would contend, is subject to change, and changes occur at the time of creation. It is this feature of Rāmānuja's theology that also distinguishes his Vedānta from the Vedānta school of Bhāskara, known as *bhedābheda*, difference-non-difference school. Though both Rāmānuja and Bhāskara advocate the *sat-kārya-vāda* theory of causation, for Bhāskara, *Brahman*, out of its own choice, transforms itself into individual selfs and manifold forms of matter, subtle and gross, like a spider weaving its web. P.N. Srinivasachari describes the position of *bhedābheda* school thus: "*Brahman*, the unconditioned, becomes the conditioned, and differentiates itself into the infinity of beings, each having its own form and function. The infinite finitizes itself and yet

6. "So in all world phenomenon one truth is being, *Brahman*, and all the phenomena that are being imposed on it are but illusory forms and names," S.N. Dasgupta, *A History of Indian Philosophy*, vol. I. p. 468.

transcends the limitation of finitude."[7] For Rāmānuja, the transformation happens only at the level of the body (*śarīra*) of *Brahman* though the action itself is initiated by *Brahman* who is the self (*śarīri*). At the point of creation, *ātman* becomes manifold embodied selves, and *prakṛti* is transformed into manifold material world. As the self, *Brahman*, though not transformed, remains the material as well as the "instrumental cause" of the created world.

Thus, with Rāmānuja's theory of causation and with the self-body relationship in place, becoming is an integral aspect of "Being" and "change" is not a marker of illusion.

Is there any purpose to creation? Rāmānuja insists that there is no purpose since to speak of purpose is to undermine the very perfection of *Brahman*; purpose would seem to point to something that remains lacking or unfulfilled in *Brahman*. To stress purposelessness, Rāmānuja describes creation as divine play (*līlā*). Rāmānuja writes in his major work, *Śrī-Bhāṣya:*

> The motive which prompts *Brahman*, all whose wishes are fulfilled and who is perfect in himself, to the creation of the world comprising of all kinds of sentient and non-sentient beings dependent on his volition, is nothing but sport, play. . . there is no objection to the view that sport only is the motive prompting creation, sustentation and destruction of this world which is easily fashioned by his mere will.[8]

S.R. Bhatt points out that *līlā* "is an expression of joyousness and super abundance of energy on the part of *Brahman*, and it must be distinguished from conscious or volitional effort. The creation follows the mere will or free choice of *Brahman*."[9]

---

7. *The Philosophy of Viśiṣṭādvaita*, p. 257.
8. II. 1. 33, Thiebaut, p. 477.
9. *Studies in Rāmānuja Vedānta*, 1975, New Delhi: Heritage Publishers, p . 99.

This act is described as "purposeless purpose" by some of the Modern scholars of Vedānta. For P.N. Srinivasachari creation as *līlā* points to an aesthetic dimension in *Brahman*.

> *Sṛṣṭi* (creation) is the creative joy of self-expression, and self-evolution of *nāma-rūpa* (names and forms) is the evolution of infinite forms of beauty from the infinite Beauty that has formless form. The world of space-time is the eternal interplay between the static and the dynamic aspects of beauty.[10]

> . . . the creative activity of God in the world of space and time or space-time is a symphony without any jarring note. Each self is like a note in the musical scale, and marks a rhythm in the dance of divine beauty. The world is a poem of beauty, and its sonorousness is imparted to every part of it and makes it vibrate with its music. The divine Artist pours beauty into nature with a view to removing the fleshly feeling and other blemishes of the finite self, beautifying it and playing the game of love with it.[11]

For Rāmānuja, "the many," at a certain point in time, returns to the One and remains dormant in it till it is propelled by the One (*Brahman*) to become many again. This is the process of periodic creation-destruction-recreation which Rāmānuja has in common with all other Hindu thinkers and Hindu theological systems. Rāmānuja writes in *Śrī Bhāṣya* commenting on 1.4.27:

> Now, when this world which forms *Brahman*'s body has been gradually reabsorbed into *Brahman*, each constituent element being refunded into its immediate cause so that in the end there remains only the highly subtle, elementary matter which Scripture calls as Darkness. . . then *Brahman*

---

10. *The Philosophy of Viśiṣṭādvaita*, p. 205.
11. *Ibid.*

> invested with this ultra-subtle body forms the resolve "May I again possess a world-body constituted by all sentient and non-sentient beings, distinguished by names and forms just as in the previous eon" and modifies (*pariṇāmāyāti*) itself by gradually evolving the world-body in the inverse order in which reaborption has taken place.[12]

For purposes of comparative study, I will focus first on the distinction between *Brahman* itself and *Brahman* as the creator and see, how it compares with the distinction between the "unnamable" and "namable" *Dao* that is made in the very first chapter of the *Daodejing*. It reads:

The Way (*Dao*) that can be followed is not the constant Way.

> The name that can be named is not the constant name.
> Nameless, it is the beginning of Heaven and Earth;
> Named, it is the mother of myriad creatures.

This chapter is considered most important to a proper understanding of the *Daodejing*. As Te-ching, a commentator of the Ming Dynasty (sixteenth and seventeenth centuries) remarks: "Lao Tzu's philosophy is all here. The remaining five thousand words only expand on this first verse."[13] In Chapter 25, we have further statements on the namable and unnamable *Dao*.

> There is a thing confused yet perfect, which arose before Heaven and earth.
> Still and indistinct, it stands alone and unchanging.
> It goes everywhere yet is never at a loss.
> One can regard it as the Mother of Heaven and earth.

---

12. Thibaut, pp. 402-03.
13. Cited in *Lao Tzu's Tao Te Ching*, tr., Red Pine, p. 3.

I do not know its proper name;
I have given it the style "the Way."
Forced to give it a proper name, I would call it "Great."

Explaining the unnamable *Dao*, Wang Bi (3rd century CE), one of the earliest commentators on the *Daodejing*, says that the *Dao* is unnamable because it has no form, and being formless it is nameless.

Anything that exists originates in nothingness (*wu*), thus before it has forms and when it is still nameless, it serves as the origin of the myriad things, and, once it has forms and is named, it grows them, rears them, ensures them in proper shapes, and matures them as their mother. In other words, the *Dao*, by being itself formless and nameless, originates and brings the myriad things to completion. They are originated and completed in this way yet do not know how it happens. This is the mystery (*xuan*) beyond mystery.[14]

A modem writer on Taoism, Holmes Welch writes: "the picture which emerges from the *Tao Te Ching* is clear in its outlines: first Tao and then the physical universe — Heaven and Earth and the Ten Thousand Creatures — arose from Something Else. This Something Else Lao Tzu variously describes as the Self-so, the Nameless, or Non-Being."[15] Chapter 21 of the *Daodejing* describes this Something Else as "hazy and nebulous," "obscure and vague." However, in spite of these characteristics, it stresses that "its essence is very real and in its midst there is genuineness." Rhett Young and Roger Ames write:

---

14. *The Classic of the Way and Virtue: A New Translation of the Tao Te Ching of Laozi as Interpreted by Wang Bi.*, tr. Richard John Lynn, 1999, New York: Columbia University Press, p. 51.

15. *Taoism The Parting of the Way*, p. 55.

> Lao Tzu states there exists a thing which heterogeneously forms one entity but that he knows of no name which can adequately express it. If forced to assign a name as discussion of it would demand, he would refer to it as "Tao." It cannot be suitably identified by name because it is both inaudible and invisible. In other words, this real entity does not have concrete form. Since designation follows from form in making its appearance, since the "Tao" has no definite form, it follows that the "Tao" is "unnamable." [16]
>
> If Lao Tzu were to admit a form as a characteristic of the "Tao," then the "Tao" would have to exist among concrete things on a particular time-space coordinate. If this were the case, the "Tao" would be subject to the transformations of birth, growth, and death, as are all constituents of the phenomenal world.[17]

Philip Ivanhoe, in his introduction to the *Daodejing*: writes about this unnamable *Dao*:

> . . . the *Dao* is *ziran*, so of itself or "spontaneous" and its unencumbered activity brings about various natural states of affairs through *wuwei*, "non-action." It is "hidden" and contains within it patterns of all we see. In the apt metaphor of the text, it is the "root" of all things.[18]

Thus the "real Tao entity not only has an existence prior to the formation of Heaven and Earth, but further, Heaven and Earth owe their very existence to the generative power of the Tao."[19] In chapter six, it is described as the "Enigmatic Female" whose portal is "called the root of Heaven and Earth."

---

16. Introduction to *Lao Tzu-Text, Notes, and Comments* by Chen Ku-ying, p. 3.
17. *Ibid.*, pp. 3-4.
18. *The Daodejing of Laozi*, p. xxii.
19. Young and Ames, *Lao Tzu-Text, Notes, and Comments*, p. 5.

In terms of our comparative study, we could first take up the very notion of the *Dao* as unnamable because it is "formless" and, being formless, it is beyond the realm of adequate conceptualization and description: "In its opening statements," Ellen Chen writes, "The *Tao Te Ching* points out the limitations of language, spoken or recorded, in conveying to us the nature of ultimate reality. Language, as Bergson points out, is invented to express and deal with the determinate and immobile. The everlasting, transcending all determinations, cannot be spoken or named."[20]

Po Chug-I, one of the famous poets of the ninth century, comments humorously on the issue whether the *Dao* as it is expounded by Laos can be expressed verbally:

Those who speak do not know;
Those who know do not speak.
This is what we are told by Lao Tzu,
Should we believe that he himself
Was the one who knew;
How could it then be that he wrote
No less than five thousand words.[21]

The Upaniṣadic attempt to describe *Brahman* as *neti neti* ("not this, not this") is something that we could find in the Hindu philosophic tradition that possibly provides "links" with the statements describing the unnamable and namable *Dao* in the first chapter of the *Daodejing*. We find that the *Kaṭha Upaniṣad* uses negative terms to describe *Brahman*, saying *Brahman* is "that which is inaudible, intangible, invisible, indestructible, which cannot be tasted, nor smelt, eternal, without beginning

20. *The Tao Te Ching: A New Translation with Commentary*, p. 52.
21. Cited in Chang Chung-yuan, *Creativity and Taoism A Study of Chinese Philosophy, Art, and Poetry*, p. 30.

or end."[22] S.N. Dasgupta comments on the *neti neti* usage in the Upaniṣads:

"They (Upaniṣadic seers) found that by whatever means they tried to give positive and definite content to the ultimate reality, *Brahman*, they failed. Positive definitions were impossible. They could not point out what *Brahman* was like in order to give an utterance to that which was unutterable, they could only say that it was not like aught that we find in experience". Yājñavalkya said:

> He the *Ātman* is not this, not this (*neti, neti*). He is inconceivable, for he cannot be conceived, unchangeable, for he is not changed, untouched, for nothing touches him; he cannot suffer by a stroke of the sword, he cannot suffer any injury.[23]

This negative usage is also reflected in the Vedānta where *Brahman*, instead of being stated to be "one," is stated to be "not-two," for the reason that one could meaningfully speak of "one" only in the context of "many." This is true particularly in the description of Śaṅkara's school of Vedānta as *a-dvaita* (not-two).

However, in spite of the recognition that *Brahman* cannot be adequately conceptualized and hence at best may be referred to only negatively, we find some positive descriptions of *Brahman*. But they are often couched in paradoxical statements. For instance, in the *Bṛhadāraṇyaka Upaniṣad*, responding to a question posed by Gārgi, sage Yājñavalkya describes *Brahman* as "neither gross nor fine, neither short nor long, neither glowing red (like fire) nor adhesive (like water)."[24] In Śaṅkara's Vedānta, *Brahman* is stated to be *sat-*

22. III. 15.
23. *A History of Indian Philosophy*, vol. 1, pp. 44-45.
24. III. 8. 8; Cf, S. Radhakrishnan, tr., *The Principal Upaniṣads*, p. 232.

cit-ānanda, that is, Being, awareness and blissfulness respectively. It is explained however that these "positive" descriptions have the purpose of *not* attributing certain negative qualities to *Brahman.* To say that *Brahman* is Being (*sat*) means that it is *not* its opposite, namely, non-being (*a-sat*); similarly *cit* states that *Brahman* is *not* inert, and *ānanda,* that it is not subject to pain and suffering. However, Rāmānuja writes of "five defining qualities" of *Brahman,* and includes the above three and adds to the list *anantatva,* and *amalatva,* infinititude and purity respectively.

The "nameable *Dao*" and the "Ten Thousand Creatures" it produced are perhaps similar, as Holmes Welch suggests, to the analogy of fire and sparks that we find in the Upaniṣads.[25] Fire in this case is the prior source for sparks, as sparks corne from fire, and yet it is not transcendent. Similarly, the scholars of the *Daodejing* would say that the (unnamable) *Dao* is not ontologically transcendent.[26] As Ames and Hall remark: "The *Daoist* does not posit the existence of some permanent reality behind appearances, some unchanging substratum behind the accidents of change."[27] Though in the theistic schools of Vedānta, *Brahman* is the source of the manifold created phenomena, fire and sparks might not be the appropriate analogy to describe the relationship between the One and Many. While Śaṅkara's Vedānta denies a real transformation of the One into many, for Rāmānuja, *Brahman* itself remains changeless, while its body is subject to change and transformation. The Bhedābheda school of Bhāskara and Yādavaprakāśa (after the time of Śaṅkara and before Rāmānuja), may come closest in expressing the spirit of the

---

25. *Taoism The Parting of the Way,* p. 58.
26. *Daodejing of Laozi,* p. xxii.
27. *A Philosophical Translation Daodejing, Making Life Significant,* p. 14.

metaphor. The Bhedābheda school presents *Brahman* in two stages: 1) The stage of *Brahman* in itself which is a pre-creational state; and 2) *Brahman* as created phenomena, where, *Brahman*, out of his own initiative and choice, transforms himself into individual selfs and manifold forms of matter. However, even here, unlike the unnamable *Dao*, *Brahman* in itself is a transcendent reality whose description may not differ much from the way *Brahman* is described in the main schools of Vedānta. This is in spite of the fact that for the Bhedābheda school, *Brahman* is marked by both "difference" (*bheda*) and "non-difference" (*a-bheda*). For Bhāskara, the state of difference arises due to limiting conditions (*upādhi*) and for Yādhavaprakāśa, difference and non-difference are essential qualities of *Brahman*. It is important to note at this point that the notion of degrees of reality is common to all schools of Vedānta. Certainly in this aspect the Vedāntic standpoint differs from the *Daoists*, whose position on this issue is summed up by Chuang Tzu thus: "There is nothing in the world greater than the tip of the hair, while Mount Tai is small." The notion that "everything is *Dao*" is taken literally; and strictly speaking, there are no hierarchies reflecting degrees of reality. A.C. Graham's comments stress this point: "For the Chinese, the purpose of seeking the one behind the many is to find, *not something more real* than what appears to the senses, but a *constant way* behind the changing and conflicting ways of life."[28] Ivanhoe explains what this quest means in the context of the *Daodejing*:

> The *Daodejing* describes a mystical ideal in the sense that those who realize the Way lose a strong sense of themselves as distinct, autonomous agents and to some extent are thought to merge into the *Dao*'s underlying patterns and processes. In such a state, one does not conceive of oneself

28. *Disputers of the Tao*, p. 223.

> as apart from and independent of the rest of the world. Since she sees herself as inextricably intertwined with the overall harmony of the *Dao*, she never assumes the perspective of narrowly self-interested agent seeking to maximize her individual well-being.[29]

Seeking the One behind the many is also the core of Hindu spirituality since the time of the Upaniṣads. The goal in both cases is to overcome the sense separation and disjointedness, by experiencing the all-pervasive real, *Brahman*, in the one case, and by experiencing and imitating the Way, the *Dao*, in the other case. However, there is one important point of difference: in the Vedānta schools there is some kind of "ontological tension" between the "One" and the "many." This is seen in the radical differences between *saṁsāra*, the state of bondage, and *mokṣa*, the state of freedom. Such radical differences and tensions tend to be mitigated in the *Daodejing* due to the notion of "circularity." Chapter 40, states this principle of circularity:

> Returning is how way-making (*Dao*) moves,
> And "weakening" is how it functions,
> The events of the world arise from the determinate (you),
> And the determinate arises from the indeterminate (*wu*).

Commenting on these verses Ames and Hall write:

> The swinging doors of the gate open and, embarking upon its initial phase of becoming increasingly determinate, the inchoate "thing" or event emerges within its already determinate context. Culminating in its full maturation, the event then begins its gradual process of decline. As the journey continues, any persisting determinate aspects are ultimately weakened and overtaken by indeterminacy,

---

29. *The Daodejing of Laozi*. pp. xx-xxi.

> concluding this sojourn into determinacy by its return to the indeterminate.[30]

"Non-Being" and "Being" are special terms in the philosophy of Lao Tzu, alluding to two aspects of Tao, write Young and Ames. "As aspects of the Tao, they are neither antithetical or contradictory. On the other hand, they are consistent and continuous with each other."[31]

Such an approach to opposites is the basis for the "complementary dualism" that we find in the *Daodejing*, and this is not the hallmark of Vedānta. At least with regard to the question of *saṁsāra* and *mokṣa*, the Vedāntic responses border on "conflicting dualism." The complementarity of opposites is a frequently stated theme in the *Daodejing*, stressing the point that the opposites need one another and they are continuous with each other. For instance, the second chapter of the *Daodejing* reads as follows:

> Everyone in the world knows that when the beautiful strives to be beautiful, it is repulsive.
> Everyone knows that when the good strives to be good, it is no good.
> And so,
> To have and to lack generate each other.
> Difficult and easy give form to each other.
> Long and short off-set each other.
> High and low incline into each other.
> Note and rhythm harmonize with each other.
> Before and after follow each other.
> That is why sages abide in the business of non-action,
> And practice the teaching that is without words.

---

30. *A Philosophical Translation Daodejing*, pp. 139-40.
31. *Lao Tzu-Text, Notes, and Comments*, p. 7.

> They work with the myriad creatures and turn none away.
> They act with no expectation of reward.
> When their work is done, they do not linger.
> And by not lingering, merit never deserts them.[32]

Thus complementary dualism is connected with the Daoist practice of non-action (*wu-wei*). A.C. Graham explains *wu-wei* thus:

> The paradox that the way to attain the goal is to cease to aim at it deliberately is most explicit in the constant appeals to "do nothing" (*wu wei*). This term, which goes back to Confucius, is often translated by such innocuous phrases as "non-action" to avoid giving the impression that the Taoists recommend idleness, but it seems better to keep the paradoxical force of the Chinese expression. *Wei* is ordinary human action, deliberated for a purpose, in contrast with the spontaneous processes of nature which are so in themselves. Man takes pride in distinguishing himself from nature by his purposive action; *Lao Tzu* by a classical reversal describes the behavior of the sage as Doing Nothing.[33]

To sum up: In terms of ultimate mystery, both *Brahman* and the *Dao* are similar. However, in terms of intrinsic dynamism, there is a significant difference. *Brahman* in the non-dual Vedānta of Śaṅkara lacks this dynamism since what is Real is ultimately One and all plurality is ultimately illusory (*māyā*). The Vedānta of Rāmānuja stresses the dynamic nature of *Brahman* by its body-self analogy. In the Bhedhābheda of Bhāskara, the one *Brahman* itself becomes many. However, there is some sort of reluctance generally in the Indian metaphysical systems to ascribe equal ontological status to

---

32. Tr. Ivenhoe, *Readings in Classical Chinese Philosophy*, pp. 159-60.
33. *Disputers of the Tao*, p. 232.

the changing phenomenon with the changeless *Brahman*. The balance is tilted in favor of the changeless. In all the Vedānta schools the goal of life is to move from the changing to the changeless.

Finally, what limits our exploration of finding similarities between the *Dao* and *Brahman* are basic differences in the world views of China and India. According to Nigosian, the "unifying principle in Chinese religion is harmony. Harmony is manifested in the cosmos, in nature, in human relationships and in one's interior life or being."[34] One could say that the unifying principle in the Vedāntic metaphysics is the quest for knowledge, particularly the knowledge of the self (*ātma-jñāna*) that enables a Hindu to transcend the world of *saṁsāra*. However, both Chinese and Indian religions deal with a common problem, namely the problem of human limitations and consequent suffering. The explanations given for such a condition and the ways to handle it are different. While *Daodejing*'s solution is focused on understanding the *Dao* and imitating its ways, the Vedāntic solution is focused on knowing the Self (*Ātman*) and thus transcending the human world of suffering.

---

34. *World Religions A Historical Approach*, 2000, Boston: Bedford/St. Marins. p. 102.

20

The Eternal Feminine in Traditional Hinduism

Patricia Reynaud

BASED on the teachings of Hinduism, three great writers-René Guénon, Ananda Coomaraswamy and Frithjof Schuon have unveiled potentialities connected to the notions of the Eternal Feminine and divine Motherhood contained in Ancient and Abrahamic metaphysics. These scholars gave an importance never possible without this incursion into India's sacred texts and into her most speculative metaphysics, what Coomaraswamy has called "the divine bi-unity:" *Brahman* and *Śakti* at the metaphysical level and *Puruṣa* and *Prakṛti* at the cosmological level. Before considering the topic of a feminine metaphysics in their writings, let's briefly introduce the authors. They are neither the founders of a new school nor fathers of a new current thought that have major philosophical implications.

René Guénon, Ananda Coomaraswamy and Frithjof Schuon are better defined as sages or masters. They are interested in spiritual realization more than in mere speculation. Only Schuon had disciples. Their action was not directed towards erudites or Western intellectuals but towards those who keep aspiring to spiritual realization in the modern world itself, those who are consumed by the desire of union with God and who can't find in the West the means to undertake this quest. The content of their teachings is impersonal, expressed without hurting the religious mentalities and appear more or less independent from any given religious form.

Depending on the circumstances, these sages speak the language of the Vedānta, of Akbarian Sufism, of Taoism and of Christian mysticism. Guénon and Schuon were Sufis and Coomaraswamy continued to live as a traditional Hindu while in the US. In essence, however, they all referred to *Sophia Perennis;* and the value of their writings is to be measured by the intrinsic orthodoxy of Perennial wisdom, neither by specific dogmatism nor postulates from any philosophical systems. Their true refuge is located on no maps: it is this Orient of the self where the mysteries of the Kingdom of heaven are forever preserved.

Similar to the popular Western thinkers' proposition of the "Transcendent Unity of Religions" these thinkers and masters insists on ultimate metaphysical principles, recognizes and stresses both the diversity and differences between religions — differences that are inscribed at the level of the Divine Word itself. This Transcendent unity is not a sentimental philosophy of universal but based on spiritual realization and inner experience.

Primordial Tradition in René Guénon's Writings

In his book *General Introduction to the Study of Hindu Doctrines,* René Guénon identifies these doctrines as the most direct branch originating from the "Great Primordial Tradition." To the somewhat relative antiquity of Greece, he opposes the staggering antiquity of the Vedas and of the *Sanātana Dharma.* The pertinence of his thesis is not from historical or archeological research. The primordial character of India derives from what Henry Corbin, a great Iranologist, called hiero-history and no chronological frieze can measure it. What characterizes Indian spirituality is that it is of a contemplative type, which provides the criterion of any possible metaphysical doctrine.

For René Guénon, while the metaphysical truths of Abrahamic religions are veiled and restricted to an esotericism only understood by an elite, in India, these truths are being exposed publicly without the risk of extreme criticisms from an esoteric authority. He provides a few characteristics of this integral intellectuality:

1. The Ultimate Principle is beyond the First Being or God as a creator (*Īśvara*): It is the One without a second, beyond any relation and apart from all relations: *Brahman Nirguṇa* or supreme Self (*Paraṁ Ātman*). This principle is going to polarize itself between active and passive perfection, the latter being identified to the Mother Goddess (*Mahā-Śakti*).
2. Active role of the Intellect[1] in knowledge and realization: This Intellect is identified to the Heart and Sojourn of *Brahman*. It is transcendent and of divine nature, located beyond the individual self (mental, *manas*).

---

1. Strictly speaking, Intellect is not only Buddi but also *cit* (the Platonic nous). The Intellectual activity is opposed to receptivity of the Heart in Sufism. The one and the other correspond to the two modalities of realization in Hinduism and Islam: Union of the Principal of the being (*Ātman*) with the Principal of Everthing (*Brahman*) for the first form and the realization of integral servitude (*ubudiyya*) implying that the unique and eternal Essence is maintained (*wujud even dhat*) for Islam.

3. Distinction between liberation and deliverance (*mokṣa*): In his book, *Man and his Becoming According to the* Vedānta, Guénon formulates a full-fledged doctrine of posthumous conditions, depending on degrees of spiritual realization, on the basis of Hindu teachings. He opposes the path of angels (*deva-yāna*) and that of the ancestors (*pitṛ-yāna*). While the latter demands a return of the being to a formal state (metempsychosis), the former leads to his perpetual continuation in a *svarga*, to the realization of the superior states of being and ultimately to the supreme identity (*mokṣa*).[2]

Guénon was neither an historian of ideas nor an Orientalist. His writings are not aimed at analyzing in detail the various *darśana*s and schools of India, but yet reminding Westerners the universal truths which India has retained and that which they have forgotten. Guénon states that the distinction between the Vedic tradition (Vedas, Upaniṣads) and the Agamic tradition (*Tantra*s, etc. . . .) is not essential.

According to Guénon, these teachings are indeed found in the esoteric doctrines of Abrahamism and, in particular, in Sufi esotericism (*Tasawwuf*) with sometimes variations in Hinduism in explicit manner without dogmatism. In Muslim esotericism for instance, a Paradise of the Essence (*jannat adh-dhati*) exists for the Gnostics as well as the heart (*qualb*) as the organ of knowledge. The doctrine of supreme Identity (*wahdat al-wujud*) however has been harshly criticized, and even attacked by the forefathers of contemporary fundamentalism such as Ibn Taymiyya. In Christianity, the development of a Christology of Incarnation contributed to make the truth of a revelation depend on some type of historicity. This is not the

---

2. Different from Śaṅkara, Guenon considers a gradual realization rather than a sudden one.

case in India and especially on the question of the divine bi-unity. On the basis of the teachings of Indian tradition, Guénon intends to recall this intellectual intuition of the Great Mother.

The Eternal Feminine: René Guénon and Frithjof Schuon

In his *The Multiple States of Being,* Guénon teaches that the Ultimate Principle, that he calls the Infinite, is ineffable. It is beyond the being, beyond ontology. Rigorously speaking, it is beyond the distinction between being and non-being. Thus Guénon opposes the active and the passive perfection of the Principle. While the passive perfection is identified to the Great Mother, *Brahman*'s *Śakti,* the active perfection is said to be masculine only by analogy. The relationship between the Principle and its manifestation is therefore made possible by the feminine pole of the Deity. The very pole includes the possibilities of manifestation, i.e., the totality of possibilities, which are going to be actualized as well as the possibilities of unmanifestation, which express the radical transcendence of the Principle. There is indeed a mystery insofar as the multiplicity of beings contradicts illusory of the unity of the Principle. In order for these beings not to be pure nothingness, this created multiplicity has to be meontologically pre-inscribed as important yet unreal multiplicity.

It is from this universal possibility that the First Being or God (*Īśvara*) as "Creator" derives the derivative second beings. From the polarization of the First Being, the two poles of universal manifestation are born: *Puruṣa* and *Prakṛti,* also called the First Intellect and Nature. Guénon mentions that manifestation is illusory only insofar as it is separated from the Principle. It is the reason why, following Coomaraswamy, he rather translates *māyā* by Construction or Measure. *Śakti* and *Prakṛti* are two designations for the feminine and maternal aspects of the Principle, in its supreme and non-supreme, transcendent and immanent aspects of manifestation. Schuon has meditated at length on the ambiguous character of *māyā* and his conclusions are the same. The feminine aspect of the Principle is one of darkness insofar as it distances second beings from the Principle. Only at the level of individual manifestation the power of projection and manifestation becomes a power of separation and distancing.

These considerations have essential implications for cyclical cosmology and Schuon develops them in detail. To be brief, for Guénon and Schuon, the entire manifestation is a process from the qualitative and formal pole *Puruṣa* toward the quantitative and substantial *Prakṛti*, the most glaring expression of the descending trend of the manifested universe.

Divine Bi-Unity in Ancient Greece and in the Traditions of the Book

It is a surprise to note that, at a time the Hindu texts were not yet available in translation, Guénon was able to come up with this essential intuition, this mystery of divine bi-unity, an intuition found at the heart of Tāntrism and in the teachings of Sri Ramakrishna. Guénon's analyses are relevant here as his followers have made pertinent connections between the Hindu teachings on divine bi-unity and some doctrines in Greek Antiquity and Abrahamism. We shall offer three instances:

Georges Vallin: Plotinus and the Two Matters

The doctrine of the two matters has been analyzed at length by the French philosopher Georges Vallin. The doctrine of the two matters — gross and intelligible, found in Plotinus' *Enneads* II, 4 is very unusual in Western metaphysics. It becomes explicit when put in relation with Śaṅkara's doctrine on the two aspects of *māyā*: power of projection and power of illusion. Plotinus requires Śaṅkara's texts to be fully meaningful. In the following passage, Plotinus distinguishes clearly between the intelligible matter from which ideas are formed and the gross matter, the determining element of instability and multiplicity are manifested.

> Matter is essentially Indefiniteness. The Matter even of the Intellectual Realm is the Indefinite (. . .) But how can Matter be common to both Spheres, be here and be There? Because even Indefiniteness has two phases. . . , the difference between the two phases is that of archetype and image.(II, 4, 15).

For Georges Vallin, if we take into consideration the metaphysics of Vedānta, Neo-Platonism and Classical Greek Ontology, the intelligible matter is upper *māyā* and gross matter is lower *māyā*. However, this comparison enables Georges Vallin to stress the difference between Greek and Hindu intellectuality, to the benefit of the latter. There is no positive concept of the Infinite in the Greek classical ontology; and the belief in the reality of individual and limited forms produces some limitations in Plotinus' perspective as he is more reluctant to speak about divine matter that produces forms (divine infinity). This limitation results in the experience of unity being attained only from an ecstatic stance, an experience less radical than the *mokṣa* of the Vedānta. Radical experience of unity remains contrary to the very nature of classical Greek ontology (Plato, Aristotle, etc. . .) centered on forms.

Frithjof Schuon: Mariology

Within Abrahamic traditions, Schuon insists on a Mariology[3] both in his written and oral teachings. His Mariology reaches the pinnacle of divine bi-unity such as it is found in the Hindu doctrines, whose intrinsic superiority from the point of view of pure metaphysics, he, like Guénon, also stresses. Although

3. i.e., the doctrines on the nature of Marie and her spiritual function.

he is most knowledgeable in Abrahamic theologies, Schuon is not confined by their limits as he grants the *Avatāra* character to Mary whose Immaculate Conception proceeds from the maternity of the divine essence itself. Mary is the *Śakti*, and beyond, the *Mahā-Śakti*.

His theological assertion is that Mary not only is the mother of Christ but also the mother of God-*Mary Theotokos* for the Eastern Church and *Mater Dei* in the Church of Rome? Be as it may, India is not, for Schuon, a distorting mirror: therefore the Immaculate Conception symbolism is fully grasped only by an encounter with Hindu doctrines.

The Abrahamic tradition is quite unwilling to admit the principle of a feminine *avatāra* or the status of a prophetess. However, for Schuon, an *avatāra* such as Christ implies a complementary descent whose divine nature had to remain invisible to the multitude, by the very fact of her feminine nature. In order for Christ to be manifested *Logos*, the Virgin Herself had to be unmanifested *Logos* since only a divine being could welcome the *Logos* made man.[4]

Schuon was a Sufi. There is no contradiction however between the teachings of Islamic *esotericism* and his Mariology. The Koran does recognize in Christ a direct manifestation of the Word of God (*Kalimat Allah*), of the Holy Spirit (*ar-ruh al-qudsi*) breathed into Mary by Gabriel (*Jibril*).[5] The Koran pays

4. Le risalah de *Seyyidna* Aissa est 1' Evangile et 1' Eucharistie son Nom(*Risalah*=fonction *de Rasul*)Le risalah de Seyyidetna Maryam est Fils; non pas le risalah de son fils, mais son Fils en soi; or ce Fils envisage en dehors de sa risalah est le Logos en tant que tel, ce que represente 1' Enfant Aissa, leLogos-Enfant etant le Logos en soi. (unpublished poem by F. Schuon)

5. From an initiatic point of view, the Sufis reproach the Christians with, and the Koran does too, if one reads it carefully, having →

also tribute to the holiness of Mary. She was one of the Saints (*wali*) and this leads some Sufis to consider her a not — lawgiver prophetess (*nabiyah*). For this reason, El-Baqli exalted her for being the "Substance of original Holiness" and the "Mother of all Prophets." In a chapter entitled "The Virginal Doctrine" in *Form and Substances in the Religions*, Schuon makes another essential connection between Mary having taken refuge in the sanctuary and the niche described in the *Surat* of Light, in which a supernatural light is burning:

> Allah is the light of the heavens and the earth; a likeness of His light is as a niche in which is a lamp, the lamp is in a glass, (and) the glass is as it were a brightly shining star, lit from a blessed olive-tree, neither eastern nor Western, the oil whereof, almost gives light though fire touch it not — light upon light. Allah guides to His light whom He pleases, and Allah sets forth parables for men, and Allah is Cognizant of all things.[6]

In his commentary Schuon stresses the connection between this olive-tree and the tree referred to in the *Surat* of Mary. The niche is Mary's heart in that she is the perfect servant. In her heart, Mary keeps the secret of her *avatāra* nature and keeps the *Logos* of her Son, before he is manifested. In order to receive the divine word, it has to be perfectly pure, devoid of any illusion of aseity. Mary is the pacified self, a self spontaneously-made vessel of God.

→ given a Son to God, thus undermining the Transcendence of the non-conditional Essence, which creates confusion between the relative and absolute aspects of the divine. But most of all, they reproach them with limiting to Christ only the immanence of God in the world, thus wanting to "localize supreme identity" (*hulul*) when, metaphysically speaking, the Being of God is the essence of all created beings.

6. Translation of the *Koran*, chapter 24, *AL-Noor* (The Light).

In his Mariology, her role is not limited to the incarnation of Christ, both in the Christian and the Islamic world, but as pacified self she symbolizes the Universal Nature that the Divine Order (Amr), that comes into form. The passivity of the self towards God, the initial condition of spiritual realization, is anticipated in the prototypical *Prakṛti* that God the male creator impregnates with forms. Schuon sees in Mary the bearer of quintessential esotericism. He identifies the "olive tree neither of the East nor of the West" to the knowledge of the Self. He writes:

> In this specific symbolism, "neither Eastern nor Western" tends to signify that the Virgin, as the personification of Universal *Śakti* and *Sophia Perennis*, belongs exclusively neither to Christianity nor Islam, but to both at the same time, or rather, she is the link between the two forms.[7]

Mary's universality operates at two levels. In Abrahamism, she comes from the house of David and is venerated by Christians and Muslims. She appears at the point of junction between the three monotheisms, the trans-historical matrix from which originated the three religions. Secondly, her universality takes us back to India. Mary's mystery is that of the *Śakti* and even *Mahā-Śakti*'s. Abrahamic theology's paradoxes converge back to her and find in her its hidden explanation.

Is not this feminine figure at the heart of the spiritual life of the Saint Ramakrishna? The *Śakti* is not, for him, substantially different from *Brahman*. He thus frames the issue of the feminine at the level of the Absolute itself, in a more daring light than Western dogmatic theology ever would:

> Thus *Brahman* and *Śakti* are identical. . . . One cannot think of *Brahman* without *Śakti*, or of *Śakti* without *Brahman*. One

7. F. Schuon, *Form and Substance in the Religions*, p. 113.

> cannot think of the Absolute without the Relative, or the Relative without the Absolute.[8]

Brahman is to *Śakti* what the One without Second is to the Universal Possibility within Guénon's doctrine of the multiple States of Being. This feminine dimension, the power of the Great Mother is to be witnessed through all manifestation as she presides over the endless effusion of what Abrahamic theology calls the Divine names:

> She is creating, preserving and destroying in play, as it were. This power is called *Kāḷi*. *Kāḷi* is verily *Brahman* and *Brahman* is verily *Kaḷi*. It is one and the same Reality. When we think of It as inactive, that is to say, not engaged in the acts of creation, preservation, and destruction, then we call it *Brahman*. But when it engages in these activities, then we call it *Kāḷi* or *Śakti*. The reality is one and the same; the difference is in name and form.[9]

In *Mahā-Śakti*, a critical text[10] from *Roots of the Human Condition*,

---

8. Ramakrishna, *The Gospal of Sri Ramakrishna*, Vivekanada Center, New York, 1942, pp. 134-35.
9. *Ibid*.
10. The term *Śakti* means fundamentally the efficient energy of the supreme Principle, envisaged in itself or at a given ontological degree. For the principle, or let us say the metacosmic Order, comprises degrees and modes in virtue of universial relativity, *māyā*, in which it reverberates. In the domain of spritual life, the same term Śakti means the celestial energy that allows man to enter into contact with the Divinity, by means of the appropritate rights and on the basis of a traditional system. Essentially, this divine *Śakti* aids and attracts: She aids as "Mother" and attracts as "Virgin"; Her aid descends upon us from Heaven, whereas her attraction raises us toward Heaven. This to say that *Śakti*, as Pontifex, on the one hand confers a second brith, and on the other offers libarating graces (F. Schuon, *Roots of the Human Conditions*, p. 29).

Schuon has expressed similar views, identifying *Mahā-Śakti* to the power of the matrix giving birth to the worlds as well as the liberating force, which ensures our reintegration in God. His Mariology has resolutely gone beyond the limits of Abrahamic esoterism and even beyond a certain type of speculative mystique. It cannot find a better ally than in the teachings of Ramakrishna on the Great Goddess:

> Bondage and liberation are both of her making. By her *māyā* worldly people become entangled in "woman and gold" and again, through Her grace they attain their liberation. She is called the Savior and the remover of the bondage that binds one to the world.[11]

In Sichuan's writings on *Mahā-Śakti*, reference is made to the duality of Mary-Eve, of which the Western theology had mentioned, with limited perspective. Eve symbolizes, for Schuon, the power of illusion and the tāmasic spiral of all beings toward Universal Substance. As for Mary, she represents the sāttvic aspiration to the One without second, a liberating and deifying force lifting some of us toward true and essential universality. Mary is this "celestial energy through which man may come in contact with the divinity" and by her power one may coincide with his/her archetype in God and may know the Self.[12]

According to this ultimate perspective, Mary as *Mahā-Śakti* is endowed with a paradoxical ontological anteriority over God as a Creator. Thus from a meontological point of view,

11. *The Gospel of Ramakrishna*, p. 136.

12. Mary is the Mother of the God-Man; She is, according to Maister Eckhart, the mother of all deified beings having attained the state of Universal Mind. His supra-theological perspective is, in part, condemned by the Church. See Maister Eckhart, *Treatises*, and *Sermons*, pp. 232-33.

the relationship masculine-feminine are reversed. As long as Mary symbolizes the pure self and by extension, Universal Nature, Mary's femininity is totally passive and subordinated to *Īśvara,* the masculine God who impregnates her. From the supreme point of view however the creative function derives from the feminine power of the Essence, which is in itself neither masculine nor feminine insofar as it is without relationship and beyond any duality. Before the *eke doe* fathering, one must conceive a creation of Platonic archetypes (or Possibility) in divines, their Immaculate Conception within Divine Infinity which itself remains unaffected by this creation, in the same way as Mary remains a Virgin after giving birth to Christ.

This mystery of the Immaculate Conception is at the centre of Jean Barilla's writings, a French philosopher who gives precision on the status of Mary from Sichuan's teachings and from the Catholic metaphysical point of view. He draws the ultimate consequences from the Hindu doctrine of the divine bi-unity, as stated below:

> The privilege which constitutes Mary, and which is constitutive of her essence is the reflection and projection in the human order of the unfathomable Mystery of the immanent fecundity of the Divine Essence. . . . According to St. Thomas of Aquinas himself, Mary is endowed with infinite grace: The Ever Happy Virgin, in her divine maternity, is bathed in an infinite grace as a result of the infinite Good that God is.[13]

The Feminine in the Akbarian Doctrine of the Wahdat al-Wujud

The Mystery of the Great Mother is to be found at the heart

13. Jean Borella, "L'esprit Saint, La Trinite et L'Immaculèe Conception" *La Pensee Catholique,* Jan-Feb. 82.

of the Wahdat al-Wujud doctrine. The Principle in itself is the Absolute Unity. It is the unconditioned Essence (*drat*). Divine Bi-Unity is subsequent to this primordial unity, at the level of the deity (*al-Aloha*). The feminine Pole of the Divine, identified by Guénon, carries different names in Ibn Arabic's teachings, such as Universal Reality, supreme *Brach* or even Nature (*Tab' air*). As Nature it corresponds to the Great Mother (*al-umm al-alias al-cobra*) and is opposed to the "second mother," daughter of the Great Nature (*al-obi' at al-unman*) who is passive with respect to the Intellect or Divine Commandment (Amr). The Universal Possibility is the Hidden Treasure of a well-known *Habit qudsi* (God speaking in the first person): "I was a Hidden Treasure. I wanted to be known so I created the world."

In his chapter, "Our superior Fathers and inferior Mothers" of *The Mecca Revelations* (*fortunate al-Mackay*), Ibn Arabic uses the symbolism of generation to describe universal manifestation. Metaphysically speaking, the Fathers are the Divine Names, the Mothers the Possibilities and the Sons the beings who have been made to exist. At the cosmological level, the Father is the Intellect, the Mother the Universal Self who engenders Nature and her sister Substance. Nature and Substance finally engenders the Universal Body.

Ibn Arabi also gives more esoteric applications to the feminine symbolism. The Primordial Man, the *Puruṣa* of the *Ṛgveda*, being created *Androgynous*, the supreme realization will consist in retrieving this bi-unity. In the chapter of his book *The Wisdom of the Prophets* (*Fusus Al-Hikam*)[14] devoted to Mohammed's wisdom, Ibn Arabi makes mention of a Great Triad composed of Allah, the Perfect Man and Woman. For the Perfect Man (*Insān Kamil*) contemplation of Allah in Woman is the most perfect because it unites passivity and activity. It

---

14. Our stransilation is based on Charles-Andre Gilis' translation of the *Fusus al-hikam*.

allows man to retrieve his feminine part and to restore his primordial *Androgynous* condition. In the same chapter, Ibn Arabi also makes direct reference to the feminine aspect of the non-conditioned essence on the basis of a famous prophetical hadith: "Three things belonging to your gross world have been made to me worthy of love: women, perfume and the ritual prayer." On the basis of Arabic grammar often used for his metaphysical commentaries, Ibn Arabi returns to the Great Triad just mentioned: "The Prophet started with women and ended with the ritual prayer, two feminine terms. Man (Adam), symbolized by perfumes, of masculine gender, is inserted between the Divine Essence (symbolized by the prayer) from where he was made to exist archetypically and Woman (Eve) whose existence derives from him, according to the Koran. This Universal Man is thus symbolically between two feminines, the Great Divine Mother and women." Women are truly of feminine gender and the prayer only so from a grammatical point of view.

Surprising exegesis, perhaps scandalous by its audacity which leads us back directly to the mystery of the Eternal Feminine and Divine Maternity in the chapter on Mohammad. It gives us a new key to interpret Ibn Arabi's works, one upon which traditional commentators have not insisted.

An in-depth comparison remains to be made between Tāntrism and Ibn Arabi. One is struck however by the fact that the same metaphysical principles underlie both doctrines. In Islam however, this symbolism did not bear the fruit it did in Hinduism: one just needs to compare the writings of Ibn Arabi on the Feminine to those of his opponent Ibn Taymyya. The latter and father of anti-akbarian polemics has also been instrumental for contemporary fundamentalists. In Ibn Arabi's writings, woman appears as an essential epiphany, the means of a contemplation enabling man to reach ultimate realization.

The writings of Ibn Taymyya on love betray the limits of a mentality opposed to any experience of non-dualism as witnessed by the radical distinction he makes between the First and the second beings, the reality of the second beings as substance, the primacy of the Will over Intelligence. . . . It is true that he opposes some theologians who criticize the idea that one can speak of the Love of God for his creature. But he is incapable of conceiving continuity between human and Divine Love, and of the possibility of transmuting sexual life into a spiritual wedding. Generally speaking however, he bears a heavy responsibility in the present decline of contemplative Intellectuality in the Muslim world, especially on the tensions with women and the feminine obfuscation.

The Death of the Divine Mother and the Development of the Modern World

The reference to India is indeed essential to understand aspects of Abrahamic theology and *esotericism*. It is also helpful to clarify some aspects of the modern world. Georges Vallin was planning to write a book on the symbolism of the Great Mother but a premature death prevented him from doing so. We are left only with notes that Jean Borella publishes in his foreword to Lumières du Non-Dualisme. In addition to the "Death of God" (the Father) loudly announced by Feuerbach and Nietzsche, another death needs to be considered: that of the Great Mother. What characterizes a late Christian intellectuality and a certain form of non-traditional Islam is the fact that the Divine Mother is hidden. But, left to himself the transcendent Creator is progressively reduced to an abstract concept for a speculative theology of Aristotelian inspiration or to an alienating force from which the modern man tries to liberate himself so that the Promethean man may emerge. In so doing man will perhaps consummate his own death: without a Father and a Divine Mother, he may surrender to the forces of nihilism. For Georges Vallin, this is a key step in the genesis of modern mentality.

The death of the Divine Mother especially has profound impact on the current ecological problems. It signifies in particular the de-socialization of Nature. S.H. Nasr, a philosopher has, after Frithjof Schuon and Georges Vallin, insisted on this issue: in traditions such as Hinduism, Nature played the role of a theophany; in the modern world however, she is progressively reduced to a collection of things designed to serve the willpower of Man. To the "Integral Nature Georges Vallin opposes the idea of a "mutilated nature" as a mere theater for human history and activity, already rooted in Hegelian philosophy.

This paper has only touched the surface of the question of the Eternal feminine. Its developments were meant to reveal how, according to the Perennialists, the Hindu texts on the *Śakti* contribute to give their ultimate meaning to some symbols and teachings of Ancient Greek philosophy and of Abrahamic theology. They were also meant to increase our awareness on the very serious implications of some tenets of the modern Western world.

Bibliography

Coomaraswamy, Ananda, *The Essential*, World Wisdom (IN), 2004.

———, *Metaphysics*, Princeton University Press, 1987.

The Gospel of Sri Ramakrishna, Ramakrishna Vivekananda Center, New York, 1942.

Guénon, René, *The multiple States of Being, Larson*, New York, 1984.

———, *Introduction to the Study of Hindu Doctrines, luzac*, London, 1945.

———, *Man and His Becoming According to the* Vedānta, *Luzac*, London, 1946.

Ibn Arabi, *Le Livre des Chatons de la Sagesse*, (fusus al-hikam), Paris: Editions Al-Bouraq, 2003, tr. by Charles André Gilis.

Nasr, Seyyed Hossein, *Knowledge and the Sacred,* Albany: State University of New York, 1989.

———, *The Need for a Sacred Science,* Albany: State University of New York, 1993.

———, *Man and Nature: The Spiritual Crisis of Modern Man,* Chicago: ABC International Group, Inc., 1993.

Schuon, Frithjof, *Transcendent Unity of Religions,* Quest Books (IL), 1984.

———, *Form and Substance in the Religions,* World Wisdom (IN), 1999.

———, *Roots of the Human Condition,* World Wisdom (IN), 2002.

———, *The Language of the Self,* World Wisdom (IN), 1999.

Vallin, Georges, *La Perspective metaphysique,* Paris: Editions Dervy, 1977.

———, *Voie de Gnose et voie d' Amour,* Sisteron: Editions Presence, 1980.

———, *Lumiéres du Non-Dualisme,* Presses Universitaires de Nancy, 1987.

Section - VI
Vedānta and Contemporary World

21

Transcendence in Modern Science and in Classical Vedānta

V.V. Raman

SINCE ancient times, two powerful and competing schools of thought have influenced our worldviews. According to one, every aspect of the phenomenal world can be understood and accounted for in terms of entities in Nature: whether by referring to the primordial elements of fire, water, earth, air, and space of ancient science, or of quarks and leptons of modern science. According to the other, above, beneath and beyond the solid substantial world of matter and energy, there is an entity, perhaps entities, that are insubstantial and spiritual, which determine the core and cause of the world.

The naturalistic framework has borne much fruit, and today the framework of the scientific establishment is governed, by and large, by the thesis that naturalistic explanations are enough to explain every aspect of physical reality, including intensely personal experiences. Yet, deep in the hearts of many people, including a number of scientists, there persists an inner voice or light, as it were, to the effect that there may be something more to the world than what our sensory faculties and instruments reveal. This something, which also provides a basic context and significance for our lives, is variously described as transcendent or supernatural or spiritual.

The term transcendence, *sa-viśeṣaṁ, atyuttaṁ, paramaṁ* (positively special, the best, the highest) has been analyzed by philosophers in many modes. In the theological sense, transcendence refers to something, which exists beyond the physical world. It is often regarded as an attribute of God. The idea of God as "wholly other" than His creation affirms God's transcendence.

Then again, transcendence is often associated with the supernatural in that it is pictured as being above the natural world. Therefore, another wording of the question, "Is there a transcendent principle?" could be: "Are the material world and its components not enough? Why does one have to accept something supernatural?"

Jaina thinkers of ancient India wisely recognized that answers to the profound questions would depend in no small measure on one's perspective. An atheist who starts from the conviction that there is no God or in the hereafter would reject transcendence no matter what proof is offered that there is. While a theist with the opposite conviction would adore a transcendent God no matter how little or weak any logical demonstration as to God's existence happens to be. The reaction to the thesis of transcendence of a naturalist who traces kindness and altruism, joy and sorrow to genes will not be the same as that of a mystic for whom the experience of the transcendental is more real than that of the fleeting panorama of the physical world. Indeed, on certain issues, it is simply not possible to arrive at unanimity.

In this lecture I propose to define transcendence in terms of science and suggest that even from this perspective one may argue for its existence.

Kṣara, Akṣara, and Avyakta: Brahman

Hindu insights on transcendence may be traced back to the Vedas which constitute the root scriptures of the mainstream tradition. The essence of Vedic visions, enriched by the spiritual experiences of later sages, are found in more than a hundred and eight Upaniṣads and other canonical texts, including the *Bhagavad-Gītā* which is the best known of them all. Thus in the *Kaṭha Upaniṣad* transcendence is affirmed explicitly as a realm beyond matter and mind in the following verse (I: 3. 10-11):

indriyebhyaḥ parā hy artha
arthebhyas ca paraṁ manaḥ
manasā ca parā buddhi
buddher ātmā mahān paraḥ
mahataḥ paraṁ avyaktaṁ
avyaktāt puruṣaḥ paraḥ
puruṣān na paraṁ kiñcit
sa kāṣṭhā, sa parah gatiḥ

(Beyond the senses are the perceived things;
Beyond these is the mind;
Beyond mind is understanding;
Beyond understanding is the supreme Self;
Beyond this is the Un-manifest;
Beyond which is the Abstract Spirit;
Beyond that there is but Naught;
This is the final destination.)

Here, transcendence is presented, not as a religious doctrine, but as a finding, which is accessible to one and all who care to seek. Transcendence is a layer of reality, a substratum, the ultimate essence of the experienced world.

This view may be clarified with an analogy. Suppose that we are enjoying a sumptuous meal. The meal was made possible through the process of cooking, which involves an array of procedures but beyond the cooking and the prepared dishes, there is the essence of the food itself: the proteins, the carbohydrates, the vitamins, the minerals, etc. Ultimately, it is the life-fuelling energy implicit in the food that is responsible for the health and well-being of the individual. This energy is too abstract to be visualized as such.

Similarly, in the course of our everyday experiences, we become aware of many things and events. The totality of all this constitutes the perceived universe. It includes everything from the most minute entities at the core of physical matter to giant stars and grand galaxies. The one common characteristic of these tangible constituents of the universe is transience: sooner or later they all transform and dissolve. This dimension of the cosmos is described as *kṣara*: that which is perishable or destructible. In the Hindu view, only that which is permanent is real, the ephemeral is but a *māyā* or appearance which creates temporally relevant states which in their fleeting persistence may seem to be real, but which are in fact illusory because of their essential impermanence.

Science explores the nature and basis of the perceived components of the universe. The investigations of science have revealed that underlying the tangible world are immutable physical laws, which are responsible for the sustenance and functioning of the world such as it is. These laws are not directly visible to us, but their nature and complexity can be grasped by the human mind. The totality of the principles and laws constitutes the *akṣara* or inerasable dimension on account of which the *kṣara* components of the universe arise. They correspond in my analogy to the cutting and boiling and spicing without which there would be no food at the table. The rules of the game are more permanent than any particular game that is played.

The Hindu world-view goes a step further. Beyond the empirical and intellectually grasped features, there is a third level. This is the ultimate substratum of the universe, like the essence of the food. This grounding is recognizable neither mentally nor perceptually because it does not manifest itself in any way. It is therefore referred to as the *avyakta* or un-manifest dimension. Yet its existence and essence can be apprehended by human consciousness by processes that transcend perceptual-mental modes.

This un-manifest root of the cosmos is *Brahman*. *Brahman* is beyond the constraints of space and time, of conservation and causality. That is why verbal discourse on its nature often leads to confusions. *Brahman* is to be apprehended, not comprehended; experienced, not described; vouched for, not proved. Those who have realized *Brahman* speak of ecstasy and bliss, not of proof and belief. *Brahman* is the transcendent principle in the Hindu framework. Thus, the Hindu world, like other traditional religious frameworks, affirms the existence of transcendence. Except at its mytho-poetic level, it does not anthropomorphize it. In other words, like electrons and matter waves, transcendence is taken as an aspect of the universe that is super-subtle and immaterial.

Individual and Cosmic Consciousness

How are we to explain these extraordinary features of human consciousness in relation to its temporal and spatial insignificance? Science's suggestion that evolution led to this extraordinarily powerful complexity is one persuasive hypothesis. The sage poets and visionaries of India probed into the ultimate nature and roots of consciousness, and they arrived at the startling conclusion that consciousness is but a pale echo of something of far grandeur dimensions. Expressed through the pithy Upaniṣadic aphorism, *tat tvaṁ asi* (That thou art) the Hindu vision is that every conscious entity is like a spark from underlying effulgence, and can flash its radiance as its source alone can.

In other words, this capacity for awareness and experience, for logical analysis and joyful interaction constitutes the intangible component in the fleeting persistence of Homo sapiens. This is the essence of what we call the human spirit. Just as there is more to a flower than soil and tree-branch, the spirit is more than neural network, heartbeat and vital breath, though these are what create and sustain it here below.

If there is splendour in the perceived world and pattern in its functioning, and if it can all result in the grand experiences of life and thought, then even prior to the advent of humans, there must have been a *puruṣa* of a vastly superior order, an Experienced, who spanned the cosmic range in space and time. Just as the expanse of water in the seas is scattered all over land in ponds and lakes and rivers and bottles, all-embracing *Brahman* finds expression in countless life forms. We are miniature lights, one and all. We have emanated from that primordial effulgence, like photons from a glorious galactic core, destined for the terrestrial experience for a brief span on the eternal time line, only to re-merge with that from which we sprang.

The Hindu spiritual vision paints individual consciousness on a cosmic canvas. It recognizes the transience of us all as separate entities, yet incorporates us into the infinity that encompasses us. It does not rule out the possibility of other manifestations of *Brahman*, sublime and subtle, carbon or silicon-based, elsewhere amidst the stellar billions. It recognizes the role of matter, and the limits of the mind, but sees subtle spirit at the core of it all. It does not speak of rewards and punishments in anthropocentric terms, or of a He-God communicating in local languages. Yet, it regards the religious expressions of humanity as echoes of the Universal Spirit, even as volcanic outbursts reveal submerged forces of far greater magnitude.

Reconciliation with the Scientific World-view

There is a way in which a spiritualist vision may be translated into the framework and terminology of current science. Consider the room in which we are. It is bathed in information-carrying electromagnetic waves from everywhere on earth. But of these, none of us are ordinarily aware. However, if we are armed with appropriate electronic gadgetry we can decode at least some of the million messages. That is what our radio receiver, TVs and cell phones do. Or again, consider the photons that pervade all space. Those that enter our eyes reveal the presence of things, their colours and shapes and relative distance.

Likewise, our universe is submerged in a sea of million meanings, which remain undetected in their mute existence. Like neutrinos that can pass through miles of matter without the slightest interaction, meaning-bits may be crisscrossing the lengths and breaths of the universe, but if and when they encounter the highly evolved system called the brain, they are deciphered. From this perspective we can understand why it took all these eons before the meaning component of the universe came to be recognized. This view explains revelation, insights, and the many other discoveries about the universe that human beings have been able to make. Just as gravitational pressure of enormous intensity was necessary for instigating nuclear fusion in the core of stars and the synthesis of heavy elements in the bowels of supernovas, the evolution of human brains was a necessary pre-condition for the manifestation of an all-pervading consciousness as individual entities.

Transcendence from Specific Theories in Physics

If nature includes all that is matter-energy in space-time, we may extend or refine the notion of transcendence to mean that which is neither matter nor energy, nor localizable in space-time. Transcendence, thus considered, may or may not be linked to the physio-energetic spacio-temporal world. From this perspective, it can be argued that some developments in twentieth century physics have made transcendence a reasonable element in a variety of contexts.

Quantum physics: Transcendence emerges as an unexpected byproduct of quantum physics in the context of an interpretation of the Heisenberg uncertainty principle. From the fact that the states of fundamental particles are inseparably intertwined with our detection of them, it has been argued that prior to any observation, electrons and other elementary particles have an existence that is not exactly physical in the conventionally accepted sense of the word. Only that which is physically observed or observable in principle has any existence. Or, as one would say in the technical jargon, the observed electron is a result of the reduction of a wave-packet. These forces us to regard unobserved electrons as epiphenomena, which are not much removed from the transcendence of the religious framework. In quantum physics one refers to the observed state of a system as one of the possible eigenstates of a mathematical operator. From this perspective, the totality of physical reality may be regarded an eigenstate of a transcendental operator.

General Relativity: Another major theory of twentieth century physics is Albert Einstein's General Relativity and the associated view of cosmo-genesis, namely the big bang. According to a fundamental theorem in this theory, space, time, matter, and energy were all co-born at the instant of the big-bang. If this be so, one could argue that what gave rise to their simultaneous genesis must have been above and beyond them: i.e., transcendent. Whether we call it God or *Brahman* or a symmetry-breaking match-stick in the metaphor of the high-energy physics, it was neither matter nor energy, nor constrained by space or time. One could say that transcendence becomes a necessary element in any world-view that specifies a time of birth for the universe, as a non-physical cause of the physical world. Laplace was right when he said he saw no need for a God-hypothesis to account for what is happening in the physical world. But we do need some hypothesis for what caused the physical world to happen. Indeed, related to this is the philosophical question of why the universe emerged with these particular laws and associated parameters. Expressed differently, who or what determined that these are to be the laws governing the physical world, and not another set. This question is circumvented by the so-called M-theory according to which this just happens to be one of countless possible perfectly valid universes, and that there is nothing intrinsically unique about it.

Higher dimensional reality: Next, consider the attempts of physics to unify the fundamental interactions described by physicists: gravitational, electromagnetic, weak, and strong. In versions known as string theories, the universe began with a far greater number of dimensions than the four in which we live: anywhere from ten to twenty-six. But soon after the emergence of the universe, all the other dimensions save the four basic ones of space-time became so curled up and minuscule that they are no longer recognizable as such. Could it be that these primordial 26 dimensions were themselves a subset of still higher dimensional realms which constitute transcendence?

Pre-big-bang entropy: Another perspective, which makes transcendence a sound principle of physics, relates to the direction of time, which is conditioned by increase in entropy. It is well known that the entropy of the universe has been steadily increasing over the eons, and will continue to do so indefinitely. We know too that living organisms are open local pockets within which entropy-decrease occurs. Going back in time, the entropy of the universe must have been less and less, but this means more and more structure. As Paul Davies put it, "It is clear that no order at all would exist unless the universe as a whole started out with a considerable stock of negative entropy. . . ." At the momentous big-bang, the entropy of the universe must have been zero. Thus the pre-big-bang state may be regarded as a state with negative entropy. Considered thus transcendence may be viewed as a state of negative entropy. That every living entity involves a diminishing of entropy could be interpreted as reflecting a striving towards that state of negative entropy. In other words, the human effort to commune with transcendence in one mode or another may be looked upon as pockets of diminishing entropy struggling in a sea of increasing entropy to regain its original status.

Transcendence from Physics and in Religion

It is important to recognize that the transcendence, which is suggested from the theories in science has little relevance to the transcendence of which religions generally speak. From the perspective of most religions, transcendence is an aspect of a divinity that is very closely linked to the human condition. The vision of God as a transcendent principle is very different from the transcendence that seems plausible from physical theories. The higher dimensional transcendence of general relativity or quantum mechanics has no glory to laud, no grace to give, no mercy to show, no heaven to welcome our selfs. The intellectual logic-derived transcendence is as bereft of meaning and love, as cold and callous to the human experience as quarks, leptons, and field bosons. At best, it could be like the rainbow which evokes awe and wonder, but like the rainbow, it is there, unperceived, whether you and I are admiring it or not.

Just as deducing free will from quantum indeterminacy will be of little guidance when we are confronted with a moral choice, the assurance of transcendence on the basis of string theories or negative pre-big-bang entropy contributes little to the peace that comes to the pious from prayer or penitence. This is not to affirm nor deny the transcendence of which religions speak, but to state that proofs for the existence of God have little connect with the coherent constructs of science.

If we wish to seek a link between a reasonable extrapolation to transcendence from physics, and an affirmation of transcendence in one of the religious traditions of humankind, the Hindu concept of *Brahman* is perhaps what comes closest. It is not unlike the God of James Jeans who imagined the Divine as pure mathematical thought governing the physical universe. For in the world of Hindu spirituality, *Brahman* is not a He or a She that prescribes or proscribes behavior, nor a principle that is compassionate to the suffering or considerate to the repentant, but a mute substratum of cosmic awareness that is at the beginning and end of a cyclical universe, and bears witness to the events and episodes that transpire during the intervening spacio-temporal phases of matter-energy transformations. It does seem reasonable to imagine that even as vapors rising from the oceans fall back as raindrops into containers, a magnificent cosmic consciousness manages to thrust itself into the complex systems of human bodies.

From this perspective, transcendence is the subtle backdrop of the physical universe. If we compare the universe to a great painting, the tiny signature in a corner is like the human spirit: a reminder of how it all came to be a witness to the creation, as it were.

It has been a slow process: the evolution of the universe from the first big-bang of creation, through the formation of atoms and molecules and stars, supernovas, and planets, to the first spark of self-replicating molecules and the gradual transformation to reflecting and restless minds. As the stamp of the artist is imprinted only after the work is done, the human spirit is manifest only at the long-end of creation.

Much of bio-diversity has been adequately accounted for in terms of the view that all its expressions are products of the first molecules and cells that were synthesized from the primordial salts and gases that permeated ancient oceans, and that the variety of life forms resulted from genetic mutations, often instigated by the sole goal of survival. However, it is not sufficiently clear what some elements of cultural evolution have to do with biological survival: such as appreciation of beauty, reverence for nature, commitment to justice, creation of music, fondness for rhyme and rhythm, and the like. It is just as reasonable, and to many even heart-warming, to suppose that just as at its most advanced stages of evolution the human mind became aware of electrons and protons, managed to measure the speed of light and the distance of galaxies, it also developed the potential for uncovering the transcendental dimensions of the universe. Homo sapiens seem to be the only species we know of, which has gone way beyond the call of duty for keeping the species alive. Much of what humans have created and uncovered are quite irrelevant to the biological survival.

The Natural, the Sub-natural, and the Trans-natural

Science deals with the natural world. This is the world beyond human lives and minds, a world, which has, to all appearances, been there for eons before the emergence of Homo sapiens. It includes plants and trees, rivers and mountains, but also stars and planets, atoms, molecules, and distant galaxies. It is the study of this nature that we call physics and science in our own times. But there are two other entities that need to be mentioned in this context, because their existence is also part of the physical world.

First, current physics has unveiled the existence of what are called virtual particles, which are responsible for all the known fundamental interactions. It is in terms of these that we explain the myriad aspects and functioning of the physical world. They are subtle and minute beyond imagination. Virtual particles come and go, and even violate during very short intervals of time the hallowed law of matter-energy conservation. It is by their fleeting appearance and disappearance, firefly-like, as it were, that current physics pictures the root-forces that give stability to the physical world. They make cosmic emptiness perpetually throb, causing the so-called vacuum fluctuations.

Virtual particles are not like the substantial entities which they engender: the world of material chunks which we observe, measure, and detect, consisting of dust bits and sand grains, mammoth stars and galaxies. Virtual particles are the ultimate units at the deepest substratum of the material world. They can never be observed, even in principle. They may well be described as sub-natural, for they are well below what we normally call nature. More densely packed than bacteria in a cesspool or sand grains on the beach, sub-natural entities throng the microcosm. They are the ground stuff of which the gross material world of our experience is the tangible result. Yet, ironically, they are no stuff at all. Nor are they like anything in the nature that we see and study.

Then again, although everything in nature is matter-energy in space-time, there also arise in the world, from electro-biochemical processes in human brains, entities that we call thoughts. Thoughts are not spacio-temporally localizable, nor are they physio-chemical entities. More tenuous than a subdued whisper, subtler by far than neutrinos and massless photons, thoughts are the only non-physical entities that arise from purely physical systems, as far as we know.

We have at present no clear knowledge of whether thoughts have independent existence and of what nature they are. But this much is clear: all our science and religion, all our society and civilization, all our knowledge and understanding, all our values and relationships, rest ultimately on insubstantial thoughts and ideas, concepts and reflections. Thoughts and ideas are trans-natural entities. The world may be natural, but its comprehension calls for the trans-natural.

Concluding Thoughts

Four centuries of science have thrown much light on the physical basis of this uncommon wonder, which may have parallels in other planetary pockets in the universe. Perhaps some day we will be able to account for it in terms of neurons, microtubules, and other matter-based principles. But as of now, it remains a fantastic anomaly in the mindless arena of mass-energy. No material link has as yet been unveiled between alphabetical permutations and sublime sonnets, nor between molecular structure and meaning and value. Perhaps the tenuous bridge between matter and mind is transcendence.

It is quite satisfying to many to regard love and laughter, acts of kindness, and the quest for truth as among the peak performances of neuron firings, as evolutionary upshots of cerebral chemistry, as readable scripts from genetic programming. It may well be that we are essentially sophisticated carnal robots which organize conferences in Star Island. But it is also plausible that some kind of transcendence is at work in the context of value and meaning and whatever else goes with what we loosely call the human spirit.

Each one of us carries within a totality that is more than the sum of our body's material substrate. Yet, many of the atoms and molecules that make up our anatomy at this hour, were not part of us not so long ago. Moreover, millions of micro-organisms thrive and perish in our saliva and alimentary canal. With all that, there is a subtle self that has been illumining everyone of us, something that etches the identity of a separate existence even within a hugely interconnected whole. This self has been with us since the first utterance of I and me, and it will be part of us until the dusk of life when, gradually or suddenly, our individual memories will falter and fade away for good.

The biochemical basis in the persistence of person-hood is clearly there. Some day, silicon configurations in plastic casings may acquire feelings and emotions, mimicking the heaves and exhilaration of the human heart. Computers create music today; they might be enjoying it tomorrow. But this is no proof there is nothing beyond matter and energy in space and time. Who is to say that silicon chips can't experience transcendence?

Nature certainly appears as a tangible manifestation of matter and energy. However, the laws of nature, which organize and sustain cannot be located here or there: they pervade the entire span of spread-out space and ceaseless time. From this perspective, transcendence is the intangible principle that breathes life into inert matter. The scientific, philosophical, and religious quest for transcendence may well be more than thirst for a fantasy. Even as a heliotrope is drawn to light, the evolved brain may be reaching out for transcendence. If it is a thirst, the thirst could well be the yearning of the human spirit to remember its own pre-physical origins.

22

Jīvan-mukti and Spiritual Awakening in Radhakrishnan

P. George Victor

THIS essay is about the essence and goal of Vedāntic vision, as commented by the great interpreter of Vedānta in the contemporary times, S. Radhakrishnan, who has made Indian thought understandable to the English world, explaining it with the words, notions and concepts familiar to the Western mind. The highest goal of man, according to Śaṅkara is liberation while living, *jīvan-mukti*, which is said to be the state of absolute freedom from ignorance (*a-vidyā*), illusion or non-cognition (*māyā*) and mundane existence (*saṁsāra*). The liberation that Śaṅkara spoke was the realization of the identity of the individual self (*ātman*) and the supreme Soul (*Brahman*) propounded in the Upaniṣads, which realization was called *mokṣa*, known as *Brahmānubhava;* and the way that helps is the path of knowledge, *jñāna-mārga*. Radhakrishnan, who is equally at home with Western philosophy and Indian thought, and also being rooted in classical tradition and being familiar with Christian texts, has interpreted Vedānta in the light of the global issues. Apart from his translation of the basic texts of Vedānta, *prasthāna-trayi*, — the Upaniṣads, the *Bhagavad-Gītā*, and the *Brahma-Sūtra*, Radhakrishnan in his other works stood for "Global understanding with Vedāntic spirit," and this motto led him to proclaim the concept of "Spiritual Awakening."

Radhakrishnan's life

Radhakrishnan's life spanned over two worlds — between the nineteenth and twentieth centuries, between Hinduism and Christianity, between colonial British India and independent India, and between his calling as an academic philosopher and an administrative "philosopher-king."

In his intellectual life of seventy years, starting from the college studies in Chennai from 1905 until his death in 1975, Radhakrishnan's life shows a continuous craving for understanding different religions and cultures. A stream of thought pervades in his mind, a message to the world, the "awakening of the spirit." His analysis of the "spirit" is found in those books, where Radhakrishnan exercised his understanding of world-religions, philosophies and traditions. Radhakrishnan proposed his *mantra* of "Spiritual Awakening" in 1929 and cherished it throughout his life. The "spirit" of Radhakrishnan had its delivery in *Kalki or the Future of Civilization*, which appeared in 1929, nurtured by *Idealist View of Life* in 1932, sustained in the *Eastern Religions and Western Thought* of 1939 and reached its full-bloom in the *Recovery of Faith*, appeared in 1956.

Spiritual Awakening as Religious Idealism

Radhakrishnan witnessed the effects and evils of the two world-wars and understood the crisis of his age and civilization. The "restlessness and uncertainty" of human life made him to herald a philosopher's voice for the redemption of the sufferings of mankind, to which his answer is "Spiritual Awakening." To overcome all the miseries of his age, including that of the individual as well as society, and the apparent variations of different religions of the world, Radhakrishnan advocated his "religion of the spirit." His *Kalki or the Future of Civilization* depicts the "Spiritual Awakening" as religious idealism. This book being the earliest and containing his views, illustrates the Hindu view of the coming age. It reflects the tragic effects of world-war I; Radhakrishnan saw the evils of modern science and the decline of traditional values; hence he expressed his concern for the survival of human civilization. He surveyed the world-history, scientific and political developments, English literature, and also extensively commented on Soviet Russia.[1] In this work Radhakrishnan asserted the need for the common code of law for all nations and the need of the League of Nations for peace and survival of human civilization, by which time the UNO was far from conception. Simultaneously, Radhakrishnan argued that it is possible more effectively on the religious lines and wrote that the "religious idealism to be the most helpful political instrument for peace which the world has ever seen."[2]

It does not mean that Radhakrishnan is advocating a particular religious doctrine. For him religious idealism does not reflect a particular type but it is the "one embracing within its scope all those who are religious-minded in sentiment, allowing them full liberty so far as creeds and thought-pictures are concerned."[3] While the subject matter of *Kalki* depicts Radhakrishnan's wide scholarship, the message of it leads us to arrive at religious idealism for the realization of the "spirit."

The Meaning of "Spirit"

The "spirit" propounded by Radhakrishnan is all-encompassing

1. Vide: Radhakrishnan refers to Gorky, Trotsky, and Bolsheviks on pages 6, 21, 24 and 72 respectively in his, *Kalki or the Future of Civilization*. Ludhiana: Kalyani Publishers, 1974.
2. *Ibid.*, p. 76.
3. *Ibid.*, p. 47.

super-mind, possessing goodness and creativity. After duly considering the wisdom of Hindus and Greeks, he is of the opinion that man strives himself to reach higher level. There is a change from the "crude stages following superstitions, animism and myth" to the "refined and complicated philosophical system and ethical cultures of today." According to Radhakrishnan the change and evolution of human social history is the "manifestation of the spirit." He states that, "our spiritual longings — expressed themselves."[4] The meaning of "spirit" is the perfectness of individual in thought and action, which consequently influence the state, society and civilization:

> When a civilization tirumphs, it is more by the might of the spirit than by physical power . . . when it falls, it is through lack of spiritual vigour and vitality. So long as we put our hope in the sword and fail to rule by the power of the spirit, the future is gloomy. An acquisitive society with competitive . . . forces . . . represents a civilization of power and not of spirit (*sattva*) and so can not endure.[5]

Fundamentally, according to Radhakrishnan, "spirit" is *sattva* or goodness; and it is understood as the temper of mind,[6] and the driving force of the human self. He says: "Broadly speaking the human self is a trinity of body, mind and spirit."[7] Radhakrishnan firmly believes in the ethical norms of the society and its order. He does not touch them either to change or modify them. For him the "spirit" has to realize its potentiality in the world process and society. Here Radhakrishnan had in mind the Indian society and its social order as it is evident from the mention of "Rajaput Warrior"

4. *Ibid.*, p. 30.
5. *Ibid.*, p. 41.
6. *Ibid.*, p. 47.
7. *Ibid.*, p. 29.

and the sayings of the *Bhagavad-Gītā* (10.41). He firmly believes that the ethical norms are the expressions of the "spirit" or sātvic mind; he writes: "We cannot reject any expression of human life, provided we have a disciplined realization of ideal in that line."[8]

Radhakrishnan follows the Hegelian perspective of analyzing the social, political and ethical norms of the society. However, we do not find in him the dialectical method as interpreted by Hegel, but only the supremacy of the spirit. Accordingly every individual in the society has to take up his own ways for the ultimate realization of the "spirit." Harmonious unity is the nature of the society and world; and the individual has to find himself a specific duty and goal. He writes: "The given has to be accepted, and on the basis of it we have to build higher."[9]

The Spirit and Cosmos

In his *An Idealist View of Life* Radhakrishnan interprets the spirit in divine terms, attributing the qualities of Upaniṣadic *Ātman* or *Brahman*. He writes under the sub-heading, "The Spirit in Man:"

> We know it, but we can not explain it. It is felt everywhere though seen nowhere, it is not the physical body or the vital organism, the mind or the will, but something which underlies them all and sustains them. It is the basis and background of our being.[10]

Radhakrishnan uses a number of words such as *Spiritual Unity* and *Spiritual Experience*. He writes that consciousness has three

---

8. *Ibid.*, p. 54.
9. *Ibid.*, p. 52.
10. Vide: Radhakrishnan *An Idealist View of Life*, London: Unwin Books, 1964, p. 162.

levels — the animal, human and super. The super consciousness is the *Spiritual Consciousness,* where new aspects of reality reveal themselves or experienced. Correspondingly there are psychological, logical and spiritual unities.[11] The *Spiritual Unity* is the state of possessing the bliss of *Spiritual Consciousness.* It is the inward nature of man disassociating himself with the outer world. The individual becomes aware of the substance of the spirit. Here Radhakrishnan had in his mind the state of *Brahman*-knower. Directly speaking, it is nothing but the Upaniṣadic realization of *Ātman* as *Brahman*:

> In the language of religion spirit is God, the ultimate reality which is one and all-comprehensive. The spiritualized man is a new genus of man exhibiting a new quality of life.[12]

The spiritual man is nothing but a human being endowed with divine qualities and subsequently becomes superman. Radhakrishnan also maintained this same trend of thought in his book *Eastern Religions and Western Thought* (1939). He maintains that spirituality is the realization of the conscious self with the cosmos as a whole:

> This is the goal of man. His evolution is a constant self transcending until he reaches his potential and ultimate nature — we are not . . ., abolishing our individuality but transforming it into a conscious term of the universal being.[13]

It is the establishment of the *Spiritual Personality* where the human body becomes illuminated with the divine spirit. Radhakrishnan argues that all the outer experiences of the waking state alienate man from the "spirit." Man is a specific

---

11. *Ibid.*, p. 239.
12. *Ibid.*, p. 240.
13. Vide: Radhakrishnan, *Eastern Religions and Western Thought*, London: Oxford University Press, 1939, p. 37.

being in the world different from plants and animals. A conscious man coordinates all different forces in him and evolves to attain "an integrated life."

Individual's happiness reflects the amount that he cultivates his consciousness with the "spirit." Radhakrishnan, in this connection brings the need of religion for man who has not realized the "spirit" and who is affraid and possesses inferiority complex. According to him religions provide "a faith and a way of life, a creed and a community." This is nothing but the restoration of "the broken relationship between him and the spiritual world above and the human world around."[14] If man believes that there is nothing after life and "nothing worth while; he cannot live." Radhakrishnan adds that man resorts to "some dream" by believing that the wicked will be punished and the innocent rewarded. In this connection he says that "our intellectual consciousness" is the root cause of all separatism,[15] therefore "by attempting to abolish altogether the reason" the "reintegration of human nature is possible."[16] Radhakrishnan writes, further:

> When we discover the secret seed of spirit which lies concealed within the coatings of our nature and live by it, life becomes a pure flame full of light and happiness. "Knowing the bliss of *Brahman*, he does not fear anything" (*Taittirīya Upaniṣad* 2-8). "By knowing Him alone, one surpasses death" (*Śvetāśvatara Upaniṣad* 6.15). "What sorrow, what delusion is there for him who perceives this unity?" (*Īśa Upaniṣad* 7)[17]

By understanding the sayings of seers one attains the identity of oneself with all. This faith gives a new meaning to

---

14. *Ibid.*, p. 39.
15. *Ibid.*, p. 40.
16. *Ibid.*, p. 44.
17. *Ibid.*, p. 45.

life and deeper significance to thought. Then every other man in the world becomes our fellow being and the difference dissolves.

Faith and Society

The manifestation of the "spirit" as well as the cultivation of "spirit," which were actively discussed by Radhakrishnan from 1929 to 1939, again assumed their relevance after 1950. His autobiographical account, *Fragments of a Confession* published as an essay in 1952, has the title *The Religion of the Spirit and the World's Need.*[18] But the ecstasy of the spirit is found in his *Recovery of Faith* published in 1955. Radhakrishnan starts this book with the following assertion:

> Sensitive and informed minds believe that the fundamental need of the world, far deeper than any social, political or economic readjustment, is a spiritual reawakening, a recovery of Faith.[19]

Radhakrishnan devoted this entire book to herald his religion of the "spirit." He discussed about the difficulties of belief and asserted the need for belief. He believed that the comparative study of the various religions gives us the clue that the universal man is essentially craving for a rational faith which gives him a new light and universal validity.[20] In this connection Radhakrishnan discussed some of the interpretations that go against "Spiritual Awakening" and the rights of the individual. He discussed elaborately the communist

18. Vide: Paul Arthur Schilpp, ed. *The Philosophy of Sarvepalli Radhakrishnan*, New York: Tudor Publishing Company, 1952, pp. 5-82.
19. Radhakrishnan, *Recovery of Faith*, London: George Allen & Unwin Ltd., 1956, p. 1.
20. *Ibid.*, p. 74.

ideals and practices. According to him, what they speak about human equality and personal liberty do not find place in their administration and society. There should be an examination of "the social philosophy of communism" and the technique that the "communist countries adopt to implement the theory."[21]

Radhakrishnan prefers religion to communism because while the religious people advocate love for all men including the enemies, the communists assert the annihilation of the enemies. The *Recovery of Faith* devotes about 20 pages for the contradictions in between the theory and practice of communism. The estimate made by Radhakrishnan should not be underestimated in this connection as he had been the ambassador of India to USSR from 1949 to 1952, and stayed in Moscow. He says:

> In a communist society, it is the human spirit that does not get a chance. . . . In communism there is little of the pursuit of truth, no passion for individual integrity, and spiritual perfection.[22]

Religion of the Spirit

Radhakrishnan analyses that the "Spiritual Awakening" alone is the way for annihilation of prejudices of race, nation and culture and for overcoming the evils of the developed science. The modern society suffers from restlessness, insecurity, social chaos and religious pluralism and the individual becomes an insignificant and depersonalized unit. To overcome this state of affairs Radhakrishnan advocates the "religion of the spirit" by considering the religious experiences propounded in different religions, i.e., *Brahmānubhava* of Hinduism, and

21. *Ibid.*, p. 58.
22. *Ibid.*, p. 68.

various experiences of Taoism, Judaism, Zoroastrianism, Buddhism, Christianity and Islam. The awakening of the spirit, in these religious lines, is the re-awakening of the spirit. It is the identification of the individual self with the supreme universal Self. Here the message of the Upaniṣads, and the meaning of Advaita revealed and asserted. For Radhakrishnan the illumination of the reawakening of the spirit pervades not only man but also the society and world. The 200 pages text of the *Recovery of Faith* recorded the rationalization and the necessity for the need of the "religion of the spirit:"

> The recognition of a Transcendent supreme, the freedom of the human individual as a manifestation of the supreme, and the unity of mankind as the goal of history are the foundations of the major religions. The religion of spirit reasserts these fundamental truths. It does not regard dogmas and rites. . . . The religion outlined in these pages may be called the *sanātana-dharma*, the eternal religion. It is not to be identified with any particular religion for it is the religion which transcends race and creed, and yet informs all races and creeds. We can so transform the religion to which we belong as to make it approximate to the religion of spirit.[23]

The "religion of the spirit," which promotes awakening in man, is the aspiration of the human soul for centuries in all nations. The followers of this religion are saints and seers, says Radhakrishnan: "They belonged to the open, unorganized community, the invisible church of spirit."[24]

Conclusion

Thus, in Radhakrishnan the "Spiritual Awakening" has its roots

---

23. *Ibid.*, p. 204.
24. *Ibid.*, p. 143.

in the Upaniṣadic teaching, which implies the cultivation of love, mercy and kindness towards all, a satisfying basis for an ethics of altruism and unselfishness. This is the eternal religion, *sanātana dharma,* no way connected to ritualism, but the enlightenment of the individual. H. Nakamura, a contemporary Japanese scholar writes:

> Finally the thinkers came to assume that the *ātman* or *Brahman* was the Absolute. Here the philosophy of the Upaniṣads reached its peak. If we were to know the *ātman* or *Brahman,* we could reach the absolute state of acceptance of what life brings in serenity of mind. That is liberation, and it cannot be reached by means of rituals — this was the teaching.[25]

He goes on to add that to assume a unique fundamental principle and to explain the manifold and diverse aspects of the phenomenal world as based upon that principle "is a common characteristic of Upaniṣadic thinking."[26] This is what is said in Yājñavalkya's teaching to Maitreyī in the *Bṛhadāraṇyaka Upaniṣad.* The translator of the Upaniṣads, Hume comments that according to it all things are the phases of the one Self; and so any affection one individual has for others is an illustration of his finding his self-hood in the larger Self which embraces everything.[27] As the Marxist writer Damodaran perceptively pointed out, the doctrine of *Brahman-ātman* identity abolishes all distinctions between man and man, and led many thinkers to accept the oneness of all men ignoring

---

25. Hajime Nakamura, *A History of Early* Vedānta *Philosophy,* Part I, Delhi: Motilal Banarsidass, 1983, p. 104.
26. Ibid., p. 106.
27. R.E. Hume, *The Thirteen Principal Upaniṣads,* London: Oxford University Press, 1962, p. 65.

the *varṇa* system.[28] This is precisely what Radhakrishnan is interpreting for the discovery of the aspects of the spirit in us, moulding the life in accordance with its directions, and making our vision in tune with the spirit, elevating ourselves, beyond the mundane world to the higher level, the *paramārthika-satya*, the divine truth, which is absolute. The "Spiritual Awakening" in Radhakrishnan is the state of *jīvan-mukti* (the living-free) propounded in the Vedāntic tradition.

---

28. K. Damodaran, *Man and Society in Indian Philosophy*, New Delhi: People's Publishing House, 1970, pp. 14, 17.

23

The Three Ākāśas of Yoga-Vāśiṣṭa as Interpreted by Sri Satya Saibaba

Klaus Witz

SRI SATYA SAIBABA mentioned the three universes or worlds (*ākāśa*s) namely — *bhūta, citta* and *cid-ākāśa* of the *Yoga-Vāśiṣṭa* in about a score of discourses during the period from 1972 to 2002. I found that he used the three *ākāśa*s in a much broader way to talk about experience/knowledge of Divinity and *Ātma*. After much reflection over several years I now believe that his approach is much more true to the realities of subjective experience and direct knowledge of Divinity.

There is only little serious scholarship on Saibaba's teachings and a few words on my approach here may be appropriate. In reading or listening to Saibaba's discourses one feels as if whatever he is talking about is immediately present to him and emerges from him completely spontaneously. He does not try to build up a concept or picture of a state of affairs in the readers' mind; he makes no efforts to be consistent in terminology and develop a detailed map of a whole field. Hence, I always interpret him as picturing, or referring to or suggesting, direct experience, such as a state, or a critical element in experience, etc. In what follows I will work primarily in an excerpt — a text of commentary format. To understand a single excerpt, or to see whether and how different excerpts from the same or different discourses are related, I intuitively listen for the essence of what each excerpt is saying, taking the whole discourse context into account. Finally, I do not know Telugu language and am working throughout with published English translations, which are known to be sometimes only paraphrases, etc.

Basic Framework

Many of the following excerpts come from a series of 34 daily talks on the *Bhagavad-Gītā*, which Saibaba gave in 1984. I will usually give the version in Drucker's (1988) edition; and the Sri Satya Sai Publications Trust (SSSPT) published in 2002 a different translation (Satya Saibaba, 2002) which I sometimes quote also:

> (1) There are three types of spaces, which can also be considered universes or worlds: *bhūta-ākāśa*, the gross physical universe, *citta-ākāśa*, the subtle universe of the mind, and the *cid-ākāśa*, the subtlest and most extensive of all three, referred to as the causal universe. Beyond these and serving as a basis for all three of them is the Divine Principle, what has been called *Brahman* or God, and what has also been called *Ātma*, the immortal Self. A devotee, who is anxious to know the Divine principle and merge with it, should have an understanding of these three types of *ākāśa*s or universes.
>
> — Drucker, 1985, p. 150

Levels of Subtle-ness

There are several important points:

(i) Although it can be in some sense felt in all three *ākāśa*s, *Ātma* is outside the system of the three *ākāśa*s.

(ii) The three *ākāśa*s are described more as "universes of

objects" in them, but they are also treated as "universes of experience."

(iii) The fundamental characterization or differentiation of the three *ākāśa*s is in terms of degrees of "subtle-ness."

In Indian tradition generally as well as in (1) stated above, physical objects are "gross" (*sthūla*) while thoughts, thinking, imagining, etc. and all "things in the mind" are "subtle" (*sūkṣma*). ("Psychic energy," which one may experience in "psychic experience," is also part of this world and is thus also subtle; this agrees with psychics' descriptions of what they are seeing as "subtle objects"). In (1), the "things in *cid-ākāśa*," or *cid-ākāśa* experience, are even more subtle. So the things experienced in the three *ākāśa*s are thought of in terms of different degrees of subtle-ness (gross, subtle, and extremely subtle). Saibaba tends to treat not only *citta-ākāśa* but all three *ākāśa*s both "objectively," as worlds of objects, aspects, and also as worlds of subjective experience, or at least that he tends to blur the distinction between the two. The above (1) exemplifies a way of thinking (in Indian tradition generally, not specific to Saibaba) which does not follow the usual categorical and ontological distinctions in the West.

One immediate consequence of this is that three universes are seen with an equal eye. They are worlds of manifestations of different degrees of subtleness. In addition there is a commonality, kinship, unity among them: "Beyond (the three universes) and serving as a basis for all three of them is the Divine Principle," God, *Brahman* or *Ātma*. ("The Divine principle," probably *Ātma-tattva*, is slightly more abstract than *Brahman* and *Ātma*). Again there is a peculiar violation of categories: Although the *bhūta-*, *citta-*, and *cid-ākāśa* are qualitatively distinct worlds, they have something like a common "basis," "the Divine principle." And although the "Divine principle" is "beyond them," there is a suggestion that it can be felt in each of them, one can be aware of it in each universe of experience, as its basis.

Perhaps Saibaba's most detailed discussion of the three *ākāśa*s occurs in a much more recent discourse; I only quote some of the most important points:

> (2) What is the *citta-ākāśa*? . . . There is a power that is invisible, silent, imperceptible and eternal. That power is the *citta-ākāśa* (space, ether of mind, *citta*). In it is reflected or imprinted everything that can be seen in *bhūta-ākāśa*. The span of the *citta-ākāśa* is very small and subtle. On the other hand the gross and visible *bhūta-ākāśa* spans a terrific extent. Yet, the entire contents of *bhūta-ākāśa* appear in the *citta-ākāśa* as small blips. For example, you see a huge mountain. When you close your eyes after seeing, you will be able to visualize the mountain from the *citta-ākāśa*. Similarly, the stars and all that is seen are permanently etched on the *citta-ākāśa*.
>
> . . . The entire visible creation is stored in *citta-ākāśa* in subtle form. Every form and sound in the *citta-ākāśa* is a reflection of some entity in the *bhūta-ākāśa*, which is physically perceptible. That which is mentally perceptible is *citta-ākāśa*.
>
> The third (*ākāśa*) is called *cid-ākāśa*. It is also called *Ātma*. *Ātma* has no form. It has no movement. It is without any attributes, ever effulgent, eternal, victorious, pure, ever unsullied and everlasting. He who has seen this *cid-ākāśa* is one who has had the experience of *Ātma*. . . .
>
> . . . The reflection of *bhūta-ākāśa* is *citta-ākāśa*. That which reflects *citta-ākāśa* itself is *cid-ākāśa*.
>
> — Summer Showers 2002, pp. 132-134

The particular description of *cid-ākāśa* in (2) refers to more advanced experience of *cid-ākāśa*; in developing an understanding of *cid-ākāśa*, the reader should initially think of it as involving divine experience or consciousness or indubitable higher knowing in one's heart or self, or in one's being.

Relationship Between the Three Ākāśas

Lack of differentiation between subjective and objective (2) makes several new points with reference to the relationships between the three *ākāśa*s. Whenever Saibaba talks about the three *ākāśa*s, he talks as if *bhūta-ākāśa* was somehow contained in *citta-ākāśa* and *citta-ākāśa* was in turn somehow contained in *cid-ākāśa*. But it is striking that he describes this apparently rather definite relationship between the *ākāśa*s in such different ways. The *bhūta*s or perceptible things in *bhūta-ākāśa* are "reflected in" and "appear in" *citta-ākāśa*. They are "imprinted in" or "etched on" *citta-ākāśa*. They are "stored in" it "in subtle form." A colour or a sound, when it is remembered, after it was once seen or heard, is gotten "from *citta-ākāśa*." These metaphors are partly contradictory or involve mutually conflicting presuppositions, but Saibaba accepts them equally. Elsewhere he elaborates: "The gross aspect takes a subtle form in the mind." That is, the *bhūta*-s (things in the *bhūta-ākāśa*, things in the gross-world) continue to live in all the conceivable thoughts of, images of, conceptions involving these things in the *citta-ākāśa* or mind-world. "Every form and sound in the *citta-ākāśa* is a reflection of some entity in the *bhūta-ākāśa*." The world of mind is infinitely vaster than the world of matter that we experience through the senses, but somehow the world of matter provides most of the material for the world of mind. Similarly, "this mental aspect takes a still finer and more subtle form in the heart." The whole world of mental things, ideas, feelings, images, is reflected in the still subtler world of the heart. And although the world of *cid-ākāśa* is infinitely more extensive than the world of mind, the world of mind provides most of the material for the world of the heart and self.

The Three *Ākāśa*s and the Experience of Divinity

ARJUNA'S EXPERINCE OF LORD KṚṢṆA'S UNIVERSAL FORM

So far we have no idea of the subjective experience of *cid-ākāśa*; and in the 22nd of the 1984 discourses on the *Bhagavad-Gītā*, Saibaba gives an example:

> (3) After having been given the vision of the cosmic form of the Lord, he (Arjuna) immediately understood its deeper meaning. He realized that it means the union of the *bhūta-ākāśa*, the *citta-ākāśa*, and the *cid-ākāśa*. After having had the vision of the cosmic form, whenever Arjuna closed his eyes thereafter, he would continuously see Kṛṣṇa, as an indelible impression on his heart. He realized that what he had seen with eyes wide open was in the *bhūta-ākāśa*. Then, after closing his eyes, whatever still registered in his mind and was seen by him internally, was in the *citta-ākāśa*. Then the indelible impression of this vision that remained in his heart was in the *cid-ākāśa*. It is something like a print on paper: Once a picture is printed it is impossible to separate it again from the paper. In this way, the cosmic form of Kṛṣṇa became a permanent impression in Arjuna's heart.
>
> — Drucker, 1985: pp. 157-58

Cid-ākāśa as involving (a) an imprint of Divinity in the heart and (b) Divine consciousness left by the experience in the heart: these are revolutionary explanations. The experience of the Lord's cosmic form caused an "indelible impression" in Arjuna which he would recall again and again many times even in his wanderings years later. In general, every experience of Divinity leaves an indelible impression in the heart. "The indelible impression of this vision that remained in his heart, was in the *cid-ākāśa*." Even when there is no detailed memory of form, and no mental image or representation, there is still an indelible impression a pervasive state or feeling "in the heart" (using the usual connotation of "in the heart" in English as well as in Sanskrit). So implicit in the passage are two points.

(a) The Divine experience leaves an imprint ("indelible impression") in the heart and *cid-ākāśa*, which (imprint) enables the experience to be recalled to some extent; and (b) this indelible impression makes it possible that when the experience is recalled later, it is experienced as a particular nuance or state of Divine consciousness.

Arjuna's experience involves the three *ākāśa*s in a unity: But there is still more in (3). When Arjuna had the vision of the Lord's cosmic form, all three *ākāśa*s were in a unity. Thus the three *ākāśa*s are not three forms or arenas of experience, which are ontologically separate. We might say they are three levels or capacities. Levels or capacities of what? Of experience, of consciousness in a larger sense, or of being. The alternative translation in the SSPT version says that Arjuna's experience was experience of Divine *Śakti*, Divine Power. It says "Arjuna realized that what he had seen with eyes wide open was in the *bhūta-ākāśa*," he realized that what he had experienced in his vision with his eyes open belonged to physical experience, or "was in physical world consciousness." "After closing his eyes, whatever still registered in his mind and was seen by him internally, was in the *citta-ākāśa*." And finally, "the indelible impression of this vision that remained in his heart, was in the *cid-ākāśa*." That is, the indelible impression that lingered on in his heart indicated that the original experience also involved (experience of) *cid-ākāśa*, and whenever that original experience is recalled, it also involves (experience of) *cid-ākāśa*.

All the Divine Experience Involves the Ākāśas in a Unity

It is true that Arjuna's experience in the *Bhagavad-Gītā* XI, is not the usual experience of Divinity — it was an experience of a kind which, as Kṛṣṇa implies, is granted to very few human beings. It was a "cosmic" experience. Nevertheless, on the basis of the discussion of Arjuna's vision in passage (4), we might set up a very general hypothesis. An experience of Divinity — particularly a person's first experience of Divinity, and if it is in the waking state and involves form — is of such a nature that it has an incalculable impact on the person. It will be forever engraved on his/her heart, completetly out of proportion with the visual, etc. or any paranormal aspects of the experience. So that what makes an experience of Divinity in the waking state which involves form an experience of Divinity or a Divine experience is that it involves the three *ākāśa*s in a unity (or *cid-ākāśa* in a unity with one or both of the other *ākāśa*s). All form-full experience of Divinity in the waking state, if it is true experience of Divinity, involves the three *ākāśa*s in a union or unity. It does not matter whether the experience is a vision of Lord in the form in which one worships him (Rāma, Kṛṣṇa, Viṣṇu, Śiva, Devī), or an experience of Kṛṣṇa's *līlā*s, or — devotees of Saibaba's including myself would add — experiences of Saibaba's *līlā*s. It may be any experience of Divinity in the waking state that involves major alterations in physical or mental consciousness. This would include Moses' experience of the burning bush, or his hearing God walk on mount Sinai, and the disciples' experience of Jesus' transfiguration, etc.

Cid-ākāśa: Formless Divinity and Divinity with Form

The above passage (3) suggests that all the experience of Divinity in the waking state, if it is true experience of Divinity, involves the three *ākāśa*s in a union or unity. In the third of the 1984 *Bhagavad-Gītā* discourses Saibaba brings in another important aspect and discusses it in terms of *cid-ākāśa*: viz. that *cid-ākāśa*, besides involving experience of Divinity that involves form, also involves experience of "formless Divinity." In effect, this brings in "formless Divinity" as a new term and aspect that manifests in subjective experience.

Saibaba begins the discourse at a very general level saying that one needs to start with worship of Divinity with a form (Viṣṇu, Śiva, Rāma, Kṛṣṇa); but then one should, and gradually, be able to change one's practice and "worship Formless Divinity." Then he continues:

> (4) During the waking state the effect of the mind and the senses will be very strong. During the dream-state there may not be the effect of the senses but there will, nevertheless, be the effect of the mind. In the causal state of deep sleep or *suṣupti,* the mind gets dissolved. The phenomenal world, which is associated with the senses is the *bhūta-ākāśa.* The *citta-ākāśa* refers to the state of the mind, which is associated with the dream-state. The *suṣupti*-state of deep-sleep is the one where there is neither mind nor sense organs; this is the *cid-ākāśa.* It is only in the *suṣupti*-state, when the mind and senses are inactive, that it is possible to experience the attributeless and formless aspects of Divinity.
>
> — Drucker, 1988, p. 15

The basic statement is that Formless Divinity is only experienced in a pure form (without "Divinity with form") in deep-sleep (*suṣupti*) and *nirvikalpa samādhi.* Saibaba continues to say:

> once you have experienced God in form, you will certainly be able to get the experience of Formless God later on. The form is momentary whereas the formless is eternal, but the formless will live on as a permanent entity for you only after having first experienced the Divine form and printed it on your heart through worship and devotion.
>
> — Drucker, 1985, p. 16

Saibaba uses to make two points: Firstly, to remember the experience you have had in the first place. And secondly, just as the experience in the hall is needed before it can be recalled later, so also, the experience of Divinity with form is needed before there can be experience of formless Divinity later on.

So it is not enough to worship God with form like Rāma, Kṛṣṇa, Viṣṇu, Śiva, and in the course of a life of such worship having Divine experience. The worship of the form "takes its support" from the worship of the formless, so the formless is the more fundamental. So we also have to worship Formless Divinity and eventually experience it.

Cid-ākāśa in Normal Consciousness of Beauty

So far *cid-ākāśa* was discussed as a part of "direct experience of Divinity." However, there is an unusual passage in the 1984, *Bhagavad-Gītā* discourses that describes how *cid-ākāśa* participates (or can be thought of as participating) in normal consciousness, in experience of beauty, sublime qualities of character, etc.

> (5) . . . Since everything in the *bhūta-ākāśa* is made up of the five elements and only the five elements, the *bhūta-ākāśa* is inert and insentient. Yet, the Divine Principle is inherent in it. Similarly, this Divine Principle is also to be found in the *citta-ākāśa*, although since the *citta-ākāśa* is made up of the same five elements (in their subtle aspects), it is also inert and insentient. But, just as the Divine Principle as indweller is inherent in the inert body, vitalizing and activating it, so also, it is inherent in these inert physical and mental worlds, the *bhūta-ākāśa* and *citta-ākāśa*, energizing and vitalizing them. This Divine principle shines forth from the *cid-ākāśa*, the subtlest of these infinite universes. To try to understand this, consider a reflection in a mirror. The image or reflection has no independent existence of its own. It moves only when the object, which is being reflected moves. All the apparent lustre of objects in the world arises from the *cid-ākāśa*, the causal world, and is then reflected by the *citta* and *bhūta-ākāśa*s, which act as mirrors. Just as the effulgence of sun is reflected in the moon, the effulgence present in the causal state of the *cid-ākāśa* gets reflected in the subtle mental state of the *citta-ākāśa* and the gross physical state of the *bhūta-ākāśa*. — Drucker, 1985, pp. 151-52

Cid-ākāśa is implicit in, and its light is subliminally perceived in, normal experience

This is a fundamental passage. All the things in the physical and mental world look as if it were they that give us happiness (and unhappiness). But in reality, all the apparent lustre of objects in the world (which inspires and give us true happiness) arises from the *cid-ākāśa*, the causal world. And Saibaba draws a picture to visualize this. The light of the *Ātma* "shines forth from the *cid-ākāśa*, the subtlest of these infinite universes," and "is then reflected in the mental and physical world that act like mirrors." So *cid-ākāśa* is implicit in the normal consciousness of the splendour, beauty and power in creation. We saw in passages (3) and (4) that in experience of Divinity, the Divine aspect was remembered as something like a formless definiteness in the heart lingering on around the form aspects or the external aspects of the experience. That was *cid-ākāśa*. But there we were intent on identifying a (figuratively speaking) locus of Divinity and trying to give an initial sense and understanding of that experience. Passage (5) expands that understanding in a fundamental way. Not only experience of Divinity, but also other feelings, perceptions — all the perceptions of lustre, beauty, splendour, glory that give us happiness — arise from *cid-ākāśa*, from the layer of Divinity-Reality in the heart. To think of *cid-ākāśa* as only manifesting at times of "seeing Divine," or when there is "more direct experience-knowledge of Divinity," gives a skewed picture both of *cid-ākāśa* and of normal experience. *Bhūta-*, *citta-* and *cid-ākāśa* refer to the three naturally existing levels of subtleness in cognition, with *cid-ākāśa* referring to experience-knowledge and being at the subtlest level. At the same time we must not think of them as ontologically different categories. Talking as if Divinity-Reality was of a completely different nature ontologically from ordinary experience is sometimes useful in worship, to fan one's yearning, to counter one's complacency (or "laziness" — so Saibaba says in *Jñāna Vāhini*). But it is only a way of talking.

Integralness of all experience

From the preceding passages it appears that the most important feature of the language of the three *ākāśa*s is that it is a language that emphasizes the integral-ness of experience of all experience, being. Even in ordinary experience the three "infinities" form a unity. In the waking state, when we look at a tree for example, we experience all three, *bhūta, citta* and *cid-ākāśa,* and we experience them as a unity. Since *bhūta-ākāśa,* the visible-world is not differentiated in terms of subjective and objective (usually *bhūta,* the elements, created things, beings, etc. is thought from the outside and thus objective, but *bhūta-ākāśa* was treated as contained in *cid-ākāśa*), when we look at the tree, it can be said that we experience both *bhūta-* and *citta-ākāśa*. In addition we are also experiencing *cid-ākāśa,* Divinity or Divinity-Reality, in the form of the beauty of the tree.

Cid-ākāśa in More Advanced Experience of Divinity

As stated above, Saibaba pointed to two aspects in experience of Divinity and connected with the *cid-ākāśa*: (a) a unity of the three *ākāśa*s, and (b) the support or participation of formless Divinity. In addition, he drew attention to the impact of the experience afterwards — the lingering impression of the experience in the heart, and the ability to recall it as experience of Divinity. Further *cid-ākāśa* provided a way of understanding and talking about the beauty and lustre of the things of the world.

> (6) (*Cid-ākāśa*) . . . corresponds to subtle experiences wherein the Self remains the witnessing consciousness. In that state you are above and apart from your body and your life. It may be compared to the dream-state. In a dream you may

> feel that someone has come and cut off your head. . . . (goes on to elaborate the simile; in reality you have not died:). You are only witnessing the subtle drama. . . . In the realm of dreams you only remain an onlooker.
>
> — *Summer Showers in Bṛndāvan* 1973, p. 245

> (7) *Cid-ākāśa* is the state when a man, without being in any way influenced by emotion, just observes and remains like an observer or a spectator. Whatever may happen to the body — it may be insulted or injured — the person is not affected by them. He is always engrossed in the higher consciousness and that is the state of *cid-ākāśa*. The pot may be broken, the pond may run dry, the canvas may be torn to shreds, but that *ākāśa* stands there. The sky reflected in the pot, the sky painted on canvas, only refer to the media, not to the great sky (*mahad-ākāśa*) itself. Though this is reflected in our body, mind and senses, this *tattva* is something that transcends all of them.
>
> — *Summer Showers in Bṛndāvan* 1972, pp. 223-24

From the context (being part of a series of five descriptions of different *ākāśa*s), these statements are intended as descriptions of general states of spiritual development. But I also feel that they describe short-term states or experience.

The light of cid-ākāśa and the light of Ātma

Finally in addition to the three *ākāśa*s we are also experiencing every moment the one *Ātma*, Reality, Truth. Going back to passage (1), there is on the one hand a sharp division: There are the three worlds (and we experience them), and there is the Divine principle beyond them. But on the other hand, the Divine principle can be experienced in the three worlds "as their basis." When we are looking at a tree, we are not only experiencing *bhūta-*, *citta-*, and *cid-ākāśa*, but we are experiencing all of them "based on the Divine principle," *Ātma*. We are experiencing a single unity — the present moment is an integral unity of the physical, the mental, the Divine-Real, and *Ātma*. Let me close with a passage that combines the Vedāntic understanding and experience of *Ātma* with *cid-ākāśa* as I have tried to portray it in this paper.

> (8) There is something that transcends both the gross and the subtle. That is the cid-ākāśa. The cid-ākāśa does not have any movement. It does not undergo any change. Within it is to be found the param-jyoti (the supreme light), the self-effulgent light of the Ātma. It is on account of this all pervasive light of the Ātma, shining in and through the cid-ākāśa that you are able to experience the citta-ākāśa and the bhūta-ākāśa. If there were no cid-ākāśa there would be no subtle and no gross worlds for you, no citta-ākāśa and no bhūta-ākāśa. Therefore you have to base your life on the cid-ākāśa, while at the same time you have to use the bhūta-ākāśa to reach the citta-ākāśa and the citta-ākāśa to reach the cid-ākāśa. — Drucker, 1985: p. 155

Bibliography

A. Drucker, 1985, *Bhagavan Sri Satya Saibaba: Discourses on the Bhagavad-Gītā*. Prashanti Nilayam: Śri Satya Sai Books and Publications Trust.

Satya Saibaba, 1981, *Summer Showers in Bṛndāvan* 1972, 2nd. ed. Prashanthi Nilayam: Śri Satya Sai Books and Publications Trust.

Satya Saibaba, 1983, *Summer Showers in Bṛndāvan* 1973, Prashanthi Nilayam: Sri Satya Sai Books and Publications Trust.

Satya Saibaba (n.d.), *Summer Showers in Bṛndāvan* 2002, Prashanti Nilayam: Sri Satya Sai Books and Publications Trust.

Satya Saibaba, 2003, *Bhagavad-Gītā: Dicourses of Bhagavān Sri Satya Saibaba*. In two parts: On *Bhakti-Yoga*, delivered during 2.8.1984 to 18.8.1984, and On *Karma* and *Jñāna-Yoga*, delivered during 19.08.1984 to 16.09.1984, Prashanthi Nilayam: Sri Satya Sai books and Publications Trust.

24

Vedānta and Environmental Ethics
Sunderlal Bahuguna

George A. James

THE Tehri Dam is a hydro-electric power project located on the principal upper tributary of the Ganges River. It is one of the most controversial projects of this kind in India and the world. The earth and rock fill dam, 260.5 metres in height, across the Bhāgirathi River will be the fifth highest in the world, the highest in Asia. Over the past century nine earthquakes measuring above 7.5 on the Richter scale have disturbed the region. Because no earthquakes have occurred recently in the Tehri region, some seismologists believe the project may be close to a seismic gap where earthquakes of a magnitude above 8 on the Richter scale could occur within the 100 year projected life of the dam. Evidence of past major landslides has also been observed along the Bhāgirathi River. If a landslide into the reservoir should breach the dam, a wall of water would quickly reach the pilgrimage cities of Rishikesh and Haridwar. The disaster would be measured in tens of thousands of lives. The reservoir of the dam will submerge the town of Tehri on the route to Gaṅgotrī, for the pilgrims, natural lovers, and traditional devotees. It will also flood 45 kms along the scenic Bhāgirathi valley with its 23 villages, and 35 kms along the Bhilangana valley and their terraced fields, sculpted over centuries of painstaking work. The dam will displace perhaps 100,000 people.[1]

The expected benefits of the project include 2400 megawatts (MW) of electric power to support industry in such lowland cities as Allahabad and Kanpur. It is expected to provide irrigation to 270,000 hectares of land in the western districts of Uttar Pradesh and 500 cubic feet per second of drinking water to Delhi. The objections include the safety hazard presented to communities down stream from the dam, the inadequacy of the rehabilitation measures which the government has so far accomplished, and the unreasonable burden the project imposes upon the villages of the region.

The Geological Survey of India first identified the location as a possible dam site in 1949. In 1965 the then Union Minister K.L. Rao visited the area and met with representatives of the local opposition to the project. The Uttar Pradesh Irrigation Department, submitted its Detailed Project Report to its Planning Commission in 1969. That report, then envisaging a generating capacity of 600 MW was approved in 1972, and received administrative approval of the Uttar Pradesh Government in 1976. (At the time of writing the dam was 90 per cent complete and electrical generation expected to begin by 2005.)

Bahuguna's Protest

There is perhaps no name with which the resistance against the Tehri Dam has been more widely associated than that of Sunderlal Bahuguna. In this agitation Bahuguna has organized acts of non-violent protest that have repeatedly halted construction on the dam. He has also undertaken extended

1. Fred Pearce, "Building a Disaster: The Monumental Folly of India's Tehri Dam." *The Ecologist*, 21: 3, May/June 1991.

fasts that have sometimes brought him close to death. One of his fasts lasted 45 days and concluded in June of 1995, with the promise of the then Prime Minister to undertake a scrupulous review of all aspects of the Tehri project. When the review did not occur Bahuguna undertook a *Prāyascit vrata*, or discipline of self-purification, for letting down the people who were looking to his long fast as the act that would finally bring them justice and safety. This time his fasts lasted seventy-four days to end in June 1996, with the assurance by the then Prime Minister to investigate all objections to the project. For the past 15 years, Sunderlal Bahuguna had been living in *Satyagraha*, a small hut, not a hundred metres from the base of the dam. In December 2001, this hut was the first human dwelling to be submerged when two of the four diversion tunnels were closed.

Bahuguna's Life

The Tehri project is but one in a long line of causes with which Bahuguna has been involved. Born in 1927, Bahuguna was imprisoned at age 17 for his activities in India's freedom struggle. After independence he became involved in the struggle for land reform associated with Gandhi. His engagement with environmental issues became internationally visible in his role in the famous Chipko movement in the 70's. Chipko, meaning "to hug," was a grassroots environmental movement committed to saving the Himālayan forests from contract felling by hugging the trees to shield them from the axe. Bahuguna underlined the principles of this movement with foot marches, fasts, and discourses on the religious significance of the forests. In 1981, invited to the UN World Energy Conference in Nairobi, he arrived at the conference centre with a load of fire wood on his back to draw attention to the precarious state of the world's forest cover. Later in 1981, Bahuguna led a *pāda-yātra* or foot march through the foothills of the Himālayas from Srinagar in Kashmir, to Kohima in Nagaland, a distance of 4870 kms, sharing the Chipko story and offering discourses to local people about the exploitation to which their forests and their own lives were subject, and raising awareness of their capacity to stop it. The success of the Chipko movement has engendered movements of a similar nature in the south of India, in Sri Lanka, and elsewhere. Bahuguna has lent much support to these movements.

At age 78, Bahuguna is associated with a number of social causes but none more than the struggle of local people against the Tehri Dam. Today he remains in the Tehri region resolved to persevere until the last of the families have been evicted. With the Dam now 90 per cent complete, the town of Tehri practically deserted, and electrical generation expected to begin early in 2005, it is appropriate to examine the thoughts behind the actions of this veteran environmental activist.

Bahuguna's Philosophy

While Sunderlal Bahuguna is practically a household name in India he is known chiefly for his activism. Even in feature articles the press has made little effort to faithfully articulate the principles of his environmental thought. In discussing the movements with which he has been involved, historians, sociologists and other experts have discussed his strategies and their outcomes but have never made his philosophy of nature the focus of their research. From my own inquires concerning his life and thought I wish to suggest that there are three components to his philosophy of nature, three interrelated strands: first is the thought of Gandhi, second the spiritual traditions of India, and the third the insights of contemporary ecology. Together these form the basis of an integrated philosophy of nature that is comprehensive, critical, and coherent.

Bahuguna and Gandhi

In my most recent extended conversation with Bahuguna in the summer of 2003, Bahuguna reminded me that both he and his wife Vimla are products of two English disciples of Gandhi Mira Behn, and Sarla Behn respectively. Like Gandhi, Bahuguna believes that every village should be self sufficient in its basic needs: the needs for clean air, clean water, food, clothing, and shelter. This, he says, was Gandhi's idea of *swarāj*. Many scholars have pointed out that the term *swarāj* has both the connotation of political independence from foreign powers, and the positive connotation of material independence at the village level.[2] Bahuguna points out that at the end of Gandhi's life, the day before his assassination, Gandhi had written that while political independence was now a historical fact, the *swarāj* of his dream had not yet materialized. He then challenged the leaders of congress to implement measures to facilitate *swarāj* at the village level. Bahuguna's purpose, he explained to me, is to continue this work of Gandhi.

As a disciple of Gandhi, Bahuguna is committed to Gandhi's famous eleven vows of life. In his peaceful *dharnās*, strenuous foot marches, arrests, fasts, and periods in jails, Bahuguna's activism has embodied his commitment to non-violence and truth.

When I visited Bahuguṇa in 1998, I raised the question whether the methods of *satyāgraha* can address issues like stopping the construction of the Tehri dam. He replied that there are three methods available to address such issues. One is the method of the establishment, through the machinery of law and order, the legislature and the judiciary. This, he said, is unacceptable because the machinery of government is breaking down. Representatives of the people no longer

---

2. Bart Gruzalski, *On Gandhi*, Belmont CA: Wadsworth, 2001, pp. 33-35.

represent them. The system fails to acknowledge the plight of the poor and disenfranchised who are most affected by its actions. The second method is that of terrorism. This, he says, is ineffective because the power of individual terrorism is no match for the collective terrorism of the state. Moreover this method claims innocent human lives and undermines human values. The only method that remains, he says, is the method of *satyāgraha*, the method of standing firmly for the truth, through peaceful protest, through foot marches, and from time-to-time, when everything else has failed, through fasting. In discussing the fasts he undertook, both in his involvement with the Chipko movement and in the protest against the Tehri Dam, Bahuguna pointed out that in fasting the motive can never be that of anger or manipulation. As with Gandhi he affirms that the fast is not a hunger strike. It is an act of devotion to God.

During the independence struggle none of the famous eleven vows of Gandhi was more celebrated than that of *swadeśī*, or self-reliance. At the time *swadeśī* was widely associated with the *khādī* movement, the production of home spun cotton cloth and the boycott of textiles manufactured in England. For Gandhi, *swadeśī* is related to the idea of *swarāj* at the village level, and the commitment to address local needs at the local level. For Gandhi this meant the support of local workers within India as well. He states that we depart from the principle of *swadeśī* when we depart from our neighbour to satisfy our wants. Speaking at a meeting in Madras, Gandhi stated "If a man comes from Bombay here and offers you wares, you are not justified in supporting the Bombay merchant or trader so long as you have got a merchant at your very door, born and bred in Madras. That. . . . is my view of *swadeśī*."[3] For Bahuguna, the effort to address real problems

3. Gandhi, *Collected Works*, vol. 15, p. 171.

like the problem of water shortage by exploiting resources at great distances, and at the cost of distant local economies is a departure from the principle of *swadeśī*.

Gandhi's principle of *asteya*, is expressed in the vow not to misappropriate what belongs to another. Gandhi explains that this vow precludes the misuse of anything one has received in trust. Gandhi makes the point that "Nature provides just enough, and no more, for our daily need."[4] In the context of this principle, it is significant that among the expected benefits of the Tehri Dam is its capacity to divert drinking water from the Bhāgirathi River to Delhi. For Bahuguna this is a critical issue. But to the rulers he has raised the critical question, "What have you done to the Yamunā?" He answers, "You have polluted the Yamunā and now you want the Ganges to wash off your sins in Delhi!"[5] He points out that the 500 cubic feet per second of drinking water that the Tehri project has promised to supply swimming pools and to flush toilets in Delhi will be bought at the cost of the homes, heritage, and habitat of hard working and productive people in the Garhwal hills. Bahuguna argues that this water is needed in Delhi because unregulated industry and its untreated effluents have so contaminated the Yamunā River that health authorities have declared its water unfit for human consump-tion. The present state of the Yamunā as it passes out of Delhi is testimony to human violence to nature.

Bahuguna and Ecology

Bahuguna's commitment to the thought of Gandhi, and his appropriation of the spiritual traditions of India is supplemented by his appreciation for the contemporary science

---

4. *Ibid.*, p. 109.
5. "In Conversation: Sunderlal Bahuguna with George James," Seminar, January, 2004.

of ecology. Ecology is the natural science that explores the relationships between living organisms and their environment. Combining the three he concludes that projects to address the needs of communities from great distances do injury to nature. Bahuguna supports the claim of E.F. Schumacher that "small is beautiful." But he also holds the corollary that "big is horrible." He argues that big dams address problems of energy and water shortage in one area of the country by creating environmental disasters in others. Big is horrible, according to Bahuguna, because it does injury to local communities and the environment upon which they depend.

During his activities with the Chipko movement, Bahuguna came to the conclusion that the long term economic needs of the people of the hills would be met neither in their employment by outside companies that extract timber for the export market nor in the development of local forest industries. Trees, he said, must be available to meet the needs of local people for food, fuel, fodder, fibre, and fertilizer. They can do so without being destroyed. Instead, he envisioned self-sufficient rural communities living in a sustainable relationship with their natural surroundings. In May 1978, at Gulmukh where the Bhāgirathi River flows from the Gaṅgotrī glacier, Sunderlal Bahuguna took a pledge to devote himself to the protection of the Himālayan environment in all its aspects.

Another of his concerns was the influx of silt carried down by the river that will eventually fill the catchment area behind the dam ending its generating capacity. This he said could limit the utility of the dam to as little as 30-40 years. The Tehri Dam, he argues, is a temporary solution to a permanent problem. He argues that a permanent solution to the need for water and for energy would not be one that displaces people from land they have worked on productively for hundreds of years, that devastates the heritage of a village culture that for centuries has celebrated the meaning of their lives, and that destroys local ecosystems, all to carry water and energy to address the needs of people hundreds and thousands of kilometres away.

It would be a great misreading of the thought of Sunderlal Bahuguna, however, to suggest that he was hostile to the accomplishments of science and technology, or to the production of energy for the needs of the nation. The problem is not with science and technology but with the use to which it has been put. In support of his position he sites the saying of Vinoba Bhave that science plus spirituality equals *Sarvodaya*, the good for all. To this insight he adds only that science plus politics equals the atom bomb. For Bahuguna science and technology possess great resources for the production of energy. But to accomplish this, the needs of all and the uplift of all ought to be considered. For Bahuguna the production of energy should be developed not by one but by a variety of means.

In Bahuguna's view, the question of man's relationship to nature and to other species is really the test of our civilization. For Bahuguna, the Bhāgirathi River is not just a source of water but an ecosystem the integrity of which is part of the wealth of the nation. He notes that ecological studies of such river systems have shown that the tempestuous agitation of a mountain river as it courses through rocky terrain absorbs oxygen that energizes and purifies it. The forests of the Himālayas constitute an integrated ecosystem that, besides supporting a vast biotic community, stabilizes the soil, and mitigates the flow of water. He argues, therefore, that what is really needed to provide permanently for the basic needs of the villages of the Himālayas, is a restoration of the native forests of the Himālayas. Among the trees that provide food, he says, priority should be given first to trees yielding nuts, like walnuts, and then trees yielding edible seeds, like almonds. The third priority should be for trees giving seeds that provide oil for cooking. Fourth is for flowering trees, for honey. And last are those providing seasonal fruit. The classification depends upon the survival period of the products. The care of such forest resources could provide employment for local people, addressing the problem that has led to the money order economy in which young people from local villages go to find employment at great distances from their homes and send money home to purchase the scarce resources needed to address the basic needs of their families. Such forests would retain and help conserve water, help purify water, and help stabilize the entire ecosystem of the Himālayas. It is a solution that would support local economies, village self-reliance, and the Gandhian hope of true and lasting *swarāj*.

Bahuguna and Indian Spirituality

While Bahuguna's protest against the Tehri Dam has focused on environmental and economic justice, it has also emphasized the religious significance of the Ganges and Bhāgirathi rivers, and other aspects of nature. Bahuguna speaks of a legend in which the ancient king Bhagiratha wanted the goddess Gaṅgā to descend from the heavens to wash off the sins of his forefathers. After his many prayers and much penance she agreed. But she warned the king that when she came down she would have to be contained. The construction of the Tehri Dam, in his view, is a further violation of the sacred Himālayan environment.

Throughout his career Bahuguna has found much support for his thoughts and actions in the religious traditions of India. He does not consider himself a religious scholar or teacher but he has a high regard for the religious life of the villages of the Himālayas in which he finds an explicit support for protection of the natural world. In his discussion with me concerning his long *pāda-yātra* through the Himālayas in 1981, Bahuguna pointed out that it was not necessary to inform the villagers about the sacred character of nature. In their daily religious life, he said, they acknowledged divinity in plants, animals, birds, rivers, forests, and mountains. His role was simply to remind them of these traditions and to draw out the conclusion that the very nature upon which their well-being depends merits their protection. His appeal to the religious significance of nature, however, does not support a narrow religious point of view. It is perhaps for this reason that he prefers the term spirituality over the term religion. He argues that when the Ganges flows in her natural course she benefits all, irrespective of caste, creed, colour, poverty or wealth. When she is dammed, she becomes the possession of the privileged and powerful who dispense her blessings on a partisan basis.

Projects like the Tehri Dam, he says, are the temples of this new religion. Jawaharlal Nehru, he says, regarded them as the new temples of India. Yet he argues that Gandhi had a different view of civilization than that of Nehru, one in which each person could be afforded the means for a decent life. Bahuguna has observed that the material wealth promised through the centralized system of material production does not make people happy. Instead it makes them greedy. It does so, he says, because it seeks to provide satisfaction through the accumulation of more and more material things. For Bahuguna, the ultimate objectives of life are happiness, peace, and fulfilment. These come from within. The materialist society offers a kind of development that provides for temporary happiness, temporary peace, and temporary fulfilment, all coming from without. Because it sees nature as a commodity to be turned into cash it makes the human being the butcher of nature. He explains that this began with the exploitation of the Himālayan forests by the British in the nineteenth century.

It continued in the policy of contract felling by the Indian Forest Department, and it obtains in the exploitation of the water resources of the Himālayas today.

True development, he says, would be directed towards conditions in which communities are able to experience peace, happiness, and fulfilment on a permanent basis. This is afforded not in a system that turns nature into cash, but one that sees divinity in all beings, not only in human beings but in birds, beasts, trees, mountains, and rivers. That, he says, is spirituality. In the view of modern Western civilization the capacity to exploit resources at great distances is seen as development. Bahuguna suggests that the term civilization belongs more appropriately to those communities that live in harmony with nature. It is supported by a tradition that sees the earth as our mother and human beings as her children, who should live close to her and recognize their dependence upon her bounty. Bahuguna finds that his views are supported by the insight of the Hindu religious tradition to which Gandhi was also committed, and that proclaims, *vasudhaiva kuṭuṁbakaṁ*, "This whole earth is my family."

Epilogue

Epilogue
Vedānta as Religion

V.N. Seshagiri Rao

I

VEDĀNTA to be dynamic should be a religion also. Otherwise it will be cold or passive. Vedānta in its varied forms like *Dvaita, Viśiṣṭādvaita, Advaita, Dvaitādvaita, Suddhādvaita,* etc. is not only a metaphysical view but also a religion. Vedānta talks of reality as *Brahman*, the highest. The systems of Vedānta logically work out this. It is religion that translates the reality, *Brahman* into practice. Values associated with Vedānta, like infinity, benignness, peace and beauty, are values only when they are practised. It goes without saying that it is only religion through which all these theoretical values are realized. It is through religion that we arrive at a direct experience of reality.

If theoretical cogitation about *Brahman* be called dry Vedānta, practical realization of *Brahman* is Vedāntic religion. If theoretical problems face a man at every step in theoretical Vedānta like, how and why the eternal and infinite reality seems to have become limited, Vedāntic religion is not interested in hair-splitting logic, but in determining a personality in relation to values taught by Vedānta. Religion is bent on the intuitional foundations of Vedānta. Religion thus embodies universal teachings of Vedānta and it is experiential to the core. Technical phraseology, scholastic diction and rigorous dialectic never interfere in religion. It is feeling that matters much to the religionist. This, however, does not mean that a Vedāntic religionist is not a well-intentioned enquirer. His is certainly not an unsuspecting and unquestioning acceptance of what lot has been said in the name of Vedānta. On the other hand, he would instantaneously brighten the inquirer with his universal Vedāntic idiom! He discredits all bitterness against such controversies. His is a form of universal communication embodying new dimensions and comprehensions and is appealing. He confesses the respect and regard to a human being. He is firmly grounded in the experience of reality whether God or Absolute. He is a man of universal affiliations and vision. His loving contemplation and illuminations are always towards the existential truth and never to the theoretical. The existential truth, in the perspective of the religionist, is the boundless, the blissful: *Yo vai bhūma tat sukhaṁ*. Nothing less than the infinite can attain the infinite! This is the Advaitic philosophy as religion.

II

Coming to Viśiṣṭādvaita perspective of philosophy as religion: Viśiṣṭādvaita, more importantly is encyclopaedic in its concern for including everything — the *jīva*s (individual selfs) and *jagat* (the world), under the umbrella of one infinite Reality, viz. *Brahman* or God. The *jīva*s and the world, in spite of their having distinct existence are inseparably and intimately related to *Brahman*. In fact, they are both from the body of *Brahman* or God. It is an organic relation that holds between God and the world of individual selfs. They find their fulfilment in being subservient to the noble intentions of God. The *jīva*s adjust their wills to the will of God. They enjoy their inherent bliss by not dissociating themselves from God, the fountain of love and kindness! This is a wonderful idea that Rāmānuja Vedānta has contributed to religious consciousness! It loosened the artificial barriers of caste and creed and enabled everyone to embrace God wholeheartedly. It is in this sense that *Viśiṣṭādvaita Vedānta* is a real religion.

III

Coming to Dvaita philosophy, which is very realistic to the aspirations of a confessed religionist: it speaks the hardest truth that the finite individual selfs should not be made to lose their distinct existence in an indeterminate entity; God infact, has so lovingly granted their existence! God is the only independent and infinite Reality. The individual selfs and the world are finite and absolutely depend on God for their everything, on the sweet will of God. But the specialty of Dvaita-Vedānta lies in its accommodative spirit. God though independent (*svatantra*) lovingly accommodates the dependent entities and in this sense the spiritual unity of mankind is upheld and well protected. The message of Dvaita Vedānta that devotion is the surest means to godly bliss is the best part of its teaching. It thus overcomes the defects of religious utopia.

IV

Today's world is a world of din and puzzle, war and crime. A thorough reconstruction of it is very much needed. And it is only through Vedāntic religion that such a reconstruction could be done. It is the Vedāntic religion, whose rapprochement goes to the intuitionalist foundations of Vedānta. What is needed of a truly religionist is the inner quality of the heart. He should be sure of his viewpoints on religion. His thirst for leading a pure life should ever increase. Reading of religious texts may be necessary, but it is not all. What is important is the meditative spirit on One God, One world and One humanity. He should live a life of spiritual pursuits. He should be the instrument of happiness, peace and tranquility. The Vedāntin is a friend of all mankind. He should see light not only in the sun and the moon but in his own heart. Peace and bliss are the inalienable qualities of a Vedāntic religionist. His devotion to truth should take precedence over all other things. Man's contact with worldliness results in spiritual ignorance. He should surrender wholeheartedly to the will of God. Sri Aurobindo says: "The divine gives itself to all those who give themselves without reserve and in all their parts to the divine." He should not be swayed by excessive emotion not supported by reason. He should have his mind well within his fist. He should be pained at the sight of the people's distress. Thus to consider Vedānta as Religion is an interesting, rewarding and educative experience.

V

The Vedāntic as a religionist never delivers a message but radiates it. The Vedāntic religionist does not stop at intellectual satisfaction of the details of the Vedāntic systems. Though the Vedāntic systems had their birth in India, their message is universal. Of course there may be differences, amongst themselves with regard to the comprehension of the highest truth, etc.

The Vedāntic systems as religion, seek to discover the unity of all existence. Pluralistic and realistic attitudes of experiences are well accommodated in Dvaita, *Viśiṣṭādvāita, Dvaitadvaita* and *Suddhādvaita* systems as Religion. But from the highest point of view, the reality for Advaita is non-relative and, hence, religion is accommodated only at the empirical level. Absolute or *Nirguṇa Brahman* cannot act and work as a religious ideal, as it is an intellectual abstraction.

When it is said that Vedānta is to be viewed as religion, what is meant is that it gives direct knowledge, whether it is of the form of aesthetic or religious. What matters in religion is participation. Religion goes beyond the analyzable and the contradictable. It is participating identity that matters in religion. If so, Vedāntic philosophy should end up in Vedāntic religion. Thus there is a fundamental religious impulse in all the systems of Vedānta. Things may appear dissimilar but one inner essence flows through all of them. It is this unity that makes social life lovable. It is an undeniable fact that man lives through society.

Further, religion is a relationship with the revealed. It is a relationship of man with God or the highest reality. When it is said that Vedānta is to be regarded as religion, it only means that, it is not mere ritualism or formalism. A man of religion must be above mechanical uttering and doing of *mantra*s, *vrata*s, *pūjā*s and other rituals. The practice of *Yoga* enables one to progress spiritually. A Vedāntic religionist never imposes but appeals, to the lived genuine experience. He is the sage, the saint who sees the reality everywhere and in everything. He is a man of credibility who pardons all those who are lost in theoretical considerations. Vedāntic religion is a great boon for our time and our needs indeed!

Contributors

Das, Ganesh Prasad : Retired Professor of Philosophy, Utkal University, Professor G.P. Das got his MA. (1970) and Ph.D (1983) degrees from Utkal University, and taught at different government colleges of Orissa from 1971 till 1984. He joined the Department of Philosophy, Utkal University where he taught from 1984 till his retirement on superannuating in 2005. He is at home both with classical Indian philosophy as well as Western philosophy especially Anglo-American philosophy of analysis. His Ph.D dissertation is *An Analytic Study of the Advaita Classic, Vedānta-paribhāṣā of Dharmarājadhvarīndra*. His articles in the critical philosophy of Kant, Wittgenstein, philosophy of value and applied philosophy presented at national and international conferences have been published in reputed journals and are judged as important contributions to philosophy. [Address : *Rutayani*, 396-Paika Nagar, Bhubaneshwar-751 003]

Das, Maya : Daughter of Upendrakumar Das, Maya Das acquired BA (Hons.) 1st class 1st rank in 1972, MA 1st class 1st rank in 1974, and Ph.D in 1984 from Viśva-Bhāratī; and also holds Diploma in German Language, Certificate in Hindi Language, and MA in Sanskrit Language. Dr. Das learned Vedānta from the traditional teachers. She is on the faculty of Philosophy and Religion, Viśva Bhāratī University, Santineketan and specializes in Indian philosophy, ethics, religion including the schools of Vedānta and Hinduism. Her doctoral dissertation *A Critical Study of the Concept of Puruṣārtha* was published as a book. She has also authored several articles in reputed research journals including The *Viśva-Bhāratī Journal of Philosophy, The Philosophical Quarterly, The Journal of Philosophical*

Studies, The Vedānta Kesari, Prabuddha Bhārat and *The Statesman.* In 1998, she delivered talks on Vedānta in Ramakrishna Vedānta Centre at Buckinghamshire, UK and participated in the Twentieth World Congress of Philosophy, Boston, USA. [Address : Sripalli, Santineketan, West Bengal-731 235].

George Victor, P. : Started his career as lecturer in 1978 for the under-graduate students in DNR College, Bhimavaram, where he had majored philosophy in BA (1976), George Victor joined the faculty of Philosophy in Andhra University at Visakhapatnam in 1981, from which he earned MA earlier (1978) and Ph.D later (1986). *Padma-vibhūṣaṇ* K. Satchidananda Murty was his mentor, under whose direction he did his doctoral dissertation on the *Social Philosophy of Vedānta, a* study of the *Prastāna-trayī* and Śaṅkara's commentaries which was published in 1991. His published books include — *Social Justice: New Hopes for a Changing India* (1993), *Life and Teachings of Ādi Śaṅkarācārya* (2002) and *Moral Science* (1994) a textbook for BA students which was reprinted. He is the editor for "Andhra University Philosophical Studies" Series and has edited — *Saints and Gurus, Social Relevance of Philosophy,* and *Teaching Philosophy in the Twenty-first Century* published in 2002. He has also served as Visiting Professor at COTR Theological Seminary, participated in some national and international seminars and conferences in India, USA and Korea. [Address: D-1 Nestles Colonial, East Point Colony, Visakhapatnam-530 017].

Jain, Pankaj : Pankaj Jain is a Ph.D student in the Department of Religious Studies, University of Iowa, Iowa City, USA since August 2004. Earlier in India, Pankaj obtained his BS in Computer Science from the Karnataka University in July 1992. He is native speaker of Hindi, fluent in Gujarati and Kannada, writes poems in Urdu and Hindi, being a student of Sanskrit for ten years. Later in the US, he finished MA Religion from Columbia University in May 2003 by studying courses in Intermediate and Advanced Sanskrit, Islam, Vedic Religion, Non-duality in Indian Philosophy, Hinduism in New York, Buddhism, South Asian History, Theory and Method for Study of Religions with focus on "A Comparative Study of Buddhism,

Jainism, Islam and Hinduism," where from September 2002 to May 2003, he worked as tutor. From August 2004 onwards, he is Teaching Assistant in the University of Iowa for undergraduate and graduate students assisting them in their homework. He presented a paper on "Jain Philosophy in Comparison with Hindu and Buddhist Philosophy" in the Graduate Student Philosophy Conference at the University of Iowa, November 2004.

JAMES, GEORGE A. : Associate Professor, Department of Philosophy and Religious Studies, University of North Texas, USA, George Alfred James received his Ph.D in History and Philosophy of Religion from Columbia University in 1983. From that time on, he has been a member of the Department of Philosophy and Religion Studies at the University of North Texas. He is the author of *Interpreting Religion,* a study of phenomenological approaches to religion, and also editor of a volume of essays entitled *Ethical Perspectives on Environmental Issues in India*. For the past 15 years he has been doing research and publishing in the areas of comparative environmental philosophy and environmental movements in India. He has contributed articles to the *Encyclopaedia of Religion* and the *Encyclopaedia of Religion and Nature*. [Address : 3213 Saint Claire Drive, Denton, Texas 76210, USA].

JANAKI, PRABALA : Janaki received her MA in Telugu Literature from Andhra University in 1995 and was awarded Ph.D from Delhi University in 2002. She was awarded *Sangita Siromani* in Karnatic Music from Delhi University, a Diploma in Acting and Play Direction from Andhra University, and also has another in Journalism. Janaki has participated in many national and international conferences and cultural seminars, and presented research articles. She is participating in radio plays since 1979 and is a "B-High" grade Artist. She served as casual news reader in All India Radio, Delhi. Several talks of Janaki were broadcast from the studio of All India Radio, Visakhapatnam. She has received the senior fellowship from Department of Culture, Government of India. Presently she is pursuing D. Litt., on "The Woman Characters in Andhra Mahābhārata". Her publications include *Bhaktipadham to Prasthāna-*

trayaṁ (Ph.D Thesis), *Saraswatī Namasthubhyāṁ* (A Collection of Essays), and *Influence of Āndhra Mahā Bhāgavata on Traditional and Performing Arts*. [Address : 206-Leiam Apartments, B-15, Vasundara Enclave, Delhi -110 096].

Jeevan Babu, N.R. : Namboothiri Jeevan Babu hails from Thoppummukku, Vattiyoorkavu, Thiruvananthapuram-695 013, and working as Adjunct faculty, Department of French, Andhra University, Visakhapatnam. He is primarily a scholar of French language and literature, in which he got MA degree from Madurai Kamaraj University. He did his M.Phil on the "Influence of Sartrean Existentialism on the Modern Malayalam Novels" in Pondicherry University, and obtained the Ph.D from the Karnataka University based on his dissertation, "Uses of the images of India in the works of Dominique Lapierre." He possesses PG Diploma in teaching of French as a foreign language from the French Embassy, New Delhi. Jeevan Babu pursued extensive studies and research at the University of Jean Monet, Saint Etienne, France. He has been the resource person for various assignments of the Government of Kerala, and participated in many national seminars. [Address : Lecturer in French, St. Joseph College for Women, Visakhapatnam].

Johnson, J. Puthenpurackal : Dr. Johnson is a specialist in the philosophy of Heidegger, and has a doctorate with 'highest distinction' from the University of Louvain (Belgium). He is resident professor at Vijnananilayam Degree College, and lectures in different Catholic institutes in India. He has published several papers in philosophy and theology, and is the President of the Association of Christian Philosophers of India since 2000. [Address : Vijnananilayam Degree College, Janampeta, Vijayarai, Eluru, West Godaveri District, AP, 534 475]:

Kar, Bijayananda : Retired Professor and Head, Department of Philosophy, Utkal University, Professor Kar holds a Ph.D, and D. Litt. He has specialized in Analytic Philosophy and Philosophy of Religion with special reference to Indian Thought. He was former Vice-Chairperson, Indian Philosophical Congress; visited UK as a British

Council Fellow, 1978; visited Greece (1987), France (2000) under Cultural Exchange Programme. On being invited, he visited USA, Trinidad and Tobago, Netherlands, Thailand, Singapore and Bangladesh (1991-1999). In addition to numerous published articles, some of his principal published books are *Indian Theories of Error; Saṁkhya Philosophy; Indian Philosophy: An Analytical Study; Value Perspectives in Indian Philosophy; Major Trends in Orissan Philosophy* (translated into Hindi), and *Sri Aurobindo and Spiritualistic Humanism.* [Address : AM-26, V.V.S. Nagar, Bhubaneswar-171 007].

Lakshmi, K.A.P. : Lakshmi is Associate Professor, Department of Politics and Public Administration, Andhra University, Visakhapatnam. She has attended several national conferences and seminars, and has visited Canada, USA and Nepal in connection with international conferences. She worked as Warden of Andhra University Ladies Hostel. Several articles written by her have been published in various journals; and many research scholars were awarded degrees under her guidance.

Mishra, Godabarisha : Mishra is Professor in the Department of Philosophy, University of Madras. Formerly he worked as Editor at Kuppuswami Sastri Research Institute, Chennai between 1985-1988. He specializes in *Advaita-Vedānta* and has published twenty research articles besides some books, including the *Anubhuti-Prakāśa of Vidyāraṇya.* He is the co-editor of the *Breaking Barriers: Essays in Asian and Comparative Philosophy* (Asian Humanities Press, California). Recently, he has co-edited two volumes, *Paramparā* of Indian Council of Philosophical Research, New Delhi. Mishra has taught at the Oriental Institute, Oxford University in 1995 on a Charles Wallace Fellowship, and lectured at Oxford University in the Fall of 2003. [Address : Flat-1, *Muralikrishna*, 38, Fifth Trust Cross Street, Mandavelipakkam, Chennai-600 028].

Narayana Moorty, JSRL. : Narayana Moorty acquired BA (Hons.) from Andhra University in 1956, and worked as Assistant Compiler (1958-59) for the *Philosophy and Religion* volume of *Telugu Encyclopaedia*, edited by K. Satchidananda Murty. He was a Lecturer in Andhra University from 1959 to 1962. Moorty got his Ph.D from the University of California-Berkeley in 1972 and started his academic career as Instructor in Philosophy in 1974 at Monterey Peninsula College, Monterey, CA where he taught till 2000. His research articles were published in *Viśva-Bhāratī Journal of Philosophy*, *Journal of Indian Council of Philosophical Research*, *Radhakrishnan Centenary Volume*, and *The Philosophy of K. Satchidananda Murty*. He has translated *Sudha*, a work by Chalam (into English language with other three collaborators) published by Motilal Banarsidass, UNESCO-1989, and also *Selected Verses of Vemana* (With Elliot Roberts), published by Sahitya Akademy, Delhi in 1995. Narayana Moorty is retired and lives in Seaside, CA., USA. [Address : 1900 Highland St, Seaside, CA 93955, USA].

Puligandla, R. : After acquiring an electrical engineering degree from Andhra University in 1951, Puligandla did his MS in physics from Purdue University in 1960, he was awarded an MA degree in philosophy from the State University of Dakota in 1962, culminating with a Ph.D in philosophy of science from Rice University in 1966. He had joined the faculty of philosophy at the University of Toledo, Toledo, Ohio, USA. He authored several books, among them *Fundamentals of Indian Philosophy* (1975), *An Encounter with Awareness* (1981), *Jñāna-Yoga: The Way of Knowledge* (1985), and *Reality and Mysticism: Perspectives in the Upaniṣads* (1997). And a Festschrift entitled *Breaking Barriers: Essays in Asian and Comparative Philosophy* was presented to him in April 2004. [Address : 4138 Beverley Drive, Toledo, OH 43614, USA].

Raman, V.V., Emeritus Professor of Physics and Humanities, Rochester Institute of Technology: Varadaraja V. Raman has authored many books and articles, and spoken at many conferences on science and religion, as also on Indian culture. He has participated in many Vedānta conferences.

Reynaud, Patricia : Reynaud graduated from the Sorbonne, and from the Institute d'Etudes Politiques in Paris. Her specialization is cultural studies. For the last five years, her research on cultural constructs has incorporated the philosophical and metaphysical dimensions of Simone Weil, René Guénon and Frithjof Schuon. She is also the co-founder of religioperennis.org a website dedicated to the Perennialist School and its perspective on the main spiritual traditions. [Address : Associate Professor, Department of French and Italian, Miami University, Oxford, Ohio, USA].

SAIBABA, V.V.S. : V.V.S. Saibaba took his Master's Degree in Philosophy in 1973; P.G. Diploma in Sanskrit in 1976 and Ph.D Degree in 1985. He joined the faculty of philosophy at Andhra University in 1981. From 1987 to 1989, he was Reader and Head for the Centre for Mahāyāna Buddhist Studies at Nagarjuna University, Guntur, Andhra Pradesh, where he taught *Buddhist Hybrid Sanskrit Texts* to M.Phil and Ph.D research scholars. Saibaba is presently Professor of Philosophy at Andhra University and teaches courses in the Philosophy of the Buddha and Scriptural Readings. He has participated in many international and national conferences, seminars and summer schools, and has contributed several research articles. His book, *Facets of Buddhist Philosophy: Theravāda and Mahāyāna* (2003) which was published by Andhra University Press, contains some of his articles published in Indian and Foreign journals. Professor Saibaba is also the author of *Theravāda Buddhist Devotionalism in Ceylon, Burma and Thailand*, and *Faith and Devotion in Theravāda Buddhism*. [Address : 3/97-Vivekananda Nagar, Endada Post, Visakhapatnam-530 045].

SESHAGIRI RAO, V.N. : Seshagiri Rao did his MA (1974) from the University of Mysore and obtained his doctorate in 1981 for his thesis, *Vācaspati Mishra's Distinctive Contribution to Advaita Vedānta*, which was published in 1984. Rao has 33 years of teaching experience and has three other books — *Samakaleena Bharateeya Tattva-śāstra*, and *Pascātya Tattvika Cintana* published by the Mysore University in 1985 and *Sarvepalli Radhakrishnan . . . Tattvajñāna* published by the Karnataka Government in 1991. He has published over 60 articles in national and international journals, and has guided many research scholars. At present Professor Seshagiri Rao is the Chairman of the Department of Philosophy, University of

Mysore, Manasa Gangotri, Mysore-570 006. [Address : LIG 112, Bhamati, Gangotri Hudco Layout, Saraswatipuram, Mysore-570 009].

Singh, Abha : Reader and Head in the Department of Philosophy, B.S. College, Danapur, Patna, Abha Singh is a National Merit Scholarship holder in Intermediate Arts (IA.) and BA Philosophy (honours) as well as a Gold Medallist in MA Philosophy from Magadh University. She was awarded Ph.D (1986) and D.Litt. (2003) from B.R. Ambedkar Bihar University, Muzaffarpur, Bihar. She has been lecturing and tutoring to post-graduate and under-graduate students for the last twenty-two years, and has also delivered lectures as resource person in UGC refresher courses. Singh has participated in several national and international seminars, conferences and symposiums, and got published one book and twenty-four articles in different journals of philosophy. She has been awarded Residential Fellowship by the Indian Council of Philosophical Research as well. [Address : 203-Jaikunj Apartment, Beside Martin's High School, Kidwaipuri, Patna, Bihar - 800 001].

Sonty, Sarada Purna : Sarada Purna Sonty is a singer, poet, writer, and editor, who received her Ph.D from Andhra University in Telugu literature, her associate degree in child psychology and early childhood education from DePaul University, Chicago, USA. She is presently pursuing her D.Litt. in musicology. To date, Sarada Sonty has published five books on poetry and translation of classical texts. She is currently visiting professor and program co-ordinator for Potti Sree Ramulu Telugu University outreach centre in Chicago, USA, and is the founder of Sri Annamacharya Project of North America (SAPNA) and Sonty Renaissance International (SRI) Foundation, a non-profit organization for the promotion of Indian cultural traditions and classical fine arts. She has lectured widely in academic departments and international conferences on the topics, such as "Un-manifest to Manifest" and *Akṣara-Nāda Brahma*, exploring the power of sound in human expression. [Address : Director, International Telugu Study Centre, Chicago, 3042, Carmel Drive, Flossmoor 1160422, USA].

Sree Jahannatha Swamy : After completing his MA and M.Phil Degrees, Sri Jahannatha obtained his Ph.D in Philosophy from the Madurai Kamaraj University, Madurai, Tamilnadu, India. Sri Jahannatha Swamy is an educationist and spiritualist. He serves for the promotion of value education among school and college students with formal curriculum and non-formal training programmes. He conducts *yoga* and meditation courses, and guides and initiates disciples in *Śrī-vidyā-path* for self-realization. [Address: Director, Sri Vidya Institute of Integral Education, Shri Lalithambiga Trust, 5- Sivakami Nagar, S.B.I. P.O., Coimbatore-641 007].

Srinivas, K. : Srinivas did his MA from Andhra University in 1976 and Ph.D from Jawaharlal Nehru University, New Delhi in 1983, and presently heading the Department of Philosophy, School of Humanities, Pondicherry University, Pondicherry. He is a prolific writer and has published a number of articles and books including *Dictionary of Philosophy* (1993), a monograph on *P.T. Raju* (2001) and *An Evolution of A.J. Ayer's Logical Positivism* (1990), his doctoral dissertation. Srinivas has participated in many national and international seminars. [Address : 57, 3rd Cross, Everest Street, Kurinji Nagar Exten., Lawspet, Pondicherry 605 008].

Srinivasa Rao : Professor of Philosophy (Retired) from Bangalore University, Professor Rao previously taught at the Mysore University, and is a well-known scholar in *Advaita* and Analytic Philosophy. Besides a few articles, his important publications include *Advaita: A Critical Investigation* (1985) and *Perceptual Error: The Indian Theories of Error* (University Press of Hawaii, Honolulu, 1998). [Address : B-406, Gagan Vihar Apartments, Raja Rajeshwari Nagar, Bangalore-560 098].

Sundararajan, K.R. : Professor of Theology, St. Bonaventure University, USA, Dr. Sundararajan received his Ph.D from the Radhakrishnan Institute of Advanced Studies in Philosophy, University of Madras, under the guidance of T.M.P. Mahadevan and V.A. Devasenapathy. He joined St. Bonaventure University in 1975 after teaching at the Department of Religious Studies, Punjabi

University, Patiala, for a few years. He has edited a volume on *Hindu Spirituality-Post Classical and Modern* under the "World Spirituality Series." His professional and academic interest is in the area of the Vedānta of Rāmānuja. [Address : 132 South First Street Olean, NY 14760, USA].

Venkata Reddy, R. : Formerly Professor in the Department of Philosophy, Osmania University, Hyderabad, Venkata Reddy holds two master degrees — one in MA Psychology from Osmania University and another MA in Philosophy from the University of Delhi. Earlier he served as a Scientist for about 18 years in the Defence Institute of Psychological Research at New Delhi; later he had taught in the Osmania University for about 18 years. He has guided 20 Ph.D and 14 M.Phil scholars; and has published 15 books. He has received the State Best Teacher Award from the Government of Andhra Pradesh. Reddy worked for two years as Professor of Philosophy in the University of Asmara, Eritrea, North East Africa. He presented articles and delivered lectures at different conferences in USA, Canada, West Indies and the State of Eritrea. [Address : C-66, Phase-I, Vanastalipuram, Hyderabad-500 070].

Witz, Klaus : Klaus Witz is Professor of Education, University of Illinois, Urbana-Champaign. He got his Ph.D, in Mathematics. He is the author of *The Supreme Wisdom of the Upaniṣads: An Introduction* (Motilal Banarsidass, 1998), and has published articles in philosophy of education, philosophy of science, qualitative research methodology in the social sciences, and the creative process in art. Currently he is completing a book "Fulfilment in Mathematics: Perspectives and Case Studies" (on what inspires undergraduates to go to graduate school and become mathematicians) and working on "Cognition and the Universal Heart: Divinity-Reality in the Words of the Upanishads and Sri Sathya Sai Baba." [Address: 901 E, Mumford Drive Apt. B, Urbana IL, 61801, USA].

Index